Portfolio Management: Theories and Practices

Portfolio Management: Theories and Practices

By

Sajjan Singh Banwait

2008

CYBER TECH PUBLICATIONS
4264/3, Ansari Road, Daryaganj, New Delhi-110002 (India)
Ph.: 011-23244078. Fax: 011-23280028
E-Mail: cybertechpublicationsdelhi@yahoo.com

PORTFOLIO MANAGEMENT: THEORIES AND PRACTICES

SAJJAN SINGH BANWAIT

First Edition 2008

Published by :

G.S. Rawat for **Cyber Tech Publications**
4264/3, Ansari Road, Daryaganj, New Delhi-110002 (India)
Ph.: 011-23244078. Fax: 011-23280028
E-Mail: cybertechpublicationsdelhi@yahoo.com

Printed at : **Amit Enterprises**, Maujpur, Delhi, (9810878184)

PREFACE

Portfolio Management is a large and important industry in its own right responsible for banking of money. Wealthy people use to keep their money in private banks to have greater interests or benefits from it. The banks invest their money in high earning businesses as they could give more interests to the owners of money. This all is not so simple, a large chain of people are working under this system in insurance, stock market, banks, and other financial institutions and are managing to derive more and more benefits on the sum of investors to return them greater interests as they could lure more investments.

However this view is contentious and indeed industrial programme management and portfolio management represent ways of administering a range of projects to fulfill an over arching strategy.

Portfolio Management like all other streams of management has its few different principles and guidelines and working system. In simple worlds we can say in a labyrinthine process it has to work.

The book in your hand deals with theories and practices of portfolio management. This book has its own special features and comprises latest changes and information of the field concerned.

Undersigned is quite sure that this book will be of immense help to the readers.

—*Author*

Contents

1

Project and Portfolio

A project is a temporary endeavor undertaken to create a unique product or service.

In the above definition "temporary" means any project will have a start date and end date, doesn't mean short in duration. Unique means the product or service at the end of the project should be some thing different than the existing (Can be an invention or an innovation.) It can also comprise an ambitious plan to define and constrain a future by limiting it to set goals and parameters. The planning, execution and monitoring of major projects sometimes involves setting up a special temporary organization, consisting of a project team and one or more work teams. A project usually needs resources.

The word project comes from the Latin word projectum from projicere, "to throw something forwards" which in turn comes from pro-, which denotes something that precedes the action of the next part of the word in time (paralleling the Greek p??) and jacere, "to throw". The word "project" thus actually originally meant "something that comes before anything else is done". When the word was initially adopted, it referred to a plan of something, not to the act of actually carrying this plan out. Something performed in accordance with a project was called an object. This use of "project" changed in the 1950s when several techniques for project management were introduced. With this advent the word slightly changed meaning to cover both projects and objects. However in certain projects there may still exist so called objects and object leaders, reflecting the older use of the words.

One may also think in terms of platonism, where ideas from the realm of ideals are projected onto the physical world.

Particularly liked by Western business, projects can subdivide into sub-projects and spawn an industrial sub-culture of project planning and project management, all oblivious to more holistic developments.

Some feel this habit of short-termism has permeated economic planning and personal growth to the detriment of cyclical and multi-cultural world views. Alternatives to project-centric planning include trend-oriented goal-setting and directional planning.

However, this view is contentious, and indeed industrial program management and portfolio management represent ways of administering a range of projects to fulfil an over-arching strategy.

Notable projects include:

- *Manhattan Project:* Developed the first nuclear weapon
- *Polaris Missile Project:* an ICBM control system
- *Human Genome Project:* To map the human genome
- *Project Apollo:* Landing a man on the moon

PROJECT ACCOUNTING

Project accounting is the practice of creating financial reports specifically designed to track the financial progress of projects, which can then be used by managers to aid project management.

Standard accounting is primarily aimed at monitoring financial progress of organizational elements (geographical or functional departments, divisions and the enterprise as a whole) over defined time periods (typically weeks, months, quarters and years).

Projects differ in that they frequently cross organizational boundaries, may last for anything from a few days or weeks to a number of years, during which time budgets may also be revised many times. They may also be one of a number of projects that make up a larger overall project or program.

Consequently, in a project management environment costs and revenues are also allocated to projects, which may be subdivided into a work breakdown structure, and grouped together into project hierarchies. Project accounting permits reporting at any such level that has been defined, and often allows comparison with historical as well as current budgets.

Percentage-of-completion is frequently independently assessed by a project manager. Funding advances and actual-to-budget cost variances are calculated using the project budget adjusted to percent-of-completion.

Where labor costs are a significant portion of overall project cost, it is usually necessary for employees to fill out a timesheet in order to generate the data to allocate project costs.

The capital budget processes of corporations and governments are chiefly concerned with major investment projects that typically have upfront costs and longer term benefits. Investment go / no-go decisions are largely based on net present value assessments. Project accounting of the costs and benefits can provide crucially important feedback on the quality of these important decisions.

An interesting specialized form of project accounting is production accounting, which tracks the costs of individual movie and television episode film production costs. A movie studio will employ production accounting to track the costs of its many separate projects.

PROJECT MANAGER

The person who has the overall responsibility for the successful planning and execution of any project. This title is used in the construction industry, architecture, software development and many different occupations that are based on production of a product or service.

The Project Manager must possess a combination of skills including an ability to ask penetrating questions, detect unstated assumptions and resolve interpersonal conflicts as well as more systematic management skills.

Key amongst his/her duties is the recognition that risk directly impacts the likelihood of success and that this risk must be both formally and informally measured throughout the lifetime of the project.

Risk arises primarily from uncertainty and the successful Project Manager is the one who focuses upon this as the main concern. Most of the issues that impact a project arise in one way or another from risk. A good Project Manager can reduce risk significantly, often by adhering to a policy of open communication, ensuring that every significant participant has an opportunity to express opinions and concerns.

It follows from the above that a Project Manager is one who is responsible for making decisions both small and large, in such a way that risk is controlled and uncertainty minimized. Every decision taken by the Project Manager should be taken in such a way that it directly benefits the project.

Project Managers often use project management software to organize their tasks and workforce and to create reports and charts.

CONSTRUCTION PROJECT MANAGER

In the past, construction Project Managers were individuals who had worked in construction or a supporting industry and were promoted into project management. This led to a profession in which it was difficult to gain knowledge.

The profession has more recently grown to accommodate several dozen Construction Management Bachelor of Science programs.

Until recently, the industry also lacked any level of standardization, with individual States determining the eligibility requirements within their jurisdiction.

However, several Trade Associations based in the USA have made strides in creating a commonly-accepted set of qualifications and tests to determine a Project Manager's competency.

1. The Project Management Institute has made some headway into being a standardizing body with its creation of the Project Management Professional (PMP) designation.
2. The Constructor Certification Commission of the American Institute of Constructors holds semiannual

nationwide tests. Eight American Construction Management programs require that students take these exams before they may receive their Bachelor of Science in Construction Management degree, and 15 other Universities actively encourage their students to consider the exams.

3. The Associated Colleges of Construction Education, and the Associated Schools of Construction have made considerable progress in developing national standards for Construction Education programs.

ARCHITECTURAL PROJECT MANAGER

An architectural Project Manager has many of the same skills as their counterpart in the construction industry. An architect will often work closely with the construction manager in the office of the General contractor (GC), and at the same time, coordinate the work of the design team and numerous consultants who contribute to a construction project, and manage communication with the client. The issues of budget, scheduling, and quality-control are the responsibility of the Project Manager in an architect's office.

Software Project Manager

A Software Project Manager has many of the same skills as their counterparts in other industries. Beyond the skills normally associated with traditional project management in industries such as construction and manufacturing, a software project manager will typically have an extensive background in software. Many software project managers hold a degree in Computer Science, Information Technology or another related field and will typically have worked in the industry as a software engineer.

In traditional project management a heavyweight, predictive methodology such as the waterfall model is often employed, but software project managers must also be skilled in more lightweight, adaptive methodologies such as DSDM, SCRUM and XP. These project management methodologies are based on the uncertainty of developing a new software system and advocate smaller, incremental development cycles. These incremental or iterative cycles are timeboxed (constrained to a known period of time, typically from one to four weeks) and produce a working subset of the entire system to be developed at the end of each iteration. The increasing adoption of lightweight approaches is due largely to the fact that software requirements are very susceptible to change, and it is extremely difficult to illuminate all the potential requirements in a single project phase before the software development commences.

The software project manager is also expected to be familiar with the Software Development Life Cycle (SDLC). This may require in depth knowledge of requirements solicitation, application development, logical and physical database design and networking. This knowledge is typically the result of the aforementioned education and experience. There is not a widely accepted certification for software project managers, but many will hold the PMP designation offered by the Project Management Institute or an advanced degree in project management, such as a MSPM or other graduate degree in technology management.

Education and Industry Certifications

Individuals wishing to obtain professional certifications may take one or more of the offerings available from a variety of organizations. The Project Management Institute offers 'Certified Associate Project Manager' (CAPM) and Project Management Professional (PMP)

EXTREME PROJECT MANAGEMENT

Extreme project management (XPM) refers to the method of managing very complex and very uncertain projects.

Extreme project management differs from traditional project management mainly in its open, elastic and undeterministic approach. The main focus of XPM is on the human side of project management (e.g. managing project stakeholders), rather than on intricate scheduling techniques and heavy formalism.

Other names for extreme project management are:

- radical project management
- agile project management.

Extreme project management is a generalization of extreme programming. Advanced approaches to extreme project management utilize the principles of human interaction management to deal with the complexities of human collaboration.

PROJECT MANAGEMENT PROCESS

A project management process is the management process of planning and controlling the performance or execution of a project.

Inputs

- Documented need to act
- Project plan templates
- Lessons learned from previous projects
- Existing project management standards
- External information
- Resources for project planning and project execution

Process

- Project initiation
- Project planning
- Project execution
- Project control
- Project closeout and evaluation

Outputs

- Project products delivered
- Project objectives achieved (as a result of the interplay among project products and the organization or its environment)
- Lessons learned documented

PROJECT PLAN

A project plan is "A formal, approved document used to guide both project execution and project control. The primary uses of the project plan are to document planning assumptions and decisions, facilitate communication among stakeholders, and document approved scope, cost, and schedule baselines. A project plan may be summary or detailed." Additionally this is defined within Prince as: "a statement of how and when a project's objectives are to be achieved, by showing the major products, milestones, activities and resources required on the project." The widespread use of computerised project management tools has led to a common use of project plan to refer to a Gantt chart which has a much narrower use than a plan as defined above.

PORTFOLIO

Finance

- Portfolio (finance), a collection of investments held by an institution or a private individual. Holding a portfolio is often part of an investment and risk-limiting strategy called diversification. By owning several assets, certain types of risk (in particular specific risk) can be reduced.

Management and Marketing

- In strategic management and marketing, a portfolio is a collection of products, projects, services, or brands that are offered for sale by a company. In building up a product portfolio a company can use various analytical techniques including B.C.G. Analysis, contribution margin analysis, G.E. Multi Factoral analysis, and Quality Function Deployment. Typically a company tries to achieve both diversification and balance in their portfolio of product offerings.

Many portfolio optimization algorithms are based on MPT or Modern Portfolio Theory. The most commonly used method is Mean-Variance optimization where portfolio allocations aim at maximizing the profit while constraining the risk.

Education and Learning

- In education, portfolio refers to a personal collection of information describing and documenting a person's achievements and learning. There is a variety of portfolios ranging from learning logs to extended collections of achievement evidence. Portfolios are used for many different purposes such as accreditation of prior experience, job search, continuing professional development, certification of competences.

Tens of millions of people across the world have already used some kind of portfolio. Alone in the UK, more than 4 million people have got a qualification (NVQ) through accreditation of prior learning or accreditation of work experience, and most of them have built a portfolio to collect the evidence required to get their certificate. The recent explosion of knowledge, information and learning technologies has led to the development of digital portfolios or electronic portfolios, commonly referred as portfolios. For example, all participants in the Mississippi Teacher Corps are required to create "digital portfolios" upon the completion of the two-year program.

MODERN PORTFOLIO THEORY

Modern portfolio theory (MPT) proposes how rational investors will use diversification to optimize their portfolios, and how a risky asset should be priced given its risk relative to a portfolio containing the entire universe of risky assets. The basic concepts of the theory are Markowitz diversification, the efficient frontier, capital asset pricing model, the alpha coefficient and beta coefficient, the Capital Market Line and the Securities Market Line.

MPT models the return of an asset as a random variable and a portfolio as a weighted combination of assets; the return of a portfolio is thus also a random variable and consequently has an expected value and a variance. Risk in this model is identified with the standard deviation of portfolio return. Rationality is modeled by supposing that an investor choosing between several portfolios with identical expected returns will prefer that portfolio which minimizes risk.

Risk and Reward

The model assumes that investors are risk averse. This means that given two assets that offer the same expected return, investors will prefer the less risky one. Thus, an investor will take on increased risk only if compensated by higher expected returns. Conversely, an investor who wants higher returns must accept more risk. The exact trade-off will differ by investor based on individual risk aversion characteristics. The implication is that a rational investor will not invest in a portfolio if a second portfolio exists with a more favourable risk-return profile-i.e. if for that level of risk an alternative portfolio exists which has better expected returns.

Mean and Variance

It is further assumed that investor's risk / reward preference can be described via a quadratic utility function. The effect of this assumption is that only the expected return and the volatility (i.e. mean return and standard deviation) matter to the investor. The investor is indifferent to other characteristics of the distribution of returns, such as its skew. Note that the theory uses a historical parameter, volatility, as a proxy for risk, while return is an expectation on the future.

Under the model:

- Portfolio return is the component-weighted return (the mean) of the constituent assets. Return changes linearly with component weightings, wi.
- Portfolio volatility is a function of the correlation of the component assets. The change in volatility is non-linear as the weighting of the component assets changes.

ACTIVE MANAGEMENT

Active management (also called active investing) refers to a portfolio management strategy where the manager makes specific investments with the goal of outperforming a benchmark index.

Ideally, the manager exploits market inefficiencies by purchasing securities that are undervalued (and/or, less frequently, short selling securities that are overvalued. Depending on the goals of the specific investment portfolio or mutual fund, active management may also strive to achieve a goal of less volatility or risk than the benchmark index instead of, or in addition to, greater long-term return. Active management is the opposite of passive management, where the manager does not seek to outperform the benchmark index.

Active portfolio managers may use a variety of strategies for picking equities. These include quantitative measures such as P/E ratios and PEG ratios, sector bets that attempt to anticipate long-term macroeconomic trends (such as a focus on energy or housing stocks), and purchasing stocks of companies that are temporarily out-of-favor or selling at a discount to their intrinsic value. Some actively managed funds also pursue strategies such as merger arbitrage, short positions, option writing, and asset allocation.

The effectiveness of an actively-managed investment portfolio obviously depends on the skill of the manager and research staff. In reality, the majority of actively managed collective investment schemes rarely outperform their index counterparts over long periods of time (assuming that they are benchmarked correctly). When all expenses are taken into account one might actually see underperformance even if the securities outperform the Market. However, if it was not for active management, passive management would become a gamble, thus the incentives for active management will aways exist. In addition, many investors find active management an attractive strategy within market segments that are less likely to be fully efficient, such as investments in small cap stocks.

Advantages of Active Management

The primary attraction of active management is that it allows selection of investments that do not echo those of the market as a whole. Investors may have a variety of motivations for following such a strategy:

- They may be skeptical of the efficient market theory, or believe that some market segments are less efficient than others.
- They may want to manage volatility by investing in less-risky, high-quality companies rather than in the market as a whole, even at the cost of slightly lower returns.

- Conversely, some investors may want to take on additional risk for the chance of higher-than-market returns.
- Investments that are not highly correlated to the market are useful as a portfolio diversifier.
- Some investors may wish to follow a strategy that avoids or underweights certain industries compared to the market as a whole, and may find an actively-managed fund more in line with their particular investment goals. (For instance, an employee of a high-technology growth company who receives company stock or stock options as a benefit might prefer not to tie up their other assets in the same industry.)

Several of the actively-managed mutual funds with strong long-term records invest in value stocks. Passively-managed funds that track broad market indices such as the S&P 500 have money invested in both growth and value stocks.

DISADVANTAGES OF ACTIVE MANAGEMENT

The most obvious disadvantage of active management is that the fund manager may make bad investment choices or follow an unsound theory in managing the portfolio. Those who are considering investing in an actively-managed mutual fund should evaluate the fund's prospectus carefully.

Active fund management strategies that involve frequent trading generate higher transaction costs which cut into the fund's return. In addition, the short-term capital gains resulting from frequent trades have an unfavorable tax treatment when such funds are held in a taxable account.

When the asset base of an actively-managed fund becomes too large, it begins to take on index-like characteristics because it must invest in an increasingly diverse set of investments instead of only those which represent the fund manager's best ideas. Many mutual fund companies close their funds before they reach this point, but there is potential for conflict of interest between the fund manager and shareholders because of the additional management fees that can be collected by keeping the fund open.

Real Active Management

Equity fund managers usually do not have board members at the firms in which they have an equity stake, and they do virtually nothing about the future performance of the firm. So buying and selling equity is not active management of the companies; it is just an active transaction of equity in the fund.

Real active management is done by the people that work at the company, every employee and manager. Private-equity is often real active management since a privately owned company have a small number of owners and usually have just one owner that make strategy decisions

PASSIVE MANAGEMENT

Passive management (also called passive investing) is a financial strategy in which a fund manager makes as few portfolio decisions as possible, in order to minimize transaction costs, including the incidence of capital gains tax. One popular method is to mimic the performance of an externally specified index-called 'index funds'. The ethos of an index fund is aptly summed up in the injunction to an index fund manager: "Don't just do something, sit there!"

Passive management is most common on the equity market, where index funds track a stock market index, but it is becoming more common in other investment types, including bonds, commodities and hedge funds. Today, there is a plethora of market indexes in the world, and thousands of different index funds tracking many of them. One of the largest equity mutual funds, the Vanguard 500, is a passive management fund. The two firms with the largest amounts of money under management: Barclay's Global Investors, and State Street, primarily engage in passive management strategies.

Rationale

The concept of passive management is counterintuitive to many investors. The rationale behind indexing stems from three concepts of financial economics:

1. The efficient markets hypothesis, which postulates that equilibrium market prices fully reflect all available

information. It is widely interpreted as suggesting that it is impossible to systematically "beat the market" through active management.

2. The principal-agent problem: an investor (the principal) who allocates money to a portfolio manager (the agent) must properly give incentives to the manager to run the portfolio in accordance with the investor's risk/return appetite, and must monitor the manager's performance.
3. The capital asset pricing model (CAPM) and related portfolio separation theorems, which imply that, in equilibrium, all investors will hold a mixture of the market portfolio and a riskless asset. That is, under suitable conditions, a fund indexed to "the market" is the only fund investors need. In simplistic term this picture sourceshould help you visualize the market risk/ volatility involve if your portfolio allocation consists of 50% active management & 50% Passive Management.
4. Another reason to utilize passive management is summarized by William F. Sharpe, entitled "The Arithmetic of Active Management".

The bull market of the 1990s helped spur the phenomenal growth in indexing observed over that decade. Investors were able to achieve desired absolute returns simply by investing in portfolios benchmarked to broad-based market indices such as the S&P 500, Russell 3000, and Wilshire 5000.

In the United States, indexed funds have outperformed the majority of active managers, especially as the fees they charge are very much lower than active managers. They are also able to have significantly greater after-tax returns.

Implementation

At the simplest, an index fund is implemented by purchasing securities in the same proportion as in the stockmarket index. It can also be achieved by sampling (e.g. buying stocks of each kind and sector in the index but not necessarily some of each individual stock), and there are sophisticated versions of sampling (e.g. those that seek to buy those particular shares that have the best chance of good performance).

Investment funds run by Investment managers who closely mirror the index in their managed portfolios and offer little "added value" as managers whilst charging fees for active management are called 'closet trackers'; that is they do not in truth actively manage the fund but furtively mirror the index.

Collective investment schemes that employ passive investment strategies to track the performance of a stockmarket index, are known as index funds. Exchange-traded funds are never actively managed and often track a specific market or commodity indices.

Statistics and Data

Over the last month perhaps 50% of all actively managed funds will "beat the market"; that percentage decreases to 0% looking back 20 or 30 years.

Many people gained 500% in their Nasdaq stocks in 1999, to lose it all the next year. Hedge fund managers that closed their funds in 2000 and 2001 included Tiger Management Corp. and Soros Fund Management.

Some capital managers that have done well for decades, for example Warren Buffett and some private-equity firms like Blackstone and KKR that probably have produced an annualized 20% for the last 20 years.

Mutual Fund Investors

Dalbar Inc., a consulting company, found that, during the 16-year period through 2000, the average stock fund returned 14 percent. During that same period, the typical mutual fund investor had a 5.3 percent return. Other studies found similar results.

GOVERNMENT FINANCIAL REPORTS

Government financial reports are an important part of democracy (or a constitutionally limited republic) but often not widely read or discussed. Online reporting by governments makes these government financial reports more accessible but not necessarily more understood by the public. Governmental financial reports can include not only the budget or "general fund" as often referred to but also several other types of government financial reports, financial statements, performance reports and audits. Many governmental financial reports are online and opened to critical review by constituents, taxpayer groups, bond rating firms and creditors. Ratio analysis is one of the ways to examine the financial conditions of a government from a revenue potential for generating bond ratings for instance. One online source for state and local financial reports (some called Comprehensive Annual Financial Reports or CAFR) is from the Governmental Accounting Standards Board (GASB)

One of the key elements in the financial statement is the Management Discussion and Analysis (MD&A). The MD&A is designed to provide a readable version of the technical financial statements. In June of 1999, the Governmental Accounting Standards Board adopted standard 34. Standard 34 requested all cities and states in the US to include a MD&A in their financial statement or CAFR.

CAFR vs. Budget

The CAFR shows more comprehensive accounting entries that budget reports do not, and also should not be confused with "rainy day funds" or required pension surpluss holdings that are generally included in many government budgetary reports and process.

A budget is for a select grouping ("general fund") of accounts showing only the more commonly known revenue income from taxes, fees, licenses, fines and a select few revenue sources. The common government budget report also includes, expenses such as salaries, police, and entitlements will be shown along with required holdings to fund pensions, insurance and bonds.

The CAFR shows not only selectively presented budget items, but also government "enterprise operations" or "enterprise funds", investments, and the return on them (or loss). These funds include but are not limited to assets and holdings to back pension and retirement obligation reserves as required by law.

Surpluses

A "Comprehensive Annual Financial Report" or "CAFR" is a government book keeping practice which started in the post

WWII economic boom and replaced what was regularly an "off-the-books" practice called the "general fixed asset account group". The various levels of government; "general government" or the federal United States, individual state governments and government agencies each began producing a CAFR in the late 1940s to early 1950s to catalog an accurate picture of institutional funds, or financial holdings, assets and total investment incomes for those government and nongovernmental entities using the report, which is above and beyond the budget process.

In 1945, the Government Corporation Control Act, began the auditing of wholly owned government corporations and mixed ownership corporations, (those that government may have controlling holdings in but operate as private corporations) all of which may come under the term "enterprise funds".

While a budget might indicate that the government or agency has financial trouble and debt, (because of excess spending within the select grouping of "general fund" accounts presented), the CAFR will normally indicate that government possesses large holdings considerably over what is shown in a budget report or "general fund" alone.

Examples from recent history include, Jessie Ventura's career, punctuated by his returning some of the government surpluses to voters as governor of Minnesota. Other rare news events have highlighted the off-the-budget holdings and "enterprise funds" of government. In one widely reported example in the late 1990s (Los Angeles) Orange County California lost $1-Billion on investments in the derivatives market.

IT PORTFOLIO MANAGEMENT

IT portfolio management is the application of systematic management to large classes of items managed by enterprise information technology (IT) capabilities. Examples of IT portfolios would be planned initiatives, projects, and ongoing IT services (e.g. application support). The promise of IT portfolio management is the quantification of previously mysterious IT efforts, enabling measurement and objective evaluation of investment scenarios.

IT portfolio management started with a project-centric bias, but is evolving to include steady-state portfolio entries such as application maintenance and support, which consume the bulk of IT spending. The challenge for including application maintenance and support in portfolios is that IT budgets tend not to track these efforts at a sufficient level of granularity for effective financial tracking.

The concept is analogous to financial portfolio management, but there are significant differences. IT investments are not liquid like stocks and bonds and are measured using both financial and non-financial yardsticks (e.g. a balanced scorecard approach); a purely financial view is not sufficient.

Financial portfolio assets typically have consistent measurement information (enabling accurate and objective comparisons), and this is at the base of the concept's usefulness in application to IT. However, achieving such universality of measurement is going to take considerable effort in the IT industry.

At its most mature, IT Portfolio management is accomplished through the creation of two portfolios:

- Application Portfolio-Management of this portfolio focuses on the spending against established systems in relation to their value. These systems may be assessed as to their contribution to corporate profitability, and also on non-financial criteria such as stability, usability, and technical obsolescence.
- Project Portfolio-Management of this portfolio focuses on the spending on two types of projects: projects to develop innovative new capabilities (which are assessed on criteria such as potential ROI) and projects to reduce the overlap that occurs during corporate acquisition or reorganization (which are assessed on criteria such as maintenance savings, data cleanliness, and suitability of resulting solution for meeting future requirements).

IT Portfolio management is distinct from IT financial management in that it has an explicitly directive, strategic goal in determining what to continue investing in versus what to divest from.

Information Technology portfolio management as a systematic discipline is more applicable to larger IT organizations; in smaller organizations its concerns might be generalized into IT planning and governance as a whole.

IT portfolio management was first proposed by McFarlan. Significant authors contributing to the discipline of IT portfolio management include Aitken, Weill and Broadbent, Maizlish and Handler, Kaplan, and Benson, Bugnitz, and Walton. The ITIL Business Perspective and Application Management volumes also cover it in depth. Various vendors have offerings explicitly branded as "IT Portfolio Management" solutions.

ISACA's Val IT framework is perhaps the first attempt at standardization of IT portfolio management principles.

2

Foreign Exchange

Foreign exchange has several meanings:

- In finance, foreign exchange means currencies, such as U.S. Dollars and Euros. These are traded on foreign exchange markets.
- In telecommunications, Foreign exchange service is a type of network service.
- Foreign student exchange is a school program in which students study in another country for a time. Usually run by student exchange programs.
- Foreign Exchange with Fareed Zakaria is a weekly Public Television show in the US, hosted by Fareed Zakaria.
- Foreign Exchange is also a rap duo consisting of North Carolina rapper Phonte and Dutch producer Nicolay.

SHARES

In finance a share is a unit of account for various financial instruments including stocks, mutual funds, limited partnerships, and REIT's. In British English, the usage of the word share alone to refer solely to stocks is so common that it almost replaces the word stock itself.

A share is one of a finite number of equal portions in the capital of a company, entitling the owner to a proportion of distributed, non-reinvested profits known as dividends and to a portion of the value of the company in case of liquidation. Shares can be voting or non-voting, meaning they either do or do not carry the right to vote on the board of directors and corporate policy. Whether this right exists often affects the value of the share.

STOCK

In financial markets, stock is the capital raised by a corporation through the issuance and distribution of shares.

A person or organisation which holds at least a partial share of stocks is called a shareholder. The aggregate value of a corporation's issued shares is its market capitalization.

In the United Kingdom and Australia, the term share is used the same way, but stocks there refer to either a completely different financial instrument, the bond, or more widely to all kinds of marketable securities.

Type of Stock

Common Stock: Common stock, also referred to as common shares or ordinary shares, are, as the name implies, the most usual and commonly held form of stock in a corporation. Shareholders of common stock have voting rights in corporate decision matters. It is the residual corporate interest that bears the ultimate risks of loss and receives the benefits of success.

Preferred Stock: Preferred stock, sometimes called preference shares, have priority over common stock in the distribution of dividends and assets.

Most preferred shares provide no voting rights in corporate decision matters. However, some preferred shares have special voting rights to approve certain extraordinary events (such as the issuance of new shares, or the approval of the acquisition of the company), or to elect directors.

Dual Class Stock: Dual class stock is shares issued for a single company with varying classes indicating different rights on voting and dividend payments. Each kind of shares has its own class of shareholders entitling different rights.

Treasury Stock: Treasury stock is shares that have been bought back from the public. Treasury Stock is considered issued, but not outstanding.

Stock Derivatives

A stock derivative is any financial claim which has a value that is dependent on the price of the underlying stock. Futures and options are the main types of derivatives on stocks. The underlying security may be a stock index or an individual firm's stock, e.g. single-stock futures.

Stock futures are contracts where the buyer, or long, takes on the obligation to buy on the contract maturity date, and the seller, or short takes on the obligation to sell. Stock index futures are generally not delivered in the usual manner, but by cash settlement.

A stock option is a class of option. Specifically, a call option is the right (not obligation) to buy stock in the future at a fixed price and a put option is the right (not obligation) to sell stock in the future at a fixed price. Thus, the value of a stock option changes in reaction to the underlying stock of which it is a derivative. The most popular method of valuing stock options is the Black Scholes model.

Apart from call options granted to employees, most stock options are transferable.

History

The first company to issue shares of stock was the Dutch East India Company, in 1602. The innovation of joint ownership made a great deal of Europe's economic growth possible following the Middle Ages.

The technique of pooling capital to finance the building of ships, for example, made the Netherlands a maritime superpower. Before adoption of the joint-stock corporation, an expensive venture such as the building of a merchant ship could be undertaken only by governments or by very wealthy individuals or families.

SHAREHOLDER

A shareholder (or stockholder) is an individual or company (including a corporation) that legally owns one or more shares of stock in a joint stock company. Companies listed at the stock market strive to enhance shareholder value.

Shareholders are granted special privileges depending on the class of stock, including the right to vote (usually one vote per share owned) on matters such as elections to the board of directors, the right to share in distributions of the company's income, the right to purchase new shares issued by the company, and the right to a company's assets during a liquidation of the company. However, shareholder's rights to a company's assets are subordinate to the rights of the company's creditors. This means that shareholders typically receive nothing if a company is liquidated after bankruptcy (if the company had enough to pay its creditors, it would not have entered bankruptcy), although a stock may have value after a bankruptcy if there is the possibility that the debts of the company will be restructured.

Shareholders are considered by some to be a partial subset of stakeholders, which may include anyone who has a direct or indirect equity interest in the business entity or someone with even a non-pecuniary interest in a non-profit organization. Thus it might be common to call volunteer contributors to an association stakeholders, even though they are not shareholders.

Although directors and officers of a company are bound by fiduciary duties to act in the best interest of the shareholders, the shareholders themselves normally do not have such duties towards each other.

However, in a few unusual cases, some courts have been willing to imply such a duty between shareholders. For example, in California, majority shareholders of closely held corporations have a duty to not destroy the value of the shares held by minority shareholders.

The largest shareholders (in terms of percentages of companies owned) are often mutual funds, and especially passively managed exchange-traded funds.

Application: The owners of a company may want additional capital to invest in new projects within the company. They may also simply wish to reduce their holding, freeing up capital for their own private use.

By selling shares they can sell part or all of the company to many part-owners. The purchase of one share entitles the owner of that share to literally share in the ownership of the company a fraction of the decision-making power, and potentially a fraction of the profits, which the company may issue as dividends.

In the common case of a publicly traded corporation, where there may be thousands of shareholders, it is impractical to have all of them making the daily decisions required to run a company. Thus, the shareholders will use their shares as votes in the election of members of the board of directors of the company.

In a typical case, each share constitutes one vote (except in a cooperative society where every member gets one vote regardless of the number of shares he holds). Corporations may, however, issue different classes of shares, which may have different voting rights. Owning the majority of the shares allows other shareholders to be out-voted-effective control rests with the majority shareholder (or shareholders acting in concert). In this way the original owners of the company often still have control of the company.

Shareholder Rights

Although ownership of 51% of shares does result in 51% ownership of a company, it does not give the shareholder the right to use a company's building, equipment, materials, or other property. This is because the company is considered a legal person, thus it owns all its assets itself. This is important in areas such as insurance, which must be in the name of the company and not the main shareholder.

In most countries, including the United States, boards of directors and company managers have a fiduciary responsibility to run the company in the interests of its stockholders. Nonetheless, as Martin Whitman writes:

"...it can safely be stated that there does not exist any publicly traded company where management works exclusively in the best interests of OPMI [Outside Passive Minority Investor] stockholders. Instead, there are both "communities of interest" and "conflicts of interest" between stockholders (principal) and management (agent). This conflict is referred to as the principal/

agent problem. It would be naive to think that any management would forego management compensation, and management entrenchment, just because some of these management privileges might be perceived as giving rise to a conflict of interest with OPMIs." [Whitman, 2004; 5]

Even though the board of directors runs the company, the shareholder has some impact on the company's policy, as the shareholders elect the board of directors. Each shareholder typically has a percentage of votes equal to the percentage of shares he or she owns.

So as long as the shareholders agree that the management (agent) are performing poorly they can elect a new board of directors which can then hire a new management team. In practice, however, genuinely contested board elections are rare. Board candidates are usually nominated by insiders or by the board of the directors themselves, and a considerable amount of stock is held and voted by insiders.

Owning shares does not mean responsibility for liabilities. If a company goes broke and has to default on loans, the shareholders are not liable in any way. However, all money obtained by converting assets into cash will be used to repay loans and other debts first, so that shareholders cannot receive any money unless and until creditors have been paid (most often the shareholders end up with nothing).

Means of Financing

Financing a company through the sale of stock in a company is known as equity financing. Alternatively, debt financing (for example issuing bonds) can be done to avoid giving up shares of ownership of the company. Unofficial financing known as trade financing usually provides the major part of a company's working capital (day-to-day operational needs). Trade financing is provided by vendors and suppliers who sell their products to the company at short-term, unsecured credit terms, usually 30 days. Equity and debt financing are usually used for longer-term investment projects such as investments in a new factory or a new foreign market. Customer provided financing exists when a customer pays for services before they are delivered, e.g. subscriptions and insurance.

Trading: A stock exchange is an organization that provides a marketplace (either physical or virtual) for trading shares, where investors (represented by stock brokers) may buy and sell shares in a wide range of companies. A given company will usually list its shares by meeting and maintaining the listing requirements of a particular stock exchange. In the United States, through the inter-market quotation system, stocks listed on one exchange can also be bought or sold on several other exchanges, including relatively new internet-only exchanges. Stocks are broadly grouped into NYSE-listed and NASDAQ-listed stocks. Exchanges where NYSE-listed stocks may be bought are generally not the same group as the exchanges where NASDAQ-listed stocks may be bought. Many large foreign companies choose to list on a U.S. exchange as well as an exchange in their home country in order to broaden their investor base. These shares are called American Depository Receipts (ADRs)--or, in the case of companies such as UBS and Daimler Chrysler--"foreign ordinary shares."

Large U.S. companies also list in foreign exchanges for the same reason. Although it makes sense for some companies to raise capital by offering stock on more than one exchange, in today's era of electronic trading, there is limited opportunity for private investors to make profit on pricing discrepancies between one stock exchange and another. As such, arbitrage opportunities disappear quickly due to the efficient nature of the market.

Buying: There are various methods of buying and financing stocks. The most common means is through a stock broker. Whether they are a full service or discount broker, they arrange the transfer of stock from a seller to a buyer. Most trades are actually done through brokers listed with a stock exchange, such as the New York Stock Exchange.

There are many different stock brokers from which to choose, such as full service brokers or discount brokers. The full service brokers usually charge more per trade, but give investment advice or more personal service; the discount brokers offer little or no investment advice but charge less for trades. Another type of broker would be a bank or credit union that may have a deal set up with either a full service or discount broker.

There are other ways of buying stock besides through a broker. One way is directly from the company itself. If at least one share is owned, most companies will allow the purchase of shares directly from the company through their investor relations departments. However, the initial share of stock in the company will have to be obtained through a regular stock broker. Another way to buy stock in companies is through Direct Public Offerings which are usually sold by the company itself. A direct public offering is an initial public offering in which the stock is purchased directly from the company, usually without the aid of brokers.

When it comes to financing a purchase of stocks there are two ways: purchasing stock with money that is currently in the buyers ownership, or by buying stock on margin. Buying stock on margin means buying stock with money borrowed against the stocks in the same account. These stocks, or collateral, guarantee that the buyer can repay the loan; otherwise, the stockbroker has the right to sell the stock (collateral) to repay the borrowed money. He can sell if the share price drops below the margin requirement, at least 50% of the value of the stocks in the account. Buying on margin works the same way as borrowing money to buy a car or a house, using the car or house as collateral. Moreover, borrowing is not free; the broker usually charges 8-10% interest.

Selling: Selling stock is procedurally similar to buying stock. Generally, the investor wants to buy low and sell high, if not in that order (short selling); although a number of reasons may induce an investor to sell at a loss, e.g., to avoid further loss.

As with buying a stock, there is a transaction fee for the broker's efforts in arranging the transfer of stock from a seller to a buyer. This fee can be high or low depending on which type of brokerage, discount or full service, handles the transaction.

After the transaction has been made, the seller is then entitled to all of the money. An important part of selling is keeping track of the earnings. Importantly, on selling the stock, in jurisdictions that have them, capital gains taxes will have to be paid on the additional proceeds, if any, that are in excess of the cost basis.

Stock Price Fluctuation: The price of a stock fluctuates fundamentally due to the theory of supply and demand. Like all commodities in the market, the price of a stock is directly proportional to the demand. However, there are many factors on basis of which the demand for a particular stock may increase or decrease. These factors are studied using methods of fundamental analysis and technical analysis to predict the changes in the stock price.

Technology's Influence on Trading: Stock trading has evolved tremendously. Since the very first Initial Public Offering (IPO) in the 13th century, owning shares of a company has been a very attractive incentive. Even though the origins of stock trading go back to the 13th century, the market as we know it today did not catch on strongly until the late 1800s.

Co-production between technology and society has led the push for effective and efficient ways of trading. Technology has allowed the stock market to grow tremendously, and society has encouraged the growth. Within seconds of an order for a stock, the transaction can now take place. Most recent advancements with trading have been due to the Internet. The Internet has allowed online trading. In contrast to the past where only those who could afford expensive stockbrokers, anyone who wishes to be active in the stock market can now do so at a very low cost per transaction. Trading can even be done through Computer-Mediated Communication (CMC) use of mobile devices such as handled computers and cellular phones. These advances in technology have made day trading possible.

WARRANT (FINANCE)

A warrant is a security that entitles the holder to buy stock of the company that issued it at a specified price, which is much higher than the stock price at time of issue. Warrants are frequently attached to bonds or preferred stock as a sweetener, allowing the issuer to pay lower interest rates or dividends. Frequently, these warrants are detachable, and can be sold independently of the bond or stock. Warrants are much like call options, but the money goes to the issuer, not an option writer, and it initially has a lifespan of many years. When the warrant is exercised the company issues new shares of stock, so the number of outstanding shares increases. When a call is exercised, the owner of the call receives an existing share from an assigned call writer (except in the case of employee stock options, where new shares are created and issued by the company upon exercise). Unlike common stock shares outstanding, warrants do not have voting rights.

Sometimes the issuer will try to establish a market for the warrant and to register it with a listed exchange. In this case, the price can be obtained from a broker. But often, warrants are privately held or not registered, which makes their prices less obvious. Once the warrants are in the secondary market, they can then be traded just like a stock. Warrants can be easily tracked by adding a "w" after the company's ticker symbol to check the warrant's price.

Another difference between a warrant and an option is the duration of the contract. A warrant's lifetime is measured in years (as long as 15 years), while options are typically measured in months. Even LEAPS (long-term equity anticipation securities), the longest stock options available, tend to expire in two or three years. Upon expiration, the warrants are worthless if not exercised unless the price of the common stock is greater than the exercised price.

In many respects, options and warrants are functionally similar, except that warrants are not standardised like ASX-listed options. While investors can write stock options on the ASX, they are not permitted to do either with ASX-listed warrants, since only companies can issue warrants, and; while each option contract is over 100 underlying ordinary shares, the number of warrants that must be exercised by the holder to buy the underlying asset depends on the conversion ratio set out in the offer documentation for the warrant issue.

Types of Warrants

Traditional: Traditional warrants are issued in conjunction with a Bond (known as a warrant-linked bond), and represent the right to acquire shares in the entity issuing the bond. In other words, the writer of a traditional warrant is also the issuer of the underlying instrument. Warrants are issued in this way as a 'sweetener' to make the bond issue more attractive, and to reduce the interest rate that must be offered in order to sell the bond issue.

Naked: Naked warrants are issued without an accompanying bond, and like traditional warrants, are traded on the stock exchange. They are typically issued by banks and securities firms.

Government Issued: Also, when a government agency issues checks which they are unable to pay (due to lack of money) but are redeemable some point in the future, usually with interest, these are also called warrants. In the late 1990s, when the State of California had a budget crisis due to a disagreement between the governor and the legislature, the state treasurer was forced to issue warrants paying 18% interest in lieu of being able to pay the state's bills with real money. The state had not had to rely on this practice since before the Depression of the 1930s. Many institutions accepted them at face value because of the interest provision. It was interesting that during this period the Controller of Los Angeles County was buying state warrants to invest the county's surplus funds because the county, on the other hand, actually had money and the interest rate was better than any bank would pay.

In some U.S. states, a warrant is a demand draft drawn on a government's treasury to pay its bills. They are essentially checks (and are often referred to as such), but a different term is used as final payment is made by the treasurer instead of a bank. Checks or electronic payments have replaced these warrants, but in Arkansas the state, and some counties and school districts uses warrants for non-electronic payments.

BONDS BY COUPON

Fixed Rate Bond: Floating rate notes (FRNs) are bonds that have a variable coupon, equal to a money market reference rate, like LIBOR or federal funds rate, plus a spread. The spread is a rate that remains constant. Almost all FRNs have quarterly coupons, i.e. they pay out interest every three months, though counter examples do exist. At the beginning of each coupon period, the coupon is calculated by taking the fixing of the reference rate for that day and adding the spread. A typical coupon would look like 3 months USD LIBOR +0.20%.

Issuers: In the U.S., government sponsored enterprises (GSEs) such as the Federal Home Loan Banks, the Federal National Mortgage Association (Fannie Mae) and the Federal Home Loan Mortgage Corporation (Freddie Mac) are important issuers. In Europe the main issuers are banks.

Variations: Some FRNs have special features such as maximum or minimum coupons, called capped FRNs and floored FRNs. Those with both minimum and maximum coupons are called collared FRNs.

FRNs can also be obtained synthetically by the combination of a fixed rate bond and an interest rate swap. This combination is known as an Asset Swap.

Risk: FRNs carry little interest rate risk. If market rates rise, a fixed rate bond declines in value. However, the expected coupons of the FRN increase in line with the increase in forward rates. This means the price remains constant. As FRNs are almost immune to interest rate risk, they are considered conservative investments for investors who believe market rates will increase. The risk that remains is credit risk.

Trading: Securities dealers make markets in FRNs. They are traded over-the-counter, instead of on a stock exchange. In Europe, most FRNs are liquid, as the biggest investors are banks. In the US, FRNs are mostly held to maturity, so the markets aren't as liquid. In the wholesale markets, FRNs are typically quoted as a spread over the reference rate.

ZERO COUPON BOND

Zero coupon bonds are bonds which do not pay periodic interest payments, or so-called "coupons". Zero coupon bonds are purchased at a discount from their value at maturity. The holder of a zero coupon bond is entitled to receive a single payment, usually of a specified sum of money at a specified time in the future. Some zero coupon bonds are inflation indexed, so the amount of money that will be paid to the bond holder is calculated to have a set amount of purchasing power rather than a set amount of money, but the majority of zero coupon bonds pay a set amount of money known as the face value of the bond.

In contrast, an investor who has a regular bond receives income from coupon payments, which are usually made semi-annually. The investor also receives the principal or face value of the investment when the bond matures. Zero coupon bonds may be long or short term investments. Long-term zero coupon maturity dates typically start at ten to fifteen years. The bonds can be held until maturity or sold on secondary bond markets.

Short term zero coupon bond generally have maturities of less than one year and are called bills. The U.S. Treasury bill market is the most active and liquid debt market in the world.

STRIP BONDS

Investment bankers or dealers may separate the coupons from the bond principal, which is known as the residue, so that different investors may receive the principal and each of the coupon payments. This creates a supply of new zero coupon bonds.

The coupons and residue are sold separately to investors. Each of these investments then pays a single lump sum. This method of creating zero coupon bonds is known as stripping and the contracts are known as strip bonds. "STRIPS" stands for Separate Trading of Registered Interest and Principal Securities.

Dealers normally purchase a block of high-quality and non-callable bonds-often government issues-to create strip bonds. A strip bond has no reinvestment risk because the payment to the investor only occurs at maturity.

The impact of interest rate fluctuations on strip bonds, known as the bond duration, is higher than for a coupon bond. A zero coupon bond always has a duration equal to its maturity, a coupon bond always has a lower duration. Strip bonds are normally available from investment dealers maturing at terms up to 30 years. For some Canadian bonds the maturity may be over 90 years.

In Canada, investors may purchase packages of strip bonds, so that the cash flows are tailored to meet their needs in a single security. These packages may consist of a combination of interest (coupon) and/or principal strips.

In New Zealand, bonds are stripped first into two pieces-the coupons and the principal. The coupons may be traded as a unit or further subdivided into the individual payment dates.

In most countries, strip bonds are primarily administered by a central bank or central securities depository. An alternative form is to use a custodian bank or trust company to hold the underlying security and a transfer agent/registrar to track ownership in the strip bonds and to administer the program. Physically created strip bonds (where the coupons are physically clipped and then traded separately) were created in the early days of stripping in Canada and the U.S., but have virtually disappeared due to the high costs and risks associated with them.

Uses: Pension funds and insurance companies like to own long maturity zero coupon bonds because of the bonds' high duration. This high duration means that these bonds' prices are particularly sensitive to changes in the interest rate, and therefore offset, or immunize the interest rate risk of these firms' long-term liabilities.

Yield curve traders and academics use zero coupon bonds to precisely analyze the yield curve. Coupon bonds inherently mix different cash flows and interest rates, but by limiting cash flows to a single payment, zero coupon bonds enable analysts to separate out the effect of a single interest rate for each time period.

Taxes: In the United States, the holder may be liable for imputed income (sometimes called phantom income), even though these bonds don't pay periodic interest. Because of this, zero coupon bonds subject to U.S. taxation should generally be held in tax-deferred retirement accounts, to avoid paying taxes on future income. Alternatively, when purchasing a zero coupon bond issued by a U.S. state or local government entity, the imputed interest is free of U.S. federal taxes, and in most cases, state and local taxes, too.

INFLATION-INDEXED BOND

Inflation-indexed bonds (also known as linkers) are bonds whose principal are indexed to inflation, cutting out inflation risk. The first known inflation-indexed bond was issued by the Massachusetts Bay Company in 1780. The market has grown dramatically since the British government began issuing inflation-linked Gilts in 1981. Today, the asset class comprises over $500 Billion of the international debt market. The market primarily consists of sovereign debt, with privately issued inflation-linked bonds constituting a small portion of the market.

Underlying Mechanism

A common misconception about these bonds is that the interest rate changes with inflation. What actually happens is that the underlying principal of the bond changes, which results in a higher interest payment when multiplied by the same rate. For example, if the coupon of a bond was 5%, and the underlying principal of the bond was 100 units, the bond would pay 5 units, assuming annual payments. If the inflation index then increased by 10%, the principal of the bond would then increase to 110 units. This is multiplied by the same coupon rate of 5%, which results in an interest payment of 5.5 units. The only known exception to this is the Australian Capital Indexed Bond, which also adjusts the interest rate.

Global Issuance

Best known in the U.S. are Treasury Inflation-Protected Securities (TIPS), a type of US Treasury security. The UK also issues Index-linked Gilts. The Australian government stopped issuing the Capital Indexed Bond in 2003. The Australian bond was unique among inflation-linked bonds in that the rate of interest and the principal were both linked to inflation. France, Canada, Greece, Italy, Japan, and Sweden also issue Inflation Indexed Bonds.

3

Stock Exchange

A stock exchange, share market or bourse is a corporation or mutual organization which provides facilities for stock brokers and traders, to trade company stocks and other securities. Stock exchanges also provide facilities for the issue and redemption of securities, as well as, other financial instruments and capital events including the payment of income and dividends. The securities traded on a stock exchange include: shares issued by companies, unit trusts and other pooled investment products and bonds.

To be able to trade a security on a certain stock exchange, it has to be listed there. Usually there is a local & central location at least for record keeping, but trade is less and less linked to such a physical place, as modern markets are electronic networks, which gives them advantages of speed and cost of transactions. Trade on an exchange is by members only & stock & share holders. The initial offering of stocks and bonds to investors is by definition done in the primary market and subsequent trading is done in the secondary market. A stock exchange is often the most important component of a stock market. Supply and demand in stock markets is driven by various factors which, as in all free markets, affect the price of stocks.

There is usually no compulsion to issue stock via the stock exchange itself, nor must stock be subsequently traded on the exchange. Such trading is said to be off exchange or over-the-counter. This is the usual way that bonds are traded. Increasingly more and more stock exchanges are part of a global market for securities.

HISTORICAL BACKDROP

In 12th century France the courtiers de change were concerned with managing and regulating the debts of agricultural communities on behalf of the banks. As these men also traded in debts, they could be called the first brokers.

Some stories suggest that the origins of the term "bourse" come from the latin bursa meaning a bag because, in 13th century Bruges, the sign of a purse (or perhaps three purses), hung on the front of the house where merchants met.

However, it is more likely that in the late 13th century commodity traders in Bruges gathered inside the house of a man called Van der Burse, and in 1309 they institutionalized this until now informal meeting and became the "Bruges Bourse". The idea spread quickly around Flanders and neighbouring counties and "Bourses" soon opened in Ghent and Amsterdam.

In the middle of the 13th century Venetian bankers began to trade in government securities. In 1351 the Venetian Government outlawed spreading rumors intended to lower the price of government funds. There were people in Pisa, Verona, Genoa and Florence who also began trading in government securities during the 14th century. This was only possible because these were independent city states ruled by a council of influential citizens, not by a duke.

The Dutch later started joint stock companies, which let shareholders invest in business ventures and get a share of their profits-or losses. In 1602, the Dutch East India Company issued the first shares on the Amsterdam Stock Exchange. It was the first company to issue stocks and bonds.

Raising Capital for Businesses

The Stock Exchange provides companies with the facility to raise capital for expansion through selling shares to the investing public.

Mobilizing Savings for Investment

When people draw their savings and invest in shares, it leads to a more rational allocation of resources because funds, which could have been consumed, or kept in idle deposits with banks, are mobilized and redirected to promote business activity with benefits for several economic sectors such as agriculture, commerce and industry, resulting in a stronger economic growth and higher productivity levels.

Facilitating Company Growth

Companies view acquisitions as an opportunity to expand product lines, increase distribution channels, hedge against volatility, increase its market share, or acquire other necessary business assets. A takeover bid or a merger agreement through the stock market is one of the simplest and most common ways for a company to grow by acquisition or fusion.

Redistribution of Wealth

By giving a wide spectrum of people a chance to buy shares and therefore become part-owners (shareholders) of profitable enterprises, the stock market may help to reduce large income inequalities. However, capital losses may also happen. Both casual and professional stock investors through stock price increases and dividends get a chance to share in the profits of promising business that were set up by other people.

Corporate Governance

By having a wide and varied scope of owners, companies generally tend to improve on their management standards and efficiency in order to satisfy the demands of these shareholders and the more stringent rules for public corporations imposed by public stock exchanges and the government. Consequently, it is alleged that public companies (companies that are owned by shareholders who are members of the general public and trade shares on public exchanges) tend to have better management records than privately-held companies (those companies where shares are not publicly traded, often owned by the company founders and/or their families and heirs, or otherwise by a small group of investors). However, some well-documented cases are known where it is alleged that there has been considerable slippage in corporate governance on the part of some public companies (e.g. Enron Corporation, MCI WorldCom, Pets.com, Webvan, or Parmalat).

Creates Investment Opportunities for Small Investors

As opposed to other businesses that require huge capital outlay, investing in shares is open to both the large and small stock investors because a person buys the number of shares they can afford. Therefore the Stock Exchange provides the opportunity for small investors to own shares of the same companies as large investors, and to enjoy similar rates of return.

Government Raises Capital for Development Projects

Governments at various levels may decide to borrow money in order to finance infrastructure projects such as sewage and water treatment works or housing estates by selling another category of securities known as bonds. These bonds can be raised through the Stock Exchange whereby members of the public buy them, thus loaning money to the government. The issuance of such municipal bonds can obviate the need to directly tax the citizens in order to finance development, although by securing such bonds with the full faith and credit of the government instead of with collateral, the result is that the government must tax the citizens or otherwise raise additional funds to make any regular coupon payments and refund the principal when the bonds mature.

BAROMETER OF THE ECONOMY

At the stock exchange, share prices rise and fall depending, largely, on market forces. Share prices tend to rise or remain stable when companies and the economy in general show signs of stability and growth. An economic recession, depression, or financial crisis could eventually lead to a stock market crash. Therefore the movement of share prices and in general of the stock indexes can be an indicator of the general trend in the economy.

INTERNATIONAL STOCK EXCHANGES

The main stock exchanges in the world include:

- American Stock Exchange
- Australian Stock Exchange

- Bombay Stock Exchange
- Euronext
- Frankfurt Stock Exchange
- Helsinki Stock Exchange
- Hong Kong Stock Exchange
- Istanbul Stock Exchange
- JASDAQ
- Johannesburg Securities Exchange
- Karachi Stock Exchange
- Korea Stock Exchange
- London Stock Exchange
- Madrid Stock Exchange
- Milan Stock Exchange
- Nagoya Stock Exchange
- National Stock Exchange of India
- NASDAQ
- New York Stock Exchange
- Osaka Securities Exchange
- São Paulo Stock Exchange
- Shanghai Stock Exchange
- Singapore Exchange
- Stockholm Stock Exchange
- Taiwan Stock Exchange
- Tokyo Stock Exchange
- Toronto Stock Exchange
- Zurich Stock Exchange

LISTING REQUIREMENTS

The listing requirements are the set of conditions imposed by a given stock exchange upon companies that want to be listed on that exchange. Such conditions sometimes include minimum number of shares outstanding, minimum market capitalization, and minimum annual income.

Requirements by Stock Exchange

Companies have to meet the requirements of the exchange in order to have their stocks and shares listed and traded there, but requirements vary by stock exchange:

- *London Stock Exchange:* The main market of the London Stock Exchange has requirements for a minimum market capitalization (£700,000), three years of audited financial statements, minimum public float (25 per cent) and sufficient working capital for at least 12 months from the date of listing.
- *NASDAQ Stock Exchange:* To be listed on the NASDAQ a company must have issued at least 1.25 million shares of stock worth at least $70 million and must have earned more than $11 million over the last three years .
- *New York Stock Exchange:* To be listed on the New York Stock Exchange (NYSE), for example, a company must have issued at least a million shares of stock worth $100 million and must have earned more than $10 million over the last three years .

Ownership: Stock exchanges originated as mutual organizations, owned by its member stock brokers. There has been a recent trend for stock exchanges to demutualize, where the members sell their shares in an initial public offering. In this way the mutual organization becomes a corporation, with shares that are listed on a stock exchange. Examples are Australian Stock Exchange (1998), Euronext (2000, as of 14 June 2006 in talks to a proposed merger process with the New York Stock Exchange), NASDAQ (2002) and the New York Stock Exchange (2005).

OTHER TYPES OF EXCHANGE

In the 19th century, exchanges were opened to trade forward contracts on commodities. Exchange traded forward contracts are called futures contracts. These commodity exchanges later started offering future contracts on other products, such as interest rates and shares, as well as options contracts. They are now generally known as futures exchanges.

The Future of Stock Exchanges

The future of stock trading is electronic, seemingly pitting the remaining traditional New York Stock Exchange specialist system against the relatively new, all Electronic Communications Networks, or ECNs. ECNs extol their speedy execution of large block trades, while specialist system proponents cite the role of specialists in maintaining orderly markets, especially under extraordinary conditions or for special types of orders.

The ECNs contend an array of special interests profits at the expense of investors from even the most mundane exchange-directed trades. Machine-based systems, on the other hand, are said to be much more efficient, improving the traditional execution mechanism and eliminating the requirement of dealing with an intermediary.

Historically, the 'market' (which, as noted, encompasses the totality of stock trading on all exchanges) has been slow to respond to technological innovation. Conversion to all-electronic trading could erode/eliminate the trading profits of floor specialists and the NYSE's "upstairs traders."

"I'd definitely say the ECNs are winning," declares William Lupien, founder of the Instinet trading system and the OptiMark system. "Things happen awfully fast once you reach the tipping point. We're now at the tipping point."

Congress mandated the establishment of a national market system of multiple exchanges in 1975. Since then, the 'electronic communications networks' have been developing rapidly.

Electronic networks, by executing large trades at lightning speed, reduce the possibility of front running, or trading ahead of a customer's order, an illegal practice for which several NYSE floor brokers were investigated and severely fined in recent years. Under the specialist system, when the market sees a large trade in a name, other buyers are immediately able to look to see how big the trader is in the name, and make inferences about why s/he is selling or buying. That is how the

Street anticipates price action. ECNs have changed ordinary stock transaction processing (like brokerage services before them) into a commodity-type business. ECNs could regulate the fairness of initial public offerings (IPOs), oversee Hambrecht's OpenIPO process, or measure the effectiveness of securities research and use transaction fees to subsidize small- and mid-cap research efforts.

Some, however, believe the answer will be some combination of the best of technology and "upstairs trading"-in other words, a hybrid model.

Trading 25,000 shares of Lucent stock (recent quote: $2.80; recent volume: 49,069,700) would be a relatively simple e-commerce transaction; trading 100 shares of Berkshire Hathaway Class A stock (recent quote: $88,710.00; recent volume: 450) may never be. The choice of system should be clear (but always that of the trader), based on the characteristics of the security to be traded.

Even with ECNs forming an important part of a national market system, opportunities presumably remain to profit from the spread between the bid and offer price. That is especially true for investment managers that direct huge trading volume, and own a stake in an ECN or specialist firm. For example, in its individual stock-brokerage accounts, Fidelity Investments runs 29% of its undesignated orders in NYSE-listed stocks, and 37% of its undesignated market orders through the Boston Stock Exchange, where an affiliate controls a specialist post.

Fidelity says these arrangements are governed by a separate brokerage "order-flow management" team, which seeks to obtain the best possible execution for customers, and that its execution is highly rated.

The "Upstairs Market"

Recent research by Kumar Venkataraman, finance professor at SMU's Cox School of Business, and Hendrik Bessembinder offers insight and evidence into new possibilities and difficult issues facing stock exchanges. In "Does an electronic stock exchange need an upstairs market?" from the July, 2003 issue of Journal of Financial Economics, the authors find that a large proportion of institutional trading in electronic exchanges is executed away from the centralized book in the informal 'upstairs market', thus presenting new challenges.

Despite the efficiencies of computerized markets, virtually every stock market is accompanied by a parallel "upstairs" market, where larger traders employ the services of brokerage firms to locate counterparties and negotiate trade terms. Upstairs markets are based on relationships. Rather than submitting an electronic order to effortlessly attract counterparties, the upstairs brokers seek out counterparties (from traders known to them who might be interested). They then negotiate transactions that might otherwise be executed at an inordinate cost or delay. An electronic trading system lowers the fixed costs of trading for relatively liquid stocks in block sizes not likely to overwhelm the current market. However, it does not allow for the informal exchange of information (?) that is important for certain types of large trades and for illiquid stocks.

In electronic markets, traders don't get a sense of who they're trading with, how much more the other party is trading, etc., and that information can be very important to some traders. Large (institutional) traders therefore seek other trading venues such as the 'upstairs market' to lower the risk of exposing their order positions, to ensure symmetric transfer of information, and to retain some of the give and take of the old open outcry market. Approximately 70% of block-size trade transactions are executed in the upstairs market in Paris.

The Paris Bourse provides an excellent illustration of the use of upstairs intermediation markets, because its electronic limit order market closely resembles the downstairs (electronic) markets envisioned by theorists. The best evidence from the Paris Bourse is that:

(1) Upstairs brokers lower the risk of adverse selection by "certifying" block orders as uninformed (i.e., as not having access to nonpublic information).

(2) Upstairs brokers are able to tap into pools of hidden or unexpressed liquidity (they frequently 'go looking' for buyers or sellers not currently in the market).

(3) Traders strategically choose across the upstairs and downstairs markets to minimize expected execution costs (including slippage, etc.).

(4) Trades are more likely to be routed upstairs if they are large or are in stocks with low overall trading activity.

The second result is the most novel and arguably the most important. The upstairs broker completes transactions by searching for institutional investors who may be interested in the stock, but who have not as yet formally expressed their trading intentions. It is documented that executions costs of transactions completed by the upstairs broker average only 35% of what they would have paid if completed against limit orders in the centralized electronic exchange, suggesting that trading relationship and the informal exchange of information between upstairs brokers and institutional traders helps lower execution costs. One major challenge facing electronic markets is the lack of a comparable mechanism of certification of traders and information exchange.

The Euronext market allows large transactions in some stocks to be executed outside the quotes. Such outside-the-quote transactions are not permitted in United States markets. For eligible stocks in Paris, market participants agree to outside-the-quote execution mainly for more difficult trades and at times when downstairs liquidity is lacking. These likely represent trades that probably could not have been otherwise completed, suggesting that market quality can be enhanced by allowing participants more flexibility to execute blocks at prices outside the quotes. These findings are particularly relevant to U.S. markets because quoted spreads and depths have decreased substantially in the wake of decimalization.

The upstairs market in the Paris Bourse completes two-thirds of block trading volume, compared with 20% on the New York Stock Exchange (NYSE). A likely explanation is that the NYSE floor allows large traders to execute customized strategies through a floor broker, while avoiding the risks of order exposure. If orders submitted to electronic markets do not allow block initiators to limit order exposure and trade strategically, then order flow is likely to migrate to alternative trading venues such as the upstairs market. If you're a liquidity trader, you don't want the system to be anonymous. If you're an informed trader you like anonymity because you can hide in the order flow.

To compete with broker-intermediated markets, the next generation of electronic trading systems needs to include features that better meet the needs of large traders, particularly the lack of anonymity. To allow large investors to manage order exposure in an electronic exchange, a wider range of order types that include state contingent exposure and execution algorithms need to be made available. The NYSE's recently introduced "Conversion and Parity" (CAP) orders which are intended to be "smart" orders for large lots of stocks that are executed gradually through the day, contingent on market conditions, are a step in this direction.

The Future Role of the Specialist

The specialist trades in circumstances when others do not or will not, and therefore takes on a risk which warrants compensation. The current debate centers on the model of compensation. The specialist at the Paris Bourse is compensated in cash and with investment banking business. In contrast, the NYSE specialist is compensated in the form of privileged information on order flow. In recent months, several U.S. institutions have alleged that the NYSE trading abuses is an outcome of this compensation structure. The Paris model overcomes this criticism and presents an alternative for the NYSE to consider. Results show, however, that there continues to be a role for the specialist (or, at least, an 'upstairs trader') in electronic markets. Investors value the presence of a specialist because they can get in and out of a stock with greater ease.

4

Management

The term "management" characterizes the process of and/ or the personnel leading and directing all or part of an organization (often a business) through the deployment and manipulation of resources (human, capital, natural, intellectual or intangible). According to the Oxford English Dictionary, the word "manage" comes from the Italian maneggiare (to handle-especially a horse), which in turn derives from the Latin manus (hand). The French word management (later management) influenced the development in meaning of the English word management in the 17th and 18th centuries.

Management has to do with power by position, whereas leadership involves power by influence.

FUNCTIONS OF MANAGEMENT

Management operates through various functions, often classified as planning, organizing, leading/motivating and controlling.

- *Planning:* deciding what has to happen in the future (today, next week, next month, next year, over the next five years, etc.) and generating plans for action.
- *Organizing:* making optimum use of the resources required to enable the successful carrying out of plans.
- *Leading / Motivating:* exhibiting skills in these areas for getting others to play an effective part in achieving plans.
- *Controlling:* monitoring-checking progress against plans, which may need modification based on feedback.

THEORETICAL SCOPE

Mary Parker Follett (1868-1933), who wrote on the topic in the early twentieth-century, defined management as "the art of getting things done through people". One can also think of management functionally, as the action of measuring a quantity on a regular basis and of adjusting some initial plan; or as the actions taken to reach one's intended goal. This applies even in situations where planning does not take place. From this perspective, Frenchman Henri Fayol considers management consists of five functions:

1. planning
2. organizing
3. leading
4. coordinating
5. controlling

Some people, however, find this definition, while useful, far too narrow. The phrase "management is what managers do" occurs widely, suggesting the difficulty of defining management, the shifting nature of definitions, and the connection of managerial practices with the existence of a managerial cadre or class.

One habit of thought regards management as equivalent to "business administration", although this then excludes management in places outside commerce, as for example in charities and in the public sector. Nonetheless, university departments which teach management usually get called "business schools".

Speakers of English may also use the term "management" or "the management" as a collective word describing the managers of an organization, for example of a corporation.

HISTORICAL DEVELOPMENT

Difficulties arise in tracing the history of management. Some see it (by definition) as a late modern (in the sense of late modernity) conceptualization. On those terms it cannot have a pre-modern history, only harbingers. Others, however, detect management-like activities in the pre-modern past. Some writers trace the development of management-thought back to Sumerian traders and to the builders of the pyramids of ancient Egypt. Slave-owners through the centuries faced the problems of exploiting/motivating a dependent but sometimes unenthusiastic or recalcitrant workforce, but many pre-industrial enterprises, given their small scale, did not feel compelled to face the issues of management systematically. However, innovations such as the spread of Hindu-Arabic numerals (5th to 15th centuries) and the codification of double-entry bookkeeping (1494) provided tools for management assessment, planning and control.

Given the scale of most commercial operations and the lack of mechanized record-keeping and recording before the industrial revolution, it made sense for most owners of enterprises in those times to carry out management functions by and for themselves. But with growing size and complexity of organizations, the split between owners (individuals, industrial dynasties or groups of shareholders) and day-to-day managers (independent specialists in planning and control) gradually became more common.

19th Century

Some argue that modern management as a discipline began as an off-shoot of economics in the 19th century. Classical economists such as Adam Smith (1723-1790) and John Stuart Mill (1806-1873) provided a theoretical background to resource-allocation, production, and pricing issues. About the same time, innovators like Eli Whitney (1765-1825), James Watt (1736-1819), and Matthew Boulton (1728-1809) developed elements of technical production such as standardization, quality-control procedures, cost-accounting, interchangeability of parts, and work-planning. Many of these aspects of management existed in the pre-1861 slave-based sector of the US economy. That environment saw 4 million people, as the contemporary usages had it, "managed" in profitable quasi-mass production.

By the late 19th century, marginal economists Alfred Marshall (1842-1924) and Léon Walras (1834-1910) and others introduced a new layer of complexity to the theoretical underpinnings of management. Joseph Wharton offered the first tertiary-level course in management in 1881.

20th Century

By about 1900 one finds managers trying to place their theories on what they regarded as a thoroughly scientific basis. Examples include Henry Towne's Science of management in the 1890s, Frederick Winslow Taylor's Scientific management (1911), Frank and Lillian Gilbreth's Applied motion study (1917), and Henry L. Gantt's charts (1910s). J. Duncan wrote the first college management textbook in 1911. In 1912 Yoichi Ueno introduced Taylorism to Japan and became first management consultant of the "Japanese-management style". His son Ichiro Ueno pioneered Japanese quality-assurance.

The first comprehensive theories of management appeared around 1920. People like Henri Fayol (1841-1925) and Alexander Church described the various branches of management and their inter-relationships. In the early 20th century, people like Ordway Tead (1891-1973), Walter Scott and J. Mooney applied the principles of psychology to management, while other writers, such as Elton Mayo (1880-1949), Mary Parker Follett (1868-1933), Chester Barnard (1886-1961), Max Weber (1864-1920), Rensis Likert (1903-1981), and Chris Argyris (1923-) approached the phenomenon of management from a sociological perspective.

Peter Drucker (1909-2005) wrote one of the earliest books on applied management: Concept of the Corporation (published in 1946). It resulted from Alfred Sloan (chairman of General Motors until 1956) commissioning a study of the organisation. Drucker went on to write 39 books, many in the same vein.

H. Dodge, Ronald Fisher (1890-1962), and Thornton C. Fry introduced statistical techniques into management-studies. In the 1940s, Patrick Blackett combined these statistical theories with microeconomic theory and gave birth to the science of operations research. Operations research, sometimes known as "management science", not to be confused with Taylor's Scientific Management, attempts to take a scientific approach to solving management problems, particularly in the areas of logistics and operations.

Some of the more recent developments include the theory of constraints, management by objectives, reengineering, and various information-technology-driven theories such as agile software development, as well as group management theories such as Cog's Ladder.

As the general recognition of managers as a class solidified during the 20th century and gave perceived practitioners of the art/science of management a certain amount of prestige, so the way opened for popularised systems of management ideas to peddle their wares. In this context many management fads may have had more to do with pop psychology than with scientific theories of management. Towards the end of the 20th century, business management came to consist of six separate branches, namely:

- Human resource management
- Operations management or production management
- Strategic management
- Marketing management
- Financial management
- Information technology management responsible for management information systems

21st Century

In the 21st century observers find it increasingly difficult to subdivide management into functional categories in this way. More and more processes simultaneously involve several categories. Instead, one tends to think in terms of the various processes, tasks, and objects subject to management. A list of some of the areas of management appears later in this article.

Branches of management theory also exist relating to nonprofits and to government: such as public administration, public management, and educational management. Further, management programs related to civil-society organizations have also spawned programs in nonprofit management and social entrepreneurship.

Note that many of the assumptions made by management have come under attack from business ethics viewpoints, critical management studies, and anti-corporate activism. As one consequence, workplace democracy has become both more common, and more advocated, in some places distributing all management functions among the workers, each of whom takes on a portion of the work. However, these models predate any current political issue, and may occur more naturally than does a command hierarchy.

All management to some degree embraces democratic principles in that in the long term workers must give majority support to management; otherwise they leave to find other work, or go on strike. Hence management has started to become less based on the conceptualisation of classical military command-and-control, and more about facilitation and support of collaborative activity, utilizing principles such as those of human interaction management to deal with the complexities of human interaction. Indeed, the concept of Ubiquitous command-and-control posits such a transformation for 21st century military management.

NATURE OF MANAGERIAL WORK

In for-profit work, management has as its primary function the satisfaction of a range of stakeholders. This typically involves making a profit (for the shareholders), creating valued products at a reasonable cost (for customers), and providing rewarding employment opportunities (for employees). In nonprofit management, add the importance of keeping the faith of donors. In most models of management/governance, shareholders vote for the board of directors, and the board then hires senior management. Some organizations have experimented with other methods (such as employee-voting models) of selecting or reviewing managers; but this occurs only very rarely.

In the public sector of countries constituted as representative democracies, voters elect politicians to public office. Such politicians hire many managers and administrators, and in some countries like the United States political appointees lose their jobs on the election of a new president/governor/mayor. Some 2500 people serve at the pleasure of the United States Chief Executive, including all of the top US government executives.

Public, private, and voluntary sectors place different demands on managers, but all must retain the faith of those who select them (if they wish to retain their jobs), retain the faith of those people that fund the organization, and retain the faith of those who work for the organization. If they fail to convince employees of the advantages of staying rather than leaving, they may tip the organization into a downward spiral of hiring, training, firing, and recruiting. Management also has the task of innovating and of improving the functioning of organizations.

THE IMPORTANCE OF CONTROL

At least two perspectives on role of control exist:

1. Top management expects to control everything, making all decisions, while middle and lower managers implement decisions, and production workers operate only as instructed
2. Top management does not decide the "right" way to do something, and lower-level staff become involved in decision-making processes.

Managerial Levels/hierarchy: The management of a large organisation may have three levels:

1. Senior management (or "top management" or "upper management")
2. Middle management
3. Low-level management (compare "team leadership")

Compare Harrington Emerson's distinction between "staff management" and "line management".

ACCOUNTING MANAGEMENT

Accounting Management (Business) is the practical application of management techniques to control and report on the financial health of the organization. This involves the analysis, planning, implementation, and control of programs designed to provide financial data reporting for managerial decision making. This includes the maintenance of bank accounts, developing financial statements, cash flow and financial performance analysis. Accounting management is a mandatory knowledge module of any MBA program.

Accounting (IT) management: Accounting is often referred to as billing management. The goal is to gather usage statistics for users.

Using the statistics the users can be billed and usage quota can be enforced.

Examples:

- Disk usage
- Link utilisation
- CPU time

RADIUS, TACACS and DIAMETER are examples of protocols commonly used for accounting.

For non-billed networks, 'Administration' replaces 'Accounting'. The goals of Administration is to administer the set of authorized users, by establishing users, passwords and permissions; and to administer the operations of the equipment such as by performing software backup and synchronization.

COMMUNICATIONS MANAGEMENT

Communications management is the systematic planning, implementing, monitoring, and revision of all the channels of communication within an organization, and between organizations; it also includes the organization and dissemination of new communication directives connected with an organization, network, or communications technology. Aspects of communications management include developing corporate communication strategies, designing internal and external communications directives, and managing the flow of information, including online communication. New technology forces constant innovation on the part of communications managers.

Introduction: Effective organizational communications are an essential precondition of effective management--without effective communication, management becomes difficult or impossible. Organizations with more than one level of management suffer from communications problems that can interfere with almost any aspect of the organization, including corrective actions.

The purpose of communications management is to ensure that both managers and workers have access to the same information. Theoretically, all parties will be able to agree on the tasks to improve the organization, and everyone will work together in a more coordinated fashion; in practice, the same incentives must apply to both managers and workers, or else groups with differing incentives will develop different goals, negating the effect of the shared information.

One of the simplest and most practical communications management methods is a straightforward, hierarchical, bidirectional communication method, with clear incentives.

ROLES OF COMMUNICATIONS MANAGERS

Communications managers:

- Design of organizational communications structures
- Define communications principles and standards
- Formulate the communications goals of the organization
- Manage and monitor information flows
- Organize crisis communications
- Implement communications strategies
- Research the communications context
- Resonance analysis of team networks
- Organize communications training for staff
- Provide corporate presentations to publics, media and cybernetic space

THE WEEKLY REPORTING METHOD

One simple and popular communications method is called the weekly reporting method: every employee composes an e-mail report, once a week, including information on their activities in the preceding week, their plans for the following week, and any other information deemed relevant to the larger group, bearing in mind length considerations. Reports are sent to managers, who summarize and report to their own managers, eventually leading to an overall summary led by the CEO, which is then sent to the board of directors. The CEO then sends the board's summary back down the ladder, where each manager can append an additional summary or note before referring it to their employees.

Eventually, each employee will receive a long e-mail, containing many or all of the above-mentioned summaries, from every level of management; reading the full result is rarely a requirement. Curious or ambitious employees are considered more likely to read the result; task-centered employees, however, are not.

Examples of the Weekly reporting Method

At Printronix (NASDAQ PTNX), a $100 manufacturing organization with five levels of management, this was applied starting in 1990. Within a week, the perennial grumbles about "bad communication" ceased. By 1994 the organization had reduced total floorspace by 40% (eventually 75%), had "found" $100m of cash, reduced backlog from 3 months to 3.5 weeks, reduced product development time (for computer printers, a complex product) from three years to six months, and doubled product service life (greatly reducing the total cost of ownership of their product). This was achieved by a series of employee-initiated, management-led activities: adoption of just-in-time manufacturing, statistical process control, corrections of product weaknesses, and a cross-product "printer architecture" permitting development of "design modules" that could be mixed and matched for niche markets.

All of the programs arose via the reporting structure, making them visible to upper management, who were then free to support proposals they felt made sense.

Another cross-hierarchical system with similar traits arose at Warburg's Bank. According to Jacques Attali's biography, Warburg used a sheet of one-to-four-line summaries of each possible new loan, on a few sheets that were copied through the entire bank each day. It spanned the entire hierarchy, and anyone with comments was asked to bring them. Warburg's grew from 16,000 pounds, to 4 billion pounds under management in less than forty years.

COST MANAGEMENT

Cost management is the process whereby companies use cost accounting to report or control the various costs of doing business.

The term CM is widely used in business today. Unfortunately there is no uniform definition. We use CM to describe the approaches and activities of managers in short run and long run planning and control decisions that increase value for customers and lower costs of products and services. For example, managers make decisions regarding the amount and kind of material being used, changes of plant processes, and changes in product designs. Information from accounting systems helps managers make such decisions, but the information and the accounting systems themselves are not cost management.

Cost management has a broad focus. It includes-but is not confined to-the continuous reduction of costs. The planning and control of costs is usually inextricably linked with revenue and profit planning. For instance, to enhance revenues and profits, managers often deliberately incur additional costs for advertising and product modifications.

Cost management is not practiced in isolation. It's an integral part of general management strategies and their implementation. Examples include programmes that enhance customer satisfaction and quality as well as programmes that promote blockbuster new product development.

CRISIS MANAGEMENT

Crisis management involves identifying a crisis, planning a response to the crisis and confronting and resolving the crisis. Crisis management can be applied in almost any field of endeavor, but it is most commonly used in international relations, political science, business and management.

Many school districts have developed crisis response guides, which identify potential situations such as fires and other disasters, bomb threats, confronting unwelcome visitors, violence (and threats thereof) and the death of a student. In general terms, the theory of crisis management can be divided into crisis bargaining and negotiation, crisis decision making, and crisis dynamics.

In Management

In business there are three main types of crisis:

- Financial crisis-short term liquidity or cash flow problems; and long term bankruptcy problems
- Public relations crisis-More commonly called "crisis communications," negative publicity that could adversely affect the success of the company
- Strategic crisis-changes in the business environment that call the viability of the company into question-for example the introduction of the automobile was a strategic crisis for buggy-whip manufacturers

Certain preliminary measures need to be taken to prevent a crisis. Companies should always plan ahead and project likely outcomes. They should avoid decisions that have the potential to turn into a crisis. They shculd know their "worst case scenarios" and have a contingency plan for it. If prevention has not been successful, then the following six steps should be undertaken immediately:

- Do an objective assessment of the cause(s) of the crisis.
- Determine whether the cause(s) will have a long term effect or whether it will be a short term phenomena.
- Project the most likely course of events.
- Focus all the most capable people (including yourself) on activities that will mitigate or eliminate the problem.
- Look for opportunities-there could be a "silver lining".
- Immediately act to guard cash flow.

If it is a cashflow crisis do not wait for further evidence before acting. Immediately take actions to maintain or increase cash flow. These could include:

- accelerating accounts receivable payments even if this requires the granting of discounts

- decelerating accounts payable payments even if this means losing discounts
- increasing short term sales
- maintaining or increasing profit margins on sales if possible
- reducing expenses:
  - o eliminating non-essential expenses
  - o selling non-mission critical assets
  - o reducing payroll
  - o outsourcing non-mission critical operations
- renegotiating loans and other debts wherever possible-obtaining interest-only loans or extended payment terms

If it is a public relations crisis, act immediately to prevent or counter the spread of the negative information. Containment may require intense media activities. Use every media available to you to provide a counter argument or question the credibility of the original negative publicity.

EMERGENCY MANAGEMENT

Emergency management (or disaster management) is the discipline dealing with and avoiding risks. It is a discipline that involves preparing, supporting, and rebuilding society when natural or man-made disasters occur. Emergency management is the continuous process by which all individuals, groups, and communities manage hazards in an effort to avoid or ameliorate the impact of disasters resulting from the hazards. Actions taken depend in part on perceptions of risk of those exposed. Effective emergency management relies on thorough integration of emergency plans at all levels of government and non-government involvement. Activities at each level (individual, group, community) affect the other levels. It is common to place the responsibility for governmental emergency management with the institutions for civil defense or within the conventional structure of the emergency services. In the private sector, emergency management is commonly referred to as business continuity management.

PHASES AND PROFESSIONAL ACTIVITIES

The process of emergency management involves four phases: mitigation, preparedness, response, and recovery.

Mitigation: Mitigation efforts attempt to prevent hazards from developing into disasters altogether, or to reduce the effects of disasters when they occur. The mitigation phase differs from the other phases because it focuses on long-term measures for reducing or eliminating risk. The implementation of mitigation strategies can be considered a part of the recovery process if applied after a disaster occurs. However, even if applied as part of recovery efforts, actions that reduce or eliminate risk over time are still considered mitigation efforts.

Mitigative measures can be structural or non-structural. Structural measures use technological solutions, like flood levees. Non-structural measures include legislation, land-use planning (e.g. the designation of nonessential land like parks to be used as flood zones), and insurance. Mitigation is the most cost-efficient method for reducing the impact of hazards. However, mitigation is not always suitable and structural mitigation in particular may have adverse effects on the ecosystem. A precursor activity to the mitigation is the identification of risks. Physical risk assessment refers to the process of identifying and evaluating hazards. In risk assessment, various hazards (e.g. earthquakes, floods, riots) within a certain area are identified. Each hazard poses a risk to the population within the area assessed. The hazard-specific risk (Rh) combines both the probability and the level of impact of a specific hazard. The equation below gives that the hazard times the populations' vulnerability to that hazard produce a risk. Catastrophe modeling tools are used to support the calculation. The higher the risk, the more urgent that the hazard specific vulnerabilities are targeted by mitigation and preparedness efforts. However, if there is no vulnerability there will be no risk, e.g. an earthquake occurring in a desert where nobody lives.

Preparedness

In the preparedness phase, emergency managers develop plans of action for when the disaster strikes. Common preparedness measures include the proper maintenance and training of emergency services, the development and exercise of emergency population warning methods combined with emergency shelters and evacuation plans, the stockpiling, inventory, and maintenance of supplies and equipment, and the development and practice of multi-agency coordination. An efficient preparedness measure is an emergency operations center (EOC) combined with a practiced region-wide doctrine for managing emergencies. Another preparedness measure is to develop a volunteer response capability among civilian populations.

Response

The response phase includes the mobilization of the necessary emergency services and first responders in the disaster area, such as firefighters, police, volunteers, and non-governmental organizations (NGOs) such as Oxfam or the Caritas Network. A well rehearsed emergency plan developed as part of the preparedness phase enables efficient coordination of rescue efforts. Emergency plan rehearsal is essential to achieve optimal output with limited resources. In the response phase, medical assets will be used in accordance with the appropriate triage of the affected victims.

Where required, search and rescue efforts commence at an early stage. Depending on injuries sustained by the victim, outside temperature, and victim access to air and water, the vast majority of those affected by a disaster will die within 72 hours after impact.

Individuals are often compelled to volunteer directly after a disaster. Volunteers can be both a help and a hindrance to emergency management and other relief agencies. A spontaneous, unaffiliated volunteer is one type that can harm recovery efforts.

Recovery

The aim of the recovery phase is to restore the affected area to its previous state. It differs from the response phase in its focus; recovery efforts are concerned with issues and decisions that must be made after immediate needs are addressed.

Recovery efforts are primarily concerned with actions that involve rebuilding destroyed property, re-employment, and the repair of other essential infrastructure. An important aspect of effective recovery efforts is taking advantage of a 'window of opportunity' for the implementation of mitigative measures that might otherwise be unpopular. Citizens of the affected area are more likely to accept more mitigative changes when a recent disaster is in fresh memory.

In the United States, the National Response Plan dictates how the resources provided by the Homeland Security Act of 2002 will be used in recovery efforts. It is the Federal government that often provides the most technical and financial assistance for recovery efforts in the United States.

PHASES AND PERSONAL ACTIVITIES

Mitigation: Personal mitigation is mainly about knowing and avoiding unnecessary risks. This includes an assessment of possible risks to personal/family health and to personal property.

An example of personal non-structural mitigation would be to avoid buying property that is exposed to hazards, e.g. in a flood plain, in areas of subsidence or landslides. Homeowners may not be aware of their home being exposed to a hazard until it strikes. Real-estate agents may not come forward with such information. However, specialists can be hired to conduct risk assessment surveys. Insurance covering the most prominent identified risks are a common measure.

Personal structural mitigation in earthquake prone areas include installation of an Earthquake Valve to instantly shut off the natural gas supply to your property, seismic retrofits of property and the securing of items inside the building to enhance household seismic safety such as the mounting of furniture, refrigerators, water heaters and breakables to the walls, and the addition of cabinet latches. In flood prone areas houses can be built on poles, like in much of southern Asia. In areas prone to prolonged electricity black-outs a generator would be an example of an optimal structural mitigation measure. The construction of storm cellars and fallout shelters are further examples of personal mitigative actions.

Preparedness: On the contrary to mitigation activities which are aimed at preventing a disaster from occurring, personal preparedness are targeted on preparing activities to be taken when a disaster occurs, i.e. planning. Preparedness measures can take many forms. Examples include the construction of shelters, warning devices, back-up life-line services (e.g. power, water, sewage), and rehearsing an evacuation plan. Two simple measures prepare you for either sitting out the event or evacuating. For evacuation, a disaster supplies kit should be prepared and for sheltering purposes a stockpile of supplies.

Response: The response phase of an emergency may commence with a search and rescue phase. However in all cases the focus will be on fulfilling the basic needs of the affected population on a humanitarian basis. This assistance may be provided by national and/or international agencies and organisations. Effective coordination of disaster assistance is often crucial particularly when many organisations respond and local emergency management agency (LEMA) capacity may be over-stretched and diminished by the disaster itself.

On a personal level the response can take the shape either of a home confinement or an evacuation. In a home confinement scenario a family should be prepared to fend for themselves in their home for many days without any form of outside support. In an evacuation scenario, a family evacuates by an automobile (or other mode of transportation) with the maximum amount of supplies, including a tent for shelter. The scenario could also include equipment for evacuation on foot with at least three days of supplies and rain-tight bedding a tarpaulin and a bedroll of blankets is the minimum.

Recovery: The recovery phase starts when the immediate threat to human life has subsided. In the reconstruction it is recommended to reconsider the location or construction material of the property.

In long term disasters the most extreme home confinement scenarios like war, famine and severe epidemics last up to a year. In this situation the recovery will take place inside the home. Planners for these usually buy bulk foods and appropriate storage and preparation equipment, and eat the food as part of normal life. A simple balanced diet can be constructed from vitamin pills, whole-meal wheat, beans, dried milk, corn, and cooking oil. One should add vegetables, fruits, spices and meats, both prepared and fresh-gardened, when possible.

Profession: Emergency managers are trained in a wide variety of disciplines that support them through out the emergency life-cycle. Professional emergency managers can focus on government and community preparedness (Continuity of Operations/Continuity of Government Planning), or private business preparedness (Business Continuity Management Planning). Training is provided by local, state, federal and private organizations. It ranges from public information and media relations to high-level incident command and tactical skills such as studying a terrorist bombing site or controlling an emergency scene.

In the past, the field of emergency management has been limited to mostly men from a military or first responder background. Currently, the field is as diverse as any with many experts from a variety of backgrounds with no military or first responder history at all. Educational opportunities are increasing for those seeking undergraduate and graduate degrees in emergency management or a related field.

Professional accreditation standards are increasing as well. Such professional certificates as the Certified Emergency Manager (CEM) and Certified Business Continuity Professional (CBCP) are becoming more common place as the need for high professional standards is recognized and accepted by the emergency management community.

INTERNATIONAL ORGANISATIONS

Red Cross/Red Crescent: National Red Cross/Red Crescent societies often have pivotal roles in responding to emergencies. Additionally, the International Federation of Red Cross and Red Crescent Societies (IFRC, or "The Federation") may deploy assessment teams to the affected country.

United Nations: Within the United Nations system responsibility for emergency response rests with the Resident Coordinator within the affected country. However, in practice international response will be coordinated, if requested by the affected country's government, by the UN Office for the Coordination of Humanitarian Affairs (UN-OCHA), by deploying a UN Disaster Assessment and Coordination (UNDAC) team.

NATIONAL ORGANISATIONS

United States

Under the Department of Homeland Security (DHS), the Federal Emergency Management Agency (FEMA) is lead agency for emergency management. The HAZUS software package developed by FEMA is central in the risk assessment process in the country. The United States and its territories are covered by one of ten regions for FEMA's emergency management purposes. Tribal, state, county and local governments develop emergency management programs/departments and operate hierarchially within each region. Emergencies are managed at the most-local level possible, utilizing mutual aid agreements with adjacent jurisdictions. If the emergency is terrorist related or if declared an "Incident of National Significance", the Secretary of Homeland Security will initiate the National Response Plan (NRP). Under this plan the involvement of federal resources will be made possible, integrating in with the local, county, state, or tribal entities. Management will continue to be handled at the lowest possible level utilizing the National Incident Management System (NIMS).

The Citizen Corps is an organization of volunteer service programs, administered locally and coordinated nationally by DHS, which seek to mitigate disaster and prepare the population for emergency response through public education, training, and outreach. Community Emergency Response Teams are a Citizen Corps program focused on disaster preparedness and teaching basic disaster response skills. These volunteer teams are utilized to provide emergency support when disaster overwhelms the conventional emergency services.

Canada

Public Safety and Emergency Preparedness Canada (PSEPC) is Canada's equivalent agency. Each province has an emergency management office and most local levels of government have similar offices. PSEPC also coordinates and supports the efforts of federal organizations ensuring national security and the safety of Canadians. They also work with other levels of government, first responders, community groups, the private sector (operators of critical infrastructure) and other nations.

PSEPC's work is based on a wide range of policies and legislation. Through the Public Safety and Emergency Preparedness Act which defines the powers, duties and functions of PSEPC are outlined. Other acts are specific to fields such as corrections, emergency management, law enforcement, and national security.

New Zealand

In New Zealand the Ministry of Civil Defence & Emergency Management has statutory authority for controlling any state of emergency declared by central government. Local government bodies such as city and regional councils have their own emergency management agencies to control localised states of emergency, but these all defer to the MCDEM in the event of a national state of emergency. The Wellington Emergency Management Office utilize a building that has been purpose built with its own water, electricity, communications and sewerage facilities to ensure operations in the event of an emergency or disaster.

5

Risk Management

Risk management is the process of measuring, or assessing, risk and developing strategies to manage it. Strategies include transferring the risk to another party, avoiding the risk, reducing the negative effect of the risk, and accepting some or all of the consequences of a particular risk. Traditional risk management focuses on risks stemming from physical or legal causes (e.g. natural disasters or fires, accidents, death, and lawsuits). Financial risk management, on the other hand, focuses on risks that can be managed using traded financial instruments.

THE EXPLANATION

In ideal risk management, a prioritization process is followed whereby the risks with the greatest loss and the greatest probability of occurring are handled first, and risks with lower probability of occurrence and lower loss are handled later. In practice the process can be very difficult, and balancing between risks with a high probability of occurrence but lower loss vs. a risk with high loss but lower probability of occurrence can often be mishandled.

Intangible risk management identifies a new type of risk- a risk that has a 100% probability of occurring but is ignored by the organization due to a lack of identification ability. For example, knowledge risk occurs when deficient knowledge is applied. Relationship risk occurs when collaboration ineffectiveness occurs. Process-engagement risk occurs when operational ineffectiveness occurs. These risks directly reduce the productivity of knowledge workers, decrease cost effectiveness, profitability, service, quality, reputation, brand value, and earnings quality. Intangible risk management allows risk management to create immediate value from the identification and reduction of risks that reduce productivity.

Risk management also faces difficulties allocating resources. This is the idea of opportunity cost. Resources spent on risk management could have been spent on more profitable activities. Again, ideal risk management minimizes spending while maximizing the reduction of the negative effects of risks.

STEPS IN THE RISK MANAGEMENT PROCESS

Establish the Context

Establishing the context includes planning the remainder of the process and mapping out the scope of the exercise, the identity and objectives of stakeholders, the basis upon which risks will be evaluated and defining a framework for the process, and agenda for identification and analysis of risk involved in the process.

Identification

After establishing the context, the next step in the process of managing risk is to identify potential risks. Risks are about events that, when triggered, cause problems. Hence, risk identification can start with the source of problems, or with the problem itself.

- Source analysis Risk sources may be internal or external to the system that is the target of risk management. Examples of risk sources are: stakeholders of a project, employees of a company or the weather over an airport.
- Problem analysis Risks are related to identified threats. For example: the threat of losing money, the threat of abuse of privacy information or the threat of accidents and casualties. The threats may exist with various entities, most important with shareholder, customers and legislative bodies such as the government.

When either source or problem is known, the events that a source may trigger or the events that can lead to a problem can be investigated. For example: stakeholders withdrawing during a project may endanger funding of the project; privacy information may be stolen by employees even within a closed network; lightning striking a Boeing 747 during takeoff may make all people on board immediate casualties.

The chosen method of identifying risks may depend on culture, industry practice and compliance. The identification methods are formed by templates or the development of templates for identifying source, problem or event. Common risk identification methods are:

- Objectives-based risk identification Organizations and project teams have objectives. Any event that may endanger achieving an objective partly or completely is identified as risk. Objective-based risk identification is at the basis of COSO's Enterprise Risk Management-Integrated Framework
- Scenario-based risk identification In scenario analysis different scenarios are created. The scenarios may be the alternative ways to achieve an objective, or an analysis of the interaction of forces in, for example, a market or battle. Any event that triggers an undesired scenario alternative is identified as risk.
- Taxonomy-based risk identification The taxonomy in taxonomy-based risk identification is a breakdown of possible risk sources. Based on the taxonomy and knowledge of best practices, a questionnaire is compiled. The answers to the questions reveal risks. Taxonomy-based risk identification in software industry can be found in CMU/SEI-93-TR-6.
- Common-risk Checking In several industries lists with known risks are available. Each risk in the list can be checked for application to a particular situation.

Assessment

Once risks have been identified, they must then be assessed as to their potential severity of loss and to the probability of occurrence. These quantities can be either simple to measure, in the case of the value of a lost building, or impossible to know for sure in the case of the probability of an unlikely event occurring. Therefore, in the assessment process it is critical to make the best educated guesses possible in order to properly prioritize the implementation of the risk management plan.

The fundamental difficulty in risk assessment is determining the rate of occurrence since statistical information is not available on all kinds of past incidents. Furthermore, evaluating the severity of the consequences (impact) is often quite difficult for immaterial assets. Asset valuation is another question that needs to be addressed. Thus, best educated opinions and available statistics are the primary sources of information. Nevertheless, risk assessment should produce such information for the management of the organization that the primary risks are easy to understand and that the risk management decisions may be prioritized. Thus, there have been several theories and attempts to quantify risks. Numerous different risk formulae exist, but perhaps the most widely accepted formula for risk quantification is:

Later research has shown that the financial benefits of risk management are less dependent on the formula used but are more dependent on the frequency and how risk assessment is performed.

In business it is imperative to be able to present the findings of risk assessments in financial terms. Robert Courtney Jr. (IBM, 1970) proposed a formula for presenting risks in financial terms. The Courtney formula was accepted as the official risk analysis method for the US governmental agencies. The formula proposes calculation of ALE (annualised loss expectancy) and compares the expected loss value to the security control implementation costs (cost-benefit analysis).

Potential Risk Treatments

Once risks have been identified and assessed, all techniques to manage the risk fall into one or more of these four major categories: (Dorfman, 1997) (remember as 4 T's)

- Tolerate (aka retention)
- Treat (aka mitigation)
- Terminate (aka elimination)
- Transfer (aka buying insurance)

Ideal use of these strategies may not be possible. Some of them may involve trade-offs that are not acceptable to the organization or person making the risk management decisions.

Risk Avoidance

Includes not performing an activity that could carry risk. An example would be not buying a property or business in order to not take on the liability that comes with it. Another would be not flying in order to not take the risk that the airplane were to be hijacked. Avoidance may seem the answer to all risks, but avoiding risks also means losing out on the potential gain that accepting (retaining) the risk may have allowed. Not entering a business to avoid the risk of loss also avoids the possibility of earning profits.

Risk Reduction

Involves methods that reduce the severity of the loss. Examples include sprinklers designed to put out a fire to reduce the risk of loss by fire. This method may cause a greater loss by water damage and therefore may not be suitable. Halon fire suppression systems may mitigate that risk, but the cost may be prohibitive as a strategy.

Modern software development methodologies reduce risk by developing and delivering software incrementally. Early methodologies suffered from the fact that they only delivered software in the final phase of development; any problems encountered in earlier phases meant costly rework and often jeopardized the whole project. By developing in iterations, software projects can limit effort wasted to a single iteration. A current trend in software development, spearheaded by the Extreme Programming community, is to reduce the size of iterations to the smallest size possible, sometimes as little as one week is allocated to an iteration.

Risk Retention

Involves accepting the loss when it occurs. True self insurance falls in this category. Risk retention is a viable strategy for small risks where the cost of insuring against the risk would be greater over time than the total losses sustained. All risks that are not avoided or transferred are retained by default. This includes risks that are so large or catastrophic that they either cannot be insured against or the premiums would be infeasible. War is an example since most property and risks are not insured against war, so the loss attributed by war is retained by the insured. Also any amounts of potential loss (risk) over the amount insured is retained risk. This may also be acceptable if the chance of a very large loss is small or if the cost to insure for greater coverage amounts is so great it would hinder the goals of the organization too much.

Risk Transfer

Means causing another party to accept the risk, typically by contract or by hedging. Insurance is one type of risk transfer that uses contracts. Other times it may involve contract language that transfers a risk to another party without the payment of an insurance premium. Liability among construction or other contractors is very often transferred this way. On the other hand, taking offsetting positions in derivatives is typically how firms use hedging to financially manage risk.

Some ways of managing risk fall into multiple categories. Risk retention pools are technically retaining the risk for the group, but spreading it over the whole group involves transfer among individual members of the group. This is different from traditional insurance, in that no premium is exchanged between members of the group up front, but instead losses are assessed to all members of the group.

Plan Creation

Decide on the combination of methods to be used for each risk. Each risk management decision should be recorded and approved by the appropriate level of management. For example, a risk concerning the image of the organization should have top management decision behind it whereas IT management would have the authority to decide on computer virus risks.

The risk management plan should propose applicable and effective security controls for managing the risks. For example, an observed high risk of computer viruses could be mitigated by acquiring and implementing anti virus software. A good risk management plan should contain a schedule for control implementation and responsible persons for those actions. The risk management concept is old but is still not very effectively measured

Implementation

Follow all of the planned methods for mitigating the effect of the risks. Purchase insurance policies for the risks that have been decided to be transferred to an insurer, avoid all risks that can be avoided without sacrificing the entity's goals, reduce others, and retain the rest.

Review and Evaluation of the Plan

Initial risk management plans will never be perfect. Practice, experience, and actual loss results will necessitate changes in the plan and contribute information to allow possible different decisions to be made in dealing with the risks being faced.

Risk analysis results and management plans should be updated periodically. There are two primary reasons for this:

1. to evaluate whether the previously selected security controls are still applicable and effective, and
2. to evaluate the possible risk level changes in the business environment. For example, information risks are a good example of rapidly changing business environment.

LIMITATIONS

If risks are improperly assessed and prioritized, time can be wasted in dealing with risk of losses that are not likely to occur. Spending too much time assessing and managing unlikely risks can divert resources that could be used more profitably. Unlikely events do occur but if the risk is unlikely enough to occur it may be better to simply retain the risk and deal with the result if the loss does in fact occur.

Prioritizing too highly the risk management processes could keep an organization from ever completing a project or even getting started. This is especially true if other work is suspended until the risk management process is considered complete.

It is also important to keep in mind the distinction between risk and uncertainty. Risk can be measured by impacts x probability.

Areas of Risk Management

As applied to corporate finance, risk management is a technique for measuring, monitoring and controlling the financial or operational risk on a firm's balance sheet. The Basel II framework breaks risks into market risk (price risk), credit risk and operational risk and also specifies methods for calculating capital requirements for each of these components.

Enterprise Risk Management

In enterprise risk management, a risk is defined as a possible event or circumstance that can have negative influences on the Enterprise in question. Its impact can be on the very existence, the resources (human and capital), the products and services, or the customers of the enterprise, as well as external impacts on society, markets, or the environment. In addition, every probable risk can have a pre-formulated plan to deal with its possible consequences (to ensure contingency if the risk becomes a liability). From the information above and the average cost per employee over time, or cost accrual ratio, a project manager can estimate

- the cost associated with the risk if it arises, estimated by multiplying employee costs per unit time by the estimated time lost (cost impact, C where C = cost accrual ratio * S).
- the probable increase in time associated with a risk (schedule variance due to risk, Rs where Rs = P * S):
  - o Sorting on this value puts the highest risks to the schedule first. This is intended to cause the greatest risks to the project to be attempted first so that risk is minimized as quickly as possible.
  - o This is slightly misleading as schedule variances with a large P and small S and vice versa are not equivalent. (The risk of the RMS Titanic sinking vs. the passengers' meals being served at slightly the wrong time).

- the probable increase in cost associated with a risk (cost variance due to risk, Rc where Rc = P*C = P*CAR*S = P*S*CAR)
  - o sorting on this value puts the highest risks to the budget first.
  - o see concerns about schedule variance as this is a function of it, as illustrated in the equation above.

Risk in a project or process can be due either to Special Cause Variation or Common Cause Variation and requires appropriate treatment. That is to re-iterate the concern about extremal cases not being equivalent in the list immediately above.

Risk Management Activities as Applied to Project Management

In project management, risk management includes the following activities:

- Planning how risk management will be held in the particular project. Plan should include risk management tasks, responsibilities, activities and budget.
- Assigning a risk officer-a team member other than a project manager who is responsible for foreseeing potential project problems. Typical characteristic of risk officer is a healthy skepticism.
- Maintaining live project risk database. Each risk should have the following attributes: opening date, title, short description, probability and importance. Optionally a risk may have an assigned person responsible for its resolution and a date by which the risk must be resolved.
- Creating anonymous risk reporting channel. Each team member should have possibility to report risk that he foresees in the project.
- Preparing mitigation plans for risks that are chosen to be mitigated. The purpose of the mitigation plan is to describe how this particular risk will be handled-what, when, by who and how will be done to avoid it or minimize consequences if it becomes a liability.

- Summarizing planned and faced risks, effectiveness of mitigation activities and effort spend for the risk management

RISK MANAGEMENT AND BUSINESS CONTINUITY

Risk management is simply a practice of systematically selecting cost effective approaches for minimising the effect of threat realization to the organization. All risks can never be fully avoided or mitigated simply because of financial and practical limitations. Therefore all organizations have to accept some level of residual risks.

Whereas risk management tends to be pre-emptive, business continuity planning (BCP) was invented to deal with the consequences of realised residual risks. The necessity to have BCP in place arises because even very unlikely events will occur if given enough time. Risk management and BCP are often mistakenly seen as rivals or overlapping practices. In fact these processes are so tightly tied together that such separation seems artificial. For example, the risk management process creates important inputs for the BCP (assets, impact assessments, cost estimates etc). Risk management also proposes applicable controls for the observed risks. Therefore, risk management covers several areas that are vital for the BCP process. However, the BCP process goes beyond risk management's pre-emptive approach and moves on from the assumption that the disaster will realise at some point.

BUSINESS CONTINUITY PLANNING

Business Continuity Planning (BCP) is an interdisciplinary peer mentoring methodology used to create and validate an exercised logistical plan for how an organization will recover and restore partially or completely interrupted critical function(s) within a predetermined time after a disaster or extended disruption.

BCP may be a part of an organizational learning effort that helps reduce operational risk associated with lax information management controls. This process may be integrated with improving information security and corporate reputation risk management practices.

British Standards Institute is planning to release a new independent standard for BCP-BS 25999. The draft of standard had been put up for public comments and the final standard is expected in early 2007. This standard would reduce the reliance on Information Security oriented standards which dealt with BCP marginally.

A completed BCP cycle results in a formal printed manual available for reference before, during, and after disruptions have occurred. Its purpose is to reduce adverse stakeholder impacts determined by both the disruption's scope and duration. Measurable Business Impact Analysis (BIA) "zones" include civil, economic, natural, technical, secondary and subsequent.

For the purposes of this article, the term disaster will be used to represent natural disaster, man-made disaster, and disruptions. Business Continuity Planning is not a new concept; plans for disasters, like Noah's Ark, are evidenced from the beginning of human history. Prior to January 1, 2000, governments anticipated computer failures, called the Y2k problem, in important public utility infrastructures like banking, power, telecommunication, health and financial industries. Since 1983, regulatory agencies like the American Bankers Association and Banking Administration Institute (BAI) required their supporting members to exercise operational continuity practices (later supported by more formal BCP manuals) that protect the public interest. Newer regulations were often based on formalized standards defined under ISO/IEC 17799 or BS 7799.

Both regulatory and global business focus on BCP arguably waned after the problem-free Y2K rollover. Some believe this lax attitude ended September 11th 2001, when simultaneous terrorist attacks devastated downtown New York City and changed the 'worst case scenario' paradigm for business continuity planning.

Introduction

BCP methodology is scalable for an organization of any size and complexity. Even though the methodology has roots in regulated industries, any type of organization may create a BCP manual, and arguably every organization should have one in order to ensure the organization's longevity. Evidence that firms do not invest enough time and resources into BCP preparations are evident in disaster survival statistics. Fires permanently close 44% of the business affected. In the 1993 World Trade Center bombing, 150 businesses out of 350 affected failed to survive the event. Conversely, the firms affected by the Sept 11 attacks with well-developed and tested BCP manuals were back in business within days.

A BCP manual for a small organization may be simply a printed manual stored safely away from the primary work location, containing the names, addresses, and phone numbers for crisis management staff, general staff members, clients, and vendors along with the location of the offsite data backup storage media, copies of insurance contracts, and other critical materials necessary for organizational survival. At its most complex, a BCP manual may outline a secondary work site, technical requirements and readiness, regulatory reporting requirements, work recovery measures, the means to reestablish physical records, the means to establish a new supply chain, or the means to establish new production centers. Firms should ensure that their BCP manual is realistic and easy to use during a crisis. As such, BCP sits along side crisis management and disaster recovery planning and is a part of an organization's overall risk management.

The development of a BCP manual has five main phases:

1. Analysis
2. Solution design
3. Implementation
4. Testing and organization acceptance
5. Maintenance.

Much of the BCP material on the internet is sponsored by consultancies who offer fee-based services for BCP solution development, however basic tutorials are freely available on the internet for properly motivated organizations.

ANALYTIVE REPORT

The analysis phase in the development of a BCP manual consists of an impact analysis, threat analysis, and impact scenarios with the resulting BCP plan requirement documentation.

Impact Analysis

An impact analysis results in the differentiation between critical and non-critical organization functions. A function may be considered critical if the implications for stakeholders of damage to the organization resulting are regarded as unacceptable. Perceptions of the acceptability of disruption may be modified by the cost of establishing and maintaining appropriate business or technical recovery solutions. A function may also be considered critical if dictated by law. Next, the impact analysis results in the recovery requirements for each critical function. Recovery requirements consist of the following information:

- The time frame in which the critical function must be resumed after the disaster
- The business requirements for recovery of the critical function, and/or
- The technical requirements for recovery of the critical function

Threat Analysis

After defining recovery requirements, documenting potential threats is recommended to detail a specific disaster's unique recovery steps. Some common threats include the following:

- Disease
- Earthquake
- Fire
- Flood
- Cyber attack
- Hurricane
- Utility outage
- Terrorism

All threats in the examples above share a common impact-the potential of damage to organizational infrastructure-except one (disease). The impact of diseases is initially purely human, and may be alleviated with technical and business solutions. During the 2002-2003 SARS outbreak, some organizations grouped staff into separate teams, and rotated the teams between the primary and secondary work sites, with a rotation frequency equal to the incubation period of the disease. The organizations also banned face-to-face contact between opposing team members during business and non-business hours. With such a split, organizations increased their resiliency against the threat of government-ordered quarantine measures if one person in a team contracted or was exposed to the disease. Damage from flooding also has a unique characteristic. If an office environment is flooded with non-salinated and contamination-free water (e.g., in the event of a pipe burst), equipment can be thoroughly dried and may still be functional.

IMPACT SCENARIOS: DEFINITION

After defining potential threats, documenting the impact scenarios that form the basis of the business recovery plan is recommended. In general, planning for the most wide-reaching disaster or disturbance is preferable to planning for a smaller scale problem, as almost all smaller scale problems are partial elements of larger disasters. A typical impact scenario like 'Building Loss' will most likely encompass all critical business functions, and the worst potential outcome from any potential threat. A business continuity plan may also document additional impact scenarios if an organization has more than one building. Other more specific impact scenarios-for example a scenario for the temporary or permanent loss of a specific floor in a building-may also be documented.

Recovery Requirement Documentation

After the completion of the analysis phase, the business and technical plan requirements are documented in order to commence the implementation phase. A good asset management program can be of great assistance here and allow for quick identification of available and re-allocateable resources. For an office-based, IT intensive business, the plan requirements may cover the following elements which may be classed as ICE (In Case of Emergency) Data:

- The numbers and types of disks, whether dedicated or shared, required outside of the primary business location in the secondary location
- The individuals involved in the recovery effort along with their contact and technical details
- The applications and application data required from the secondary location desks for critical business functions
- The manual workaround solutions
- The maximum outage allowed for the applications
- The peripheral requirements like printers, copier, fax machine, calculators, paper, pens etc.

Other business environments, such as production, distribution, warehousing etc will need to cover these elements, but are likely to have additional issues to manage following a disruptive event.

Solution Design

The goal of the solution design phase is to identify the most cost effective disaster recovery solution that meets two main requirements from the impact analysis stage. For IT applications, this is commonly expressed as:

1. The minimum application and application data requirements
2. The time frame in which the minimum application and application data must be available

Disaster recovery plans may also be required outside the IT applications domain, for example in preservation of information in hard copy format, or restoration of embedded technology in process plant. This BCP phase overlaps with Disaster recovery planning methodology. The solution phase determines:

- the crisis management command structure
- the location of a secondary work site (where necessary)
- telecommunication architecture between primary and secondary work sites

- data replication methodology between primary and secondary work sites
- the application and software required at the secondary work site, and
- the type of physical data requirements at the secondary work site.

Implementation

The implementation phase, quite simply, is the execution of the design elements identified in the solution design phase. Work package testing may take place during the implementation of the solution, however; work package testing does not take the place of organizational testing.

Testing and Organizational Acceptance

The purpose of testing is to achieve organizational acceptance that the business continuity solution satisfies the organization's recovery requirements. Plans may fail to meet expectations due to insufficient or inaccurate recovery requirements, solution design flaws, or solution implementation errors. Testing may include:

- Crisis command team call-out testing
- Technical swing test from primary to secondary work locations
- Technical swing test from secondary to primary work locations
- Application test
- Business process test

At minimum, testing is generally conducted on a biannual or annual schedule. Problems identified in the initial testing phase may be rolled up into the maintenance phase and retested during the next test cycle.

Maintenance

Maintenance of a BCP manual is broken down into three periodic activities. The first activity is the confirmation of information in the manual. The second activity is the testing and verification of technical solutions established for recovery operations. The third activity is the testing and verification of documented organization recovery procedures. A biannual or annual maintenance cycle is typical.

Information update and Testing

All organizations change over time, therefore a BCP manual must change to stay relevant to the organization. Once data accuracy is verified, normally a call tree test is conducted to evaluate the notification plan's efficiency as well as the accuracy of the contact data. Some types of changes that should be identified and updated in the manual include:

- Staffing changes
- Staffing persona
- Changes to important clients and their contact details
- Changes to important vendors/suppliers and their contact details
- Departmental changes like new, closed or fundamentally changed departments.

Technical Solutions

As a part of ongoing maintenance, any specialized technical deployments must be checked for functionality. Some checks include:

- Virus definition distribution
- Application security and service patch distribution
- Hardware operability check
- Application operability check
- Data verification

Organization Recovery Procedures

As work processes change over time, the previously documented organizational recovery procedures may no longer be suitable. Some checks include:

- Are all work processes for critical functions documented?

- Have the systems used in the execution of critical functions changed?
- Are the documented work checklists meaningful and accurate for staff?
- Do the documented work process recovery tasks and supporting disaster recovery infrastructure allow staff to recover within the predetermined recovery time objective?

Treatment of Test Failures

As suggested by the diagram included in this article, there is a direct relationship between the test and maintenance phases and the impact phase. When establishing a BCP manual and recovery infrastructure from scratch, issues found during the testing phase often must be reintroduced to the analysis phase.

ENTERPRISE RISK MANAGEMENT

In business Enterprise Risk Management (ERM) are the methods and processes used to manage those risks, possible events or circumstances that can have influence on the enterprise in question. By identifying and proactively treating such potential effectors, one protects the very existence, the resources (human and capital), the products and services, or the customers of the enterprise, as well as external effects on society, markets or the environment.

ERM is similar to operational risk management (ORM) but also includes credit risk and market risk.

INFORMATION QUALITY MANAGEMENT

Information Quality Management is an information technology management discipline, which encompasses the COBIT Information Criteria of efficiency, effectiveness, confidentiality, integrity, availability, compliance, and reliability.

It is held by some that the separation of software engineering, infrastructure management, and information security management leads to difficulties and failures. Examples abound where frustrated information security professionals are confronted with newly developed applications that lack the most fundamental security controls, and that have taken no notice in the requirements gathering of the information risks that the application might introduce.

Thus, leading edge companies are starting to integrate these information quality management disciplines along with the discipline of information risk management. This will guarantee that the software engineering frameworks of the future ensure that the information risks are established and that appropriate information security controls are designed in at the start of projects.

OPERATIONAL RISK MANAGEMENT

In business, the term operational risk management (ORM) is the oversight of many forms of day-to-day operational risk including the risk of loss resulting from inadequate or failed internal processes, people and systems, or from external events. Operational risk does not include market risk or credit risk.

Benefits of ORM

1. Reduction of operational loss.
2. Lower compliance/auditing costs.
3. Early detection of unlawful activities.
4. Reduced exposure to future risks.

Categories of Risk

The Basel Committee on Banking Supervision breaks down loss events into seven general categories:

Internal Fraud: Loss due to acts of a type intended to defraud, misappropriate property or circumvent regulations, the law or company policy, excluding diversity, discrimination events, which involves at least one internal party.

External Fraud: Losses due to acts of a type intended to defraud, misappropriate property or circumvent the law, by a third party. These activities include theft, robbery, hacking or phishing attacks.

Employment Practices and Workplace Safety: Losses arising from acts inconsistent with employment, health or safety laws or agreements, from payment of personal injury claims, or from diversity/discrimination.

Clients, Products and Business Practice: Losses arising from unintentional or negligent failure to meet a professional obligation to specific clients (including fiduciary and suitability requirements), or from the nature of design of a product.

Damage to Physical Assets: Losses arising from loss or damage to physical assets from natural disaster or other events.

Business Disruption and Systems Failures: Losses arising from disruption of business or system failures. This includes loss of due to failure of computer hardware, computer software, telecommunications failure or utility outage and disruptions.

Execution, Delivery and Process Management: Losses from failed transaction processing or process management, from relations with trade suppliers and vendors.

This includes Transaction Capture, Execution & Maintenance Miscommunication, Data entry, maintenance or loading error Missed deadline or responsibility, Model/system misoperation Accounting error, entity attribution error, Delivery failure, Collateral management failure Reference data maintenance, Monitoring & Reporting Failed mandatory reporting obligation, Inaccurate external report (loss incurred), Customer Intake & Documentation Client permissions/ disclaimers missed Legal documents missing/incomplete, Customer/Client Account Management Unapproved access given to accounts, Incorrect client records (loss incurred), Negligent loss or damage of client assets, Trade partners, non-client vendor misperformance and vendor disputes.

ORM Software: The impact of the Enron failure and the implementation of the Sarbanes-Oxley Act has caused several software development companies to create enterprise-wide software packages to manage risk. These software systems allow the financial audit to be executed at lower cost.

Up till now there is not much software focusing on operational risk management. Only some consulting firm provide temporary solution, such as Loss Event Management. Because operational management is very business oriented, it is closely related with each organization's structure and business, the common software is difficult to satisfy the customer requirement.

ENVIRONMENTAL RISK MANAGEMENT AUTHORITY

The Environmental Risk Management Authority (ERMA) is a New Zealand government agency which controls the introduction of hazardous substances and new organisms.

ERMA is principally responsible for implementing the Hazardous Substances and New Organisms Act 1996 (HSNO).

The aim of ERMA is stated as: "Achieve effective prevention or management of risks to the environment, public health and safety associated with importing or manufacturing hazardous substances and introducing new organisms, and their use."

FINANCIAL RISK MANAGEMENT

Financial risk management is the practice of creating value in a firm by using financial instruments to manage exposure to risk. Similar to general risk management, financial risk management requires identifying the sources of risk, measuring risk, and plans to address them. As a specialization of risk management, financial risk management focuses on when and how to hedge using financial instruments to manage costly exposures to risk.

In the banking sector worldwide, Basel Accord are generally adopted by internationally active banks to tracking, reporting and exposing operational, credit and market risks.

When to use Financial Risk Management

Finance theory (i.e. financial economics) prescribes that a firm should take on a project when it increases shareholder value. Finance theory also shows that firm managers cannot create value for shareholders, also called its investors, by taking on project that shareholders could do for themselves at the same cost. When applied to financial risk management, this implies that firm managers should not hedge risks that investors can hedge for themselves at the same cost. This notion is captured by the hedging irrelevance proposition: In a perfect market, the firm cannot create value by hedging a risk when the price of bearing that risk within the firm is the same as the price of bearing it outside of the firm. In practice, financial markets are not likely to be perfect markets.

This suggests that firm managers likely have many opportunities to create value for shareholders using financial risk management. The trick is to determine which risks are cheaper for the firm to manage than the shareholders. A general rule of thumb, however, is that market risks that result in unique risks for the firm are the best candidates for financial risk management.

6

Corporate Behaviour

Corporate Behaviour (or corporate behavior) is the behaviour of a corporation or corporations (or company or companies). The corporate behaviour of for-profit (capitalist) corporations and not-for-profit (non-capitalist) corporations differ due to the fundamental drive for profit in for-profit corporations, compared to the non-monetary goals often held by not-for-profit corporations.

The Characteristics of for-profit (Capitalist) Corporate Behaviour

Corporate behaviour of for-profit corporations has characteristics. These characteristics are unlikely to remain fixed for various reasons, but key characteristics are discernable from the history of for-profit corporations. Some of the key characteristics may not apply to individual for-profit corporations at a point in time and space, though some key characteristics are probably present at all times. The best example is the drive for profit. The strength or importance of a key characteristic will also vary in time and space for many reasons. For instance a for-profit corporation may be able to grow at a faster rate if it has subsidiaries in other countries.

Reasons are numerous as to why key characteristics are absent or vary in strength or importance. Some reasons could be as follows:

- Economic decline
- Poor performance
- Size of for-profit corporation

- Management decisions
- Type of for-profit corporation
- Competition

Certain individuals and groups have proposed and described the characteristics of corporate behaviour. Read: These attempts, whilst a useful contribution, are not objective and should be read with this in mind.

- *Profit:* Profitability is the ultimate driver of corporate decisions. Corporations prefer higher profits to lower profits, at least in the long-run. Profitability is not necessarily the same as community well-being, though a profitable company is more likely to, for example, employ more people than an unprofitable company. Conflicts can exist, however, between what's good for a corporation and what's good for the environment, for example, or its employees or even the good of the state. A corporation is a complex organism and there has been much debate about what drives it. There is an argument that the divorce of ownership from decision-taking means that profitability isn't the main drive-senior managers may have other imperatives like keeping their jobs and avoiding being taken-over (which might run counter to the interests of share-holders). Corporations often like to grow, if only because they fear a bigger competitor having cost advantages. This is not always true, however: there have been cases where corporations have been broken up into constituent parts.
- *Amorality:* Not being human, corporations as such do not have morals or altruistic goals. Neither, though, does any other organisation. Corporations are, though, run by people who are subject to law and rules of morality.
- *Hierarchy:* Corporations are usually hierarchical, though the structure of the hierarchy varies. Some are relatively flat with a wide layer of middle managers answerable to a few individuals while others are like a pyramid. A very few corporations have a great degree of democracy to them. Ricardo Semmler owns corporations in Brazil

but allows all his staff to pick managers and decide strategy. He puts himself up for election as a chief executive.

Characteristics of not-for-profit Corporate Behaviour

As non-capitalist corporations such as NGO's or charities are not driven by the fundamentals of profit and economic growth, these do not show many of the characteristics of capitalist corporations. The behaviour of non-capitalist corporations is however often influenced by these characteristics of capitalist corporations, in similar ways to the influence of corporate behaviour on individuals. Due to this influence non-capitalist corporations can sometimes be seen to exhibit the characteristics of hierarchy, competition and ephemerality.

The Influence of Corporate Behaviour on Individuals and Society

Due to the dominance of capitalist corporations in Western societies the behaviour of corporations can be seen to have significant impacts on individuals and society. A person or group of people can have links to a corporation or corporations that range from weak to strong, if a person or group of people exhibit corporate behaviour that does not mean the person or group of people is employed by a corporation or corporations. A person or group of people may show corporate behaviour for different lengths of time, for some people they exhibit this behaviour at their place of work; for others it is exhibited at work, home and outside the home. Many people display corporate behaviour but do not agree with actions and outcomes that result from it. The fact that individuals may not agree with the outcomes of corporate behaviour is central to the concept in itself, the characteristics of capitalist corporations do not reflect the characteristics of any individual or group of individuals but are the characteristics required for the survival of capitalist corporations due to the nature of the system within which corporations operate.

Ethics

Under the law, corporations are treated in many ways as persons. However, in other ways, they are not. One example is as follows. The thought of being put in prison acts as a powerful deterrent for most people: it prevents people from committing many crimes. But this powerful deterrent to harming people or society has no effect on a corporation, for a corporation cannot be put in prison.

CORPORATE BENEFIT

Corporate benefit (sometimes referred to as commercial benefit) is the requirement under some legal systems that the directors of a company must exercise the powers of the company for the commercial benefit of the company and its members. At common law, transactions which were not ostensibly beneficial to the company were set aside as being void as against the company.

Perhaps the best illustration of this principle is to be found in Hutton v West Cork Railway Co (1883) 23 Ch D 654, where the English Court of Appeal held that the paying of a gratuity to employees prior to their dismissal was an improper exercise of the powers of the company, because the company was no longer a going concern, and thus stood to obtain no benefit (and no furtherance of its objects) through the payment of the gratuity; as Bowen L.J. memorably remarked: "there are to be no cakes and ale except such as are required for the benefit of the company."

Any transaction which the directors enter into which is outside the powers of the company (and thus outside the scope of their authority) may nonetheless be ratified by the shareholders of the company, and will thereby be binding upon the company.

Modern Developments

The rule is generally seen to be particularly harsh towards both third parties and against directors, who are regarded as being in breach of their duty only be acting with what others might regard as common human decency. Where the company's property could not be recovered from the third party, the directors would be personally liable to recompense the company.

There were also concerns that running companies ruthless for the financial benefit of the shareholders had a countervailing cost, making directors unwilling to participate in programmes that were beneficial to the community generally, or to the environment. It also meant that companies became much less willing to make donations to political parties, which may have had more impetus in bringing about legislative change than concern for communities or the environment.

Most legal systems have now abrogated by statute the rule that as against third parties the transaction may be void if it has insufficient commercial benefit to the company.

In some countries, statutes now expressly provide for the directors to consider interests other than the pure financial interests of the shareholders.

However, in some jurisdictions there are proposals to make the power to act otherwise than for the financial benefit of the company even wider. For example, in the United Kingdom, the Companies Act 2006, when brought into force, will require that directors have to consider the impact of their actions on a much wider range of stakeholders. That Act would require a director "to promote the success of the company for the benefit of its members as a whole", but sets out six factors to which a director must have regards in fulfilling the duty to promote success. These are:

- the likely consequences of any decision in the long term
- the interests of the company's employees
- the need to foster the company's business relationships with suppliers, customers and others
- the impact of the company's operations on the community and the environment
- the desirability of the company maintaining a reputation for high standards of business conduct, and
- the need to act fairly as between members of a company

The proposed new duties have been subject to some criticism, both from those who argue that the new duties do not have sufficient bite, and also from those who fear that it diverts directors' focus from what it is that they are meant to be doing (viz., generating profits), and there are fears of widespread litigation, and increase in director's insurance premiums.

However, because the new duties are expressed in non-imperative terms, and there is no sanction, the likelihood is that although they will empower the board of directors to take decisions that do not appear to directly financially benefit the company, they are unlikely to ever be required to do so.

Distinction from other Legal Concepts

Conceptually, it is important to distinguish failure of a transaction for want of corporate benefit from other related legal concepts. These include:

- Failure of consideration: Under contract law in most common law legal systems, to be enforceable a contract requires both parties to provide consideration (ie. something of value). However, the consideration does not need to be equal, and the gratuity given in Hutton v West Cork Railway Co would still have failed for want of corporate benefit if, for example, the company had allowed employees to purchase company property at a discount.
- Transactions at an undervalue: Although most examples of failure for want of corporate benefit involve transactions which were either a gift, or were made at a substantial undervalue, the concept is different in purpose and effect from provisions of insolvency law which prohibit undervalue transactions at a time when the company is insolvent.

CORPORATE CRIME

In criminology, corporate crime refers to crimes either committed by a corporation, i.e. a business entity having a separate legal personality from the natural persons that manage its activities, or by individuals that may be identified with a corporation or other business entity. This type of crime therefore overlaps with:

- white-collar crime because the majority of individuals who may act as or represent the interests of the corporation will be employees or professionals of a higher social class;

- organized crime because criminals can set up corporations either for the purposes of crime or as vehicles for laundering the proceeds of crime. Organized crime has become a branch of big business and is simply the illegal sector of capital. It has been estimated that, by the middle of the 1990s, the "gross criminal product" of organised crime made it the twentieth richest organisation in the world and richer than 150 sovereign states (Castells 1998: 169). The world's gross criminal product has been estimated at 20 percent of world trade. (de Brie 2000); and
- state-corporate crime because, in many contexts, the opportunity to commit crime emerges from the relationship between the corporation and the state.

DEFINITIONAL ISSUES

Legal Person: The Fourteenth Amendment to the U.S. Constitution stipulates that, "No State shall make or enforce any law which shall abridge the privileges or immunities of citizens of the United States; nor shall any State deprive any person of life, liberty, or property, without due process of law; nor deny to any person within its jurisdiction the equal protection of the laws."

In Santa Clara County v. Southern Pacific Railroad, 118 U.S. 394 (1886) the United States Supreme Court declared that a corporation was a "person" as interpreted by the Fourteenth Amendment. In a preface to the Court's argument, Chief Justice Morrison R. Waite stated the unanimous opinion that the Fourteenth Amendment applied equally to persons and "applied to these corporations." In English law, this was matched the decision in Salomon v Salomon & Co [1897] AC 22.

Function of Law

History shows that laws have sometimes been used as instruments of repression, exclusion, and marginalisation; and that certain criminal justice policies may sometimes be intended to serve the interests of particular groups or to undermine other groups. Thus, the definition of crime and the nature of criminal justice policies in society usually reflect the structures of power in that society. Also, while mainstream criminologists tend to focus mostly on street crimes and crimes of marginalised groups, the less obvious crimes of states, corporate organisations, and powerful groups are often ignored or under-emphasised. Lea (2001) argues that whereas crime used to be the exceptional event, disrupting the otherwise normal socio-economic processes, as crime becomes more frequent it lost its status as an exceptional event and became "a standard, background feature of our lives-a taken for granted element of late modernity." (Garland 1996: 446)

Policy to Enforce the Law against Corporations

Corporate crime has become politically sensitive in some countries. For example, in the United Kingdom following a number of fatal disasters on the rail network and at sea, the term is used to refer to corporate manslaughter and to involve a more general discussion about the technological hazards posed by business enterprises and consider incidents such as the 1985 Union Carbide accident in Bhopal, India (Pearce & Tombs: 1993) and the behaviour of the pharmaceutical industry (Braithwaite: 1984). The Law Reform Commission of New South Wales puts it thus:

Corporate crime poses a significant threat to the welfare of the community. Given the pervasive presence of corporations in a wide range of activities in our society, and the impact of their actions on a much wider group of people than are affected by individual action, the potential for both economic and physical harm caused by a corporation is great.

Similarly, Mokhiber and Weismann (1999) assert: At one level, corporations develop new technologies and economies of scale. These may serve the economic interests of mass consumers by introducing new products and more efficient methods of mass production. On another level, given the absence of political control today, corporations serve to destroy the foundations of the civic community and the lives of people who reside in them.

BEHAVIOUR TO CRIMINALISE

Behaviour can be regulated by the civil law (including administrative law) or the criminal law. In deciding to criminalise particular behaviour, the legislature is making the political judgment that this behaviour is sufficiently culpable to deserve the stigma of being labelled as a crime. In law, corporations can commit the same offences as natural persons. Simpson (2002) avers that this process should be straightforward because a state should simply engage in victimology to identify which behaviour causes the most loss and damage to its citizens, and then represent the majority view that justice requires the intervention of the criminal law. But states depend on the business sector to deliver a stable economy, so the politics of regulating the individuals and corporations that supply that stability become more complex. For the views of Marxist criminology, for Left realism, and for Right Realism. More specifically, the historical tradition of sovereign state control of prisons is ending through the process of privatisation. Corporate profitability in these areas therefore depends on building more prison facilities, managing their operations, and selling inmate labour. In turn, this requires a steady stream of prisoners able to work. (Kicenski: 2002)

The majority of crimes are committed because the offender has the "right" opportunity, i.e. where the offender simply sees the chance and thinks that he or she will be able to commit the crime and not be detected. For the most part, greed, rather than conceit, is the motive, and the rationalisation for choosing to break the law usually arises out of a form of contempt for the victim, namely that he, she or it will be powerless to prevent it, and has it coming for some reason. For these purposes, the corporation is the vehicle for the crime. This may be a short-term crime, i.e. the corporation is set up as a shell to open credit trading accounts with manufacturers and wholesalers, trades for a short period of time and then disappears with the revenue and without paying for the inventory. Alternatively and most commonly, the primary purpose of the corporation is as a legitimate business, but criminal activity is secretly intermixed with legal activity to escape detection. To achieve a suitable level of secrecy, senior managers will usually be involved. The explanations and exculpations may therefore centre around rogue individuals who acted outside the organisational structures, or there may be a serious examination of the occupational and organisational structures that facilitated the crime and around the socio-economic system, gender, racism and age.

While bribery and corruption are problems in the developed world, the corruption of public officials is one of the main causes of crime in developing societies because it is a precondition for much of the state, corporate, and organised crime which occurs. Peèar (1996) discussing the implications for policing in Eastern Europe as it seeks to adapt its laws to match a capitalist model, pointing to the difficulty of distinguishing between lack of morality and criminality in economic crimes that tend to emerge from the structural relationships in modern commerce.

PENALTY TO BE IMPOSED

In part, this will be a function of the public perception of the degree of culpability involved. Weissman and Mokhiber (1999) catalogue the silence and indifference of the major media in the face of the widespread corporate corruption. Only in part is this justifiable. The news media find it difficult to respond to corporate crime both because reporting may compromise the trial by tainting the jury's perceptions, or because of the danger of defamation proceedings. Further, major corporate crime is often complicated and more difficult to explain to the lay public, as against street crime which may provide visuals of victims injured or of property damaged in spectacular fashion. But, more significantly, the news media are owned by large corporations which may also own prisons. Thus, the political decisions on the resources to allocate to investigate and prosecute will tend to match the electorate's understanding of the dangers posed by "crime". In sentencing, the fact that the convicted individuals may have had an impeccable character as presidents, CEOs, chairmen, directors and managers is likely to be a mitigating factor.

Examples of criminal behaviour in most jurisdictions include: insider trading, antitrust violations, fraud (usually involving the consumers), damage to the environment, exploitation of labour in violation of labour and health and safety laws, and the failure to maintain a fiduciary responsibility towards shareholders.

CORPORATE LAW ECONOMIC REFORM PROGRAM ACT 2004

Corporate Law Economic Reform Program (Audit Reform & Corporate Disclosure) Act 2004, commonly called CLERP 9, is the most recent reform to the Corporations Act 2001 (Commonwealth) which governs corporations law in Australia. It was enacted in July 2004.

It is based on the reform proposals contained in the CLERP 9 discussion paper, Corporation disclosure-strengthening the financial reporting framework, which was released by the Australian government in September 2002. The CLERP Act also contains a number of reforms flowing from the recommendations contained in the report of the HIH Insurance Royal Commission released in April 2003.

The CLERP Act proposes three bodies to represent a range of interests:

1. the Financial Reporting Council to oversee standard setting for audit and accounting;
2. the Australian Stock Exchange's Corporate Governance Council to oversee the development of best practice guidelines for corporate governance within listed companies;
3. and the Shareholders and Investors Advisory Council to provide a forum for the consideration of retail investors' concerns.

CPA Australia suggested that the legislation should build a framework that also identifies the conduct and practices of boards of directors, staff who prepare financial reports and internal and external audit functions. It also suggested including the roles of institutional investors, credit rating agencies, financial analysts and investment banks.

7

Marketing and Materials Management

INTRODUCTION

Marketing management is a business discipline focused on the practical application of marketing techniques and the management of a firm's marketing resources and activities. Marketing managers are often responsible for influencing the level, timing, and composition of customer demand in a manner that will achieve the company's objectives.

DEFINITION AND SCOPE

There is no universally accepted definition of the term. In part, this is due to the fact that the role of a marketing manager can vary significantly based on a business' size, corporate culture, and industry context.

For example, in a large consumer products company, the marketing manager may act as the overall general manager of his or her assigned product category or brand with full profit & loss responsibility. In contrast, a small law firm may have no marketing personnel at all, requiring the firm's partners to make marketing management decisions on a largely ad-hoc basis.

In the widely used text Marketing Management (2006), Philip Kotler and Kevin Lane Keller define marketing management as "the art and science of choosing target markets and getting, keeping and growing customers through creating, delivering, and communicating superior customer value."

From this perspective, the scope of marketing management is quite broad. The implication of such a definition is that any activity or resource the firm uses to acquire customers and manage the company's relationships with them is within the purview of marketing management. Additionally, the Kotler and Keller definition encompasses both the development of new products and services and their delivery to customers.

Noted marketing expert Regis McKenna expressed a similar viewpoint in his influential 1991 Harvard Business Review article "Marketing is Everything." McKenna argued that because marketing management encompasses all factors that influence a company's ability to deliver value to customers, it must be "all-pervasive, part of everyone's job description, from the receptionists to the Board of Directors."

This view is also consistent with the perspective of management guru Peter Drucker, who wrote: "Because the purpose of business is to create a customer, the business enterprise has two--and only these two--basic functions: marketing and innovation. Marketing and innovation produce results; all the rest are costs. Marketing is the distinguishing, unique function of the business."

But because many businesses operate with a much more limited definition of marketing, such statements can appear controversial, or even ludicrous to some business executives. This is especially true in those companies where the marketing department is responsible for little more than developing sales brochures and executing advertising campaigns.

The broader, more sophisticated definitions of marketing management from Drucker, Kotler and other scholars are therefore juxtaposed against the narrower operating reality of many businesses. The source of confusion here is often that inside any given firm, the term marketing management may be interpreted to mean whatever the marketing department happens to do, rather than a term that encompasses all marketing activities--even those marketing activities that are actually performed by other departments, such as the sales, finance, or operations departments. If, for example, the finance department of a given company makes pricing decisions (for deals, proposals, contracts, etc.), that finance department has responsibility for an important component of marketing management--pricing.

ACTIVITIES AND FUNCTIONS

Marketing management therefore encompasses a wide variety of functions and activities, although the marketing department itself may be responsible for only a subset of these. Regardless of the organizational unit of the firm responsible for managing them, marketing management functions and activities include the following:

Marketing Research and Analysis

In order to make fact-based decisions regarding marketing strategy and design effective, cost-efficient implementation programs, firms must possess a detailed, objective understanding of their own business and the market in which they operate. In analyzing these issues, the discipline of marketing management often overlaps with the related discipline of strategic planning.

Traditionally, marketing analysis was structured into three areas: Customer analysis, Company analysis, and Competitor analysis (so-called "3Cs" analysis). More recently, it has become fashionable in some marketing circles to divide these further into five "Cs": Customer analysis, Company analysis, Collaborator analysis, Competitor analysis, and analysis of the industry Context.

The focus of customer analysis is to develop a scheme for market segmentation, breaking down the market into various constituent groups of customers, which are called customer segments or market segments. Marketing managers work to develop detailed profiles of each segment, focusing on any number of variables that may differ among the segments: demographic, psychographic, geographic, behavioral, needs-benefit, and other factors may all be examined. Marketers also attempt to track these segments' perceptions of the various products in the market using tools such as perceptual mapping.

In company analysis, marketers focus on understanding the company's cost structure and cost position relative to competitors, as well as working to identify a firm's core competencies and other competitively distinct company resources. Marketing managers may also work with the accounting department to analyze the profits the firm is generating from various product lines and customer accounts. The company may also conduct periodic brand audits to assess the strength of its brands and sources of brand equity.

The firm's collaborators may also be profiled, which may include various suppliers, distributors and other channel partners, joint venture partners, and others. An analysis of complementary products may also be performed if such products exist. Marketing management employs various tools from economics and competitive strategy to analyze the industry context in which the firm operates. These include Porter's five forces, analysis of strategic groups of competitors, value chain analysis and others. Depending on the industry, the regulatory context may also be important to examine in detail.

In Competitor analysis, marketers build detailed profiles of each competitor in the market, focusing especially on their relative competitive strengths and weaknesses using SWOT analysis. Marketing managers will examine each competitor's cost structure, sources of profits, resources and competencies, competitive positioning and product differentiation, degree of vertical integration, historical responses to industry developments, and other factors.

Marketing management often finds it necessary to invest in research to collect the data required to perform accurate marketing analysis. As such, they often conduct market research (alternately marketing research) to obtain this information. Marketers employ a variety of techniques to conduct market research, but some of the more common include:

- Qualitative marketing research, such as focus groups
- Quantitative marketing research, such as statistical surveys
- Experimental techniques such as test markets
- Observational techniques such as ethnographic (on-site) observation.

Marketing managers may also design and oversee various environmental scanning and competitive intelligence processes to help identify trends and inform the company's marketing analysis.

MARKETING STRATEGY

Once the company has obtained an adequate understanding of the customer base and its own competitive position in the industry, marketing managers are able to make key strategic decisions and develop a marketing strategy designed to maximize the revenues and profits of the firm. The selected strategy may aim for any of a variety of specific objectives, including optimizing short-term unit margins, revenue growth, market share, long-term profitability, or other goals.

To achieve the desired objectives, marketers typically identify one or more target customer segments which they intend to pursue. Customer segments are often selected as targets because they score highly on two dimensions: 1) The segment is attractive to serve because it is large, growing, makes frequent purchases, is not price sensitive (i.e. is willing to pay high prices), or other factors; and 2) The company has the resources and capabilities to compete for the segment's business, can meet their needs better than the competition, and can do so profitably. In fact, a commonly cited definition of marketing is simply "meeting needs profitably."

The implication of selecting target segments is that the business will subsequently allocate more resources to acquire and retain customers in the target segment(s) than it will for other, non-targeted customers. In some cases, the firm may go so far as to turn away customers that are not in its target segment. The doorman at a swanky nightclub, for example, may deny entry to unfashionably dressed individuals because the business has made a strategic decision to target the "high fashion" segment of nightclub patrons.

In conjunction with targeting decisions, marketing managers will identify the desired positioning they want the company, product, or brand to occupy in the target customer's mind. This positioning is often an encapsulation of a key benefit the company's product or service offers that is differentiated and superior to the benefits offered by competitive products. For example, Volvo has traditionally positioned its products in the automobile market in North America in order to be perceived as the leader in "safety", whereas BMW has traditionally positioned its brand to be perceived as the leader in "performance."

Ideally, a firm's positioning can be maintained over a long period of time because the company possesses, or can develop, some form of sustainable competitive advantage. The positioning should also be sufficiently relevant to the target segment such that it will drive the purchasing behavior of target customers.

IMPLEMENTATION PLANNING

After the firm's strategic objectives have been identified, the target market selected, and the desired positioning for the company, product or brand has been determined, marketing managers focus on how to best implement the chosen strategy. Traditionally, this has involved implementation planning across the "4Ps" of marketing: Product management, Pricing, Place (i.e. sales and distribution channels), and Promotion.

Taken together, the company's implementation choices across the 4Ps are often described as the marketing mix, meaning the mix of elements the business will employ to "go to market" and execute the marketing strategy. The overall goal for the marketing mix is to consistently deliver a compelling value proposition that reinforces the firm's chosen positioning, builds customer loyalty and brand equity among target customers, and achieves the firm's marketing and financial objectives.

In many cases, marketing management will develop a marketing plan to specify how the company will execute the chosen strategy and achieve the business' objectives. The content of marketing plans varies from firm to firm, but commonly includes:

- An executive summary
- Situation analysis to summarize facts and insights gained from market research and marketing analysis
- The company's mission statement or long-term strategic vision.

- A statement of the company's key objectives, often subdivided into marketing objectives and financial objectives
- The marketing strategy the business has chosen, specifying the target segments to be pursued and the competitive positioning to be achieved
- Implementation choices for each element of the marketing mix (the 4Ps)
- A summary of required investments (in people, programs, IT systems, etc.)
- Financial analysis, projections and forecasted results
- A timeline or high-level project plan
- Metrics, measurements and control processes
- A list of key risks and strategies for managing these risks.

PROJECT, PROCESS, AND VENDOR MANAGEMENT

Once the key implementation initiatives have been identified, marketing managers work to oversee the execution of the marketing plan. Marketing executives may therefore manage any number of specific projects, such as sales force management initiatives, product development efforts, channel marketing programs and the execution of public relations and advertising campaigns. Marketers use a variety of project management techniques to ensure projects achieve their objectives while keeping to established schedules and budgets.

More broadly, marketing managers work to design and improve the effectiveness of core marketing processes, such as new product development, brand management, marketing communications, and pricing. Marketers may employ the tools of business process reengineering to ensure these processes are properly designed, and use a variety of process management techniques to keep them operating smoothly.

Effective execution may require management of both internal resources and a variety of external vendors and service providers, such as the firm's advertising agency. Marketers may therefore coordinate with the company's Purchasing department on the procurement of these services.

LEADERSHIP AND ORGANIZATIONAL MANAGEMENT

Marketing management usually requires leadership of a department or group of professionals engaged in marketing activities. Often, this oversight will extend beyond the company's marketing department itself, requiring the marketing manager to provide cross-functional leadership for various marketing activities. This may require extensive interaction with the human resources department on issues such as recruiting, training, leadership development, performance appraisals, compensation, and other topics.

Marketing management may spend a fair amount of time building or maintaining a marketing orientation for the business. Achieving a market orientation, also known as "customer focus" or the "marketing concept", requires building consensus at the senior management level and then driving customer focus down into the organization.

Cultural barriers may exist in a given business unit or functional area that the marketing manager must address in order to achieve this goal. Additionally, marketing executives often act as a "brand champion" and work to enforce corporate identity standards across the enterprise.

In larger organizations, especially those with multiple business units, top marketing managers may need to coordinate across several marketing departments and also resources from finance, R&D, engineering, operations, manufacturing, or other functional areas to implement the marketing plan. In order to effectively manage these resources, marketing executives may need to spend much of their time focused on political issues and inter-departmental negotiations.

The effectiveness of a marketing manager may therefore depend on his or her ability to make the internal "sale" of various marketing programs equally as much as the external customer's reaction to such programs.

REPORTING, MEASUREMENT AND CONTROL SYSTEMS

Marketing management employs a variety of metrics to measure progress against objectives. It is the responsibility of marketing managers in the marketing department or elsewhere--to ensure that the execution of marketing programs achieves the desired objectives and does so in a cost-efficient manner.

Marketing management therefore often makes use of various organizational control systems, such as sales forecasts, sales force and reseller incentive programs, sales force management systems, and customer relationship management tools (CRM).

Recently, some software vendors have begun using the term "marketing operations management" or "marketing resource management" to describe systems that facilitate an integrated approach for controlling marketing resources. In some cases, these efforts may be linked to various supply chain management systems, such as enterprise resource planning (ERP), material requirements planning (MRP), efficient consumer response (ECR), and inventory management systems.

Measuring the return on investment (ROI) of and marketing effectiveness various marketing initiatives is a significant problem for marketing management. Various market research, accounting and financial tools are used to help estimate the ROI of marketing investments.

Brand valuation, for example, attempts to identify the percentage of a company's market value that is generated by the company's brands, and thereby estimate the financial value of specific investments in brand equity. Another technique, integrated marketing communications (IMC), is a CRM database-driven approach that attempts to estimate the value of marketing mix executions based on the changes in customer behavior these executions generate.

MATERIALS MANAGEMENT

Materials management is the branch of logistics that deals with the tangible components of a supply chain. Speficially, this covers the acquisition of spare parts and replacements, quality control of purchasing and ordering such parts, and the standards involved in ordering, shipping, and warehousing said parts.

Areas of Concentration

Materials management can be broken down into three areas: acquisition, quality control, and standards.

Acquisition: The bulk of materials management deals with the same sort of concepts as supply chain management, but the difference is that materials management deals with surplus material or material that is warehoused for future use.

A materials management operation thus conducts a large amount of the acquisition of parts and material used by supply chain operations "down the line". Some studies in SCM indicate that a poorly organized materials management program can cripple supply efforts more so than inefficiencies in the supply chain itself.

Quality Control: Materials management also ensures that parts and materials used in the supply chain meet minimum requirements by performing quality control. While most of the writing and discussion about materials management is on acquisition and standards, much of the day to day work conducted in materials management deals with QA issues.

Parts and material are tested, both before purchase orders are placed and during use, to ensure there are no short or long term issues that would disrupt the supply chain.

Standards: The final component of materials management is standards compliance.

There are standards that are followed in supply chain management that are critical to a supply chain's function. For example, a supply chain that uses just-in-time or lean replenishment requires absolute perfection in the shipping of parts and material from purchasing agent to warehouse to place of destination.

Systems reliant on vendor-managed inventories must have up-to-date computerized inventories and robust ordering systems for outlying vendors to place orders on. Materials management typically insures that the warehousing and shipping of such components as are needed follows the standards required to avoid problems. This component of materials management is the fastest changing part, due to recent innovations in SCM and in logistics in general, including outsourced management of warehousing, mobile computing, and real-time logistical inventories.

OPERATIONS MANAGEMENT

Operations management is an area of business that is concerned with the production of goods and services, and involves the responsibility of ensuring that business operations are efficient and effective. It is also the management of resources and the distribution of goods and services to customers.

Operations also refers to the production of goods and services, the set of value-added activities that transform inputs into many outputs. Fundamentally, these value-adding creative activities should be aligned with market opportunity for optimal enterprise performance.

Origins: Historically, the body of knowledge stemming from industrial engineering formed the basis of the first MBA programs, and is central to operations management as used across diverse business sectors, industry, consulting and non-profit organizations.

Organizations: A number of professional organizations have been formed to promote operations management profession.

Institute for Operations Research and Management Sciences [INFORMS] has a subdivision called The Manufacturing and Service Operations Management Society [MSOM]. This division has the following objective: The Manufacturing and Service Operations Management Society (MSOM) promotes the enhancement and dissemination of knowledge, and the efficiency of industrial practice, related to the operations function in manufacturing and service enterprises.

Another organization, Production and Operations Management Society (POMS), is an international professional organization representing the interests of POM professionals from around the world.

A third organization, The Association for Operations Management (APICS-the acronym comes from the original name: ~~American~~ Production and Inventory Control Society) defines operations management as "the field of study that focuses on the effective planning, scheduling, use and control of a manufacturing or service organization through the study of concepts from design engineering, industrial engineering, management information systems, quality management, production management, inventory management, accounting, and other functions as they affect the organization" (APICS Dictionary, 11th edition).

PROGRAM MANAGEMENT

Program management is the process of managing a portfolio of multiple ongoing inter-dependent projects. An example would be that of designing, manufacturing and providing support infrastructure for an automobile manufacturer.

This requires hundreds, or even thousands, of separate projects. In an organization or enterprise, Program Management also reflects the emphasis on coordinating and prioritizing resources across projects, departments, and entities to insure that resource contention is managed from a global focus.

The UK government has invested heavily in program management. In Europe, the term normally refers to multiple change projects: projects that are designed to deliver benefits to the host organization. Program management provides a layer above project management focusing on selecting the best group of programs, defining them in terms of their constituent projects and providing an infrastructure where projects can be run successfully but leaving project management to the project management community.

Program management responsibilities can vary. For instance, manufacturing program management responsibilities will be much different than program management responsibilities for a pharmaceutical trial and data collection program.

Key Factors in Program Management

Governance: Programs need a more robust structure and control because of the larger impact their failure can have:

Management: At the lowest level project managers coordinate individual projects. They are overseen by the Program Manager who accounts to the Program Sponsor (or board).

Finances: Tracking of finances is an important part of Program Management and basic costs together with wider costs of administering the program are all tracked.

Infrastructure: Allocation of resources influences the cost and success of the program. The Program Management office monitors overall and project specific resource usage.

Planning: Each project manager creates a plan which fits in with the wider plan of the Program itself.

8

Project Management

Project management is the discipline of organizing and managing resources in such a way that these resources deliver all the work required to complete a project within defined scope, time, and cost constraints. A project is a temporary and one-time endeavor undertaken to create a unique product or service. This property of being a temporary and a one-time undertaking contrasts with processes, or operations, which are permanent or semi-permanent ongoing functional work to create the same product or service over and over again. The management of these two systems is often very different and requires varying technical skills and philosophy, hence requiring the development of project management.

The first challenge of project management is ensuring that a project is delivered within the defined constraints. The second, more ambitious, challenge is the optimized allocation and integration of the inputs needed to meet those pre-defined objectives. The project, therefore, is a carefully selected set of activities chosen to use resources (time, money, people, materials, energy, space, provisions, communication, quality, risk, etc.) to meet the pre-defined objectives.

THE PROJECT MANAGER

Project management is quite often the province and responsibility of an individual project manager. This individual seldom participates directly in the activities that produce the end result, but rather strives to maintain the progress and productive mutual interaction of various parties in such a way that overall risk of failure is reduced.

A project manager is often a client representative and has to determine and implement the exact needs of the client, based on knowledge of the firm he/she is representing. The ability to adapt to the various internal procedures of the contracting party, and to form close links with the nominated representatives, is essential in ensuring that the key issues of cost; time; quality; and, above all, client satisfaction, can be realized. In whatever field, a successful project manager must be able to envisage the entire project from start to finish and to have the ability to ensure that this vision is realized.

Any type of product or service--buildings, vehicles, electronics, computer software, financial services, etc. may have its implementation overseen by a project manager and its operations by a product manager.

THE TRADITIONAL TRIPLE CONSTRAINTS

Like any human undertaking, projects need to be performed and delivered under certain constraints. Traditionally, these constraints have been listed as scope, time, and cost. This is also referred to as the Project Management Triangle, where each side represents a constraint. One side of the triangle cannot be changed without impacting the others. A further refinement of the constraints separates product 'quality' or 'performance' from scope, and turns quality into a fourth constraint.

The time constraint refers to the amount of time available to complete a project. The cost constraint refers to the budgeted amount available for the project. The scope constraint refers to what must be done to produce the project's end result. These three constraints are often competing constraints: increased scope typically means increased time and increased cost, a tight time constraint could mean increased costs and reduced scope, and a tight budget could mean increased time and reduced scope.

The discipline of project management is about providing the tools and techniques that enable the project team (not just the project manager) to organize their work to meet these constraints.

Time: Broken down for analytical purposes into the time required to complete the components of the project, which is then further broken down into the time required to complete each task contributing to the completion of each component. When performing tasks using project management, it is important to cut the work into several smaller pieces so that it is easy to follow.

Costing: Cost to develop a project depends on several variables including (chiefly): labor rates, material rates, risk management, plant (buildings, machines, etc.), equipment, and profit. When hiring an independent consultant for a project, cost will typically be determined by the consultant's or firm's per diem rate multiplied by an estimated quantity for completion.

Scope and Significance: Requirements specified for the end result. The overall definition of what the project is supposed to accomplish, and a specific description of what the end result should be or accomplish. A major component of scope is the quality of the final product. The amount of time put into individual tasks determines the overall quality of the project. Some tasks may require a given amount of time to complete adequately, but given more time could be completed exceptionally. Over the course of a large project, quality can have a significant impact on time and cost (or vice versa).

PROJECT MANAGEMENT ACTIVITIES

Project Management is composed of several different types of activities such as:

1. Planning the work or objectives
2. Analysis & Design of objectives
3. Assessing and controlling risk (or Risk Management)
4. Estimating resources
5. Allocation of resources
6. Organizing the work
7. Acquiring human and material resources
8. Assigning tasks

9. Directing activities
10. Controlling project execution
11. Tracking and Reporting progress
12. Analyzing the results based on the facts achieved
13. Defining the products of the project
14. Forecasting future trends in the project
15. Quality Management
16. Issues Management
17. Issues solving
18. Defect prevention
19. Project Closure meet

THE ARTIFACTS

All successful projects adequately document objectives and deliverables. These documents are a mechanism to align sponsors, clients, and project team's expectations.

1. Project Charter
2. Business case/Feasibility Study
3. Scope Statement / Terms of reference
4. Project Management Plan / Project Initiation Document
5. Work Breakdown Structure
6. Change Control Plan
7. Risk Management Plan
8. Communications Plan
9. Governance Model
10. Risk Register
11. Issue Log
12. Action Item List
13. Resource Management Plan
14. Project Schedule
15. Status Report

16. Responsibility assignment matrix
17. Database of risks
18. Database of lessons learned
19. Stakeholder Analysis

These documents are normally hosted on a shared resource (i.e., Intranet web page) and are available for review by the project's stakeholders. Changes or updates to these documents are explicitly outlined in the project's configuration management (or change control plan).

CONTROL VARIABLES

Project Management tries to gain control over variables such as risk:

Risk: Potential points of failure. Most negative risks (or potential failures) can be overcome or resolved, given enough planning capabilities, time, and resources. According to some definitions (including PMBOK Third Edition) risk can also be categorized as "positive--" meaning that there is a potential opportunity, e.g., complete the project faster than expected.

Customers (either internal or external project sponsors), external organizations (such as government agencies and regulators) can dictate the extent of three variables: time, cost, and scope. The remaining variable (risk) is managed by the project team, ideally based on solid estimation and response planning techniques. Through a negotiation process among project stakeholders, an agreement defines the final objectives, in terms of time, cost, scope, and risk, usually in the form of a charter or contract.

To properly control these variables a good project manager has a depth of knowledge and experience in these four areas (time, cost, scope, and risk), and in six other areas as well: integration, communication, human resources, quality assurance, schedule development, and procurement.

HISTORICAL VIEW

As a discipline, Project Management developed from several different fields of application, including construction, mechanical engineering, military projects, etc. In the United States, the forefather of project management is Henry Gantt, called the father of planning and control techniques, who is famously known for his use of the "bar" chart as a project management tool, for being an associate of Frederick Winslow Taylor's theories of scientific management, and for his study of the work and management of Navy ship building. His work is the forerunner to many modern project management tools, including the work breakdown structure (WBS) and resource allocation.

The 1950s mark the beginning of the modern project management era. Again, in the United States, prior to the 1950s, projects were managed on an ad hoc basis using mostly Gantt Charts, and informal techniques and tools. At that time, two mathematical project scheduling models were developed: (1) the "Program Evaluation and Review Technique" or PERT, developed as part of the United States Navy's (in conjunction with the Lockheed Corporation) Polaris missile submarine program; and (2) the "Critical Path Method" (CPM) developed in a joint venture by both DuPont Corporation and Remington Rand Corporation for managing plant maintenance projects. These mathematical techniques quickly spread into many private enterprises.

In 1969, the Project Management Institute (PMI) was formed to serve the interest of the project management industry. The premise of PMI is that the tools and techniques of project management are common even among the widespread application of projects from the software industry to the construction industry. In 1981, the PMI Board of Directors authorized the development of what has become the The Guide to the Project Management Body of Knowledge, containing the standards and guidelines of practice that are widely used throughout the profession.

THE APPROACHES

There are several approaches that can be taken to managing project activities including agile, interactive, incremental, and phased approaches.

Regardless of the approach employed, careful consideration needs to be given to clarify surrounding project objectives, goals, and importantly, the roles and responsibilities of all participants and stakeholders.

The Traditional Approach

A traditional phased approach identifies a sequence of steps to be completed. In the traditional approach, we can distinguish 5 components of a project (4 stages plus control) in the development of a project:

1. project initiation stage;
2. project planning or design stage;
3. project execution or production stage;
4. project monitoring and controlling systems;
5. project completion stage.

Not all the projects will visit every stage as projects can be terminated before they reach completion. Some projects probably don't have the planning and/or the monitoring. Some projects will go through steps 2, 3 and 4 multiple times.

Many industries utilize variations on these stages. For example, in bricks and mortar architectural design, projects typically progress through stages like Pre-Planning, Conceptual Design, Schematic Design, Design Development, Construction Drawings (or Contract Documents), and Construction Administration. In software development, this approach is often known as 'waterfall development' i.e. one series of tasks after another in linear sequence. In software development many organizations have adapted the Rational Unified Process (RUP) to fit this methodology, although RUP does not require or explicitly recommend this practice. Waterfall development can work for small tightly defined projects, but for larger projects of undefined or unknowable scope, it is less suited. Because software development is often the realization of a new or novel product, this method has been widely accepted as ineffective for software projects where requirements are largely unknowable up front and susceptible to change. While the names may differ from industry to industry, the actual stages typically follow common steps to problem solving--defining the problem, weighing options, choosing a path, implementation and evaluation.

THE CRITICAL CHAIN

Critical chain is an extension to the traditional critical path method.

In critical studies of project management, it has been noted that several of these fundamentally PERT-based models are not well suited for the multi-project company environment of today. Most of them are aimed at very large-scale, one-time, non-routine projects, and nowadays all kinds of management are expressed in terms of projects. Using complex models for "projects" (or rather "tasks") spanning a few weeks has been proven to cause unnecessary costs and low maneuverability in several cases. Instead, project management experts try to identify different "lightweight" models, such as, for example Extreme Programming for software development and Scrum techniques. The generalization of Extreme Programming to other kinds of projects is extreme project management, which may be used in combination with the process modeling and management principles of human interaction management.

Process-based Management

Also furthering the concept of project control is the incorporation of process-based management. This area has been driven by the use of Maturity models such as the CMMI (Capability Maturity Model Integration) and ISO/IEC15504 (SPICE-Software Process Improvement and Capability Determination), which have been far more successful.

Agile project management approaches based on the principles of human interaction management are founded on a process view of human collaboration. This contrasts sharply with traditional approach. In the agile software development or flexible product development approach, the project is seen as a series of relatively small tasks conceived and executed as the situation demands in an adaptive manner, rather than as a completely pre-planned process.

PROJECT SYSTEMS

As mentioned above, traditionally, project development includes five elements: control systems and four stages.

Project Control Systems

Project control is that element of a project that keeps it on-track, on-time, and within budget. Project control begins early in the project with planning and ends late in the project with post-implementation review, having a thorough involvement of each step in the process. Each project should be assessed for the appropriate level of control needed, too much control is too time consuming, too little control is too costly. Clarifying the cost to the business if the control is not implemented in terms of errors, fixes, and additional audit fees.

Control systems are needed for cost, risk, quality, communication, time, change, procurement, and human resources. In addition, auditors should consider how important the projects are to the financial statements, how reliant the stakeholders are on controls, and how many controls exist. Auditors should review the development process and procedures how they are implemented. The process of development and the quality of the final product may also be assessed if needed or requested. A business may want the auditing firm to be involved throughout the process to catch problems earlier on so that they can be fixed more easily. An auditor can serve as a controls consultant as part of the development team or as an independent auditor as part of an audit. Businesses sometimes use formal systems development processes. These help assure that systems are developed successfully. A formal process is more effective in creating strong controls, and auditors should review this process to confirm that it is well designed and is followed in practice. A good formal systems development plan outlines:

- A strategy to align development with the organization's broader objectives
- Standards for new systems
- Project management policies for timing and budgeting
- Procedures describing the process

Stages of Project Development

Regardless of the methodology used, the project development process will have the same major stages: initiation, development, production or execution, and closing/maintenance.

Initiation: The initiation stage determines the nature and scope of the development. If this stage is not performed well, it is unlikely that the project will be successful in meeting the business's needs. The key project controls needed here is an understanding of the business environment and making sure that all necessary controls are incorporated into the project. Any deficiencies should be reported and a recommendation should be made to fix them.

The initiation stage should include a cohesive plan that encompasses the following areas:

- Study analyzing the business needs in measurable goals.
- Review of the current operations.
- Conceptual design of the operation of the final product.
- Equipment requirement.
- Financial analysis of the costs and benefits including a budget.
- Select stake holders, including users, and support personnel for the project.
- Project charter including costs, tasks, deliverables, and schedule.

Planning and Design

After the initiation stage, the system is designed. Occasionally, a small prototype of the final product is built and tested. Testing is generally performed by a combination of testers and end users, and can occur after the prototype is built or concurrently. Controls should be in place that ensure that the final product will meet the specifications of the project charter. The results of the design stage should include a product design that:

- Satisfies the project sponsor, end user, and business requirements.
- Functions as it was intended.
- Can be produced within quality standards.
- Can be produced within time and budget constraints.

Production or Execution

The execution stage includes the actual implementation of the design or plan. In software systems, this includes conversion (transfer of data from an old system to a new system), documentation, and training.

From an auditor's perspective, training is also important because it helps users use the software correctly. The bulk of the project's work and largest capital expenditure is realized in this stage.

CLOSING AND MAINTENANCE

Closing includes the formal acceptance of the project and the ending thereof. Administrative activities include the archiving of the files and documenting lessons learned.

Maintenance is an ongoing process, and it includes:

- Continuing support of end users
- Correction of errors
- Updates of the software over time

In this stage, auditors should pay attention to how effectively and quickly user problems are resolved.

Over the course of any construction project, the work scope changes. Change is a normal and expected part of the construction process. Changes can be the result of necessary design modifications, differing site conditions, material availability, contractor-requested changes, value engineering and impacts from third parties, to name a few. Beyond executing the change in the field, the change normally needs to be documented to show what was actually constructed.

Hence, the owner usually requires a final record to show all changes or, more specifically, any change that modifies the tangible portions of the finished work. The record is made on the contract documents-usually, but not necessarily limited to, the design drawings. The end product of this effort is what the industry terms as-built drawings, or more simply, "asbuilts." The requirement for providing them is a norm in construction contracts.

PROJECT MANAGEMENT ASSOCIATIONS

Several national and professional associations exist which has as their aim the promotion and development of project management and the project management profession. The most prominent associations include:

- The Association for Project Management (UK) (APM)
- The Australian Institute of Project Management (AIPM)
- The International Project Management Association (IPMA)
- The Project Management Institute (PMI)
- The International Association of Project and Program Management (IAPPM)
- The International Project Management Commission (IPMC)

9

Quality and Time Management

Quality management is a method for ensuring that all the activities necessary to design, develop and implement a product or service are effective and efficient with respect to the system and its performance.

QUALITY IMPROVEMENT

W. Edwards Deming is best known for his management philosophy establishing quality, productivity, and competitive position. He has formulated 14 points of attention for managers, some of these points are more appropriate for service management:

- Break down barriers between departments;
- Management should learn their responsibilities, and take on leadership;
- Improve constantly;
- Institute a programme of education and self-improvement.

The following diagram is the Shewhart cycle (PDCA) for quality improvement, made popular by Deming.

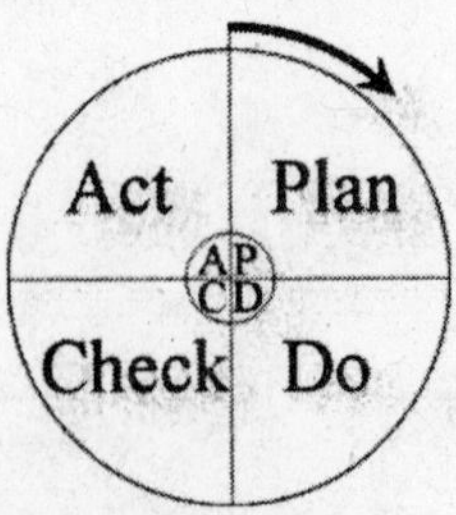

Shewhart Cycle

The philosophy is to keep improving the quality of an organization. It is defined by four keys:

- *Plan:* Design or revise business process components to improve results
- *Do:* Implement the plan and measure its performance
- *Check:* Assess the measurements and report the results to decision makers
- *Act:* Decide on changes needed to improve the process

The consolidation phase enables the organization to take stock of what has been taking place and to ensure made to processes that require documentation (both to allow processes to be repeatable and to facilitate recognition of the achievement of some form of quality standard).

QUALITY STANDARDS

The International Organization for Standardization created the Quality Management System (QMS) standards in 1987. These were the ISO 9000:1987 series of standards comprising ISO 9001:1987, ISO 9002:1987 and ISO 9003:1987; which were applicable in different types of industries, based on the type of activity: designing, production or service delivery. The standards have been regularly reviewed every few years by the International Organization for Standardization (ISO). The version of these standards was revised in 1994 and was called the ISO 9000:1994 series; comprising of the ISO 9001:1994, 9002:1994 and 9003:1994 versions. The last revision was in the year 2000 and the series was called ISO 9000:2000 series. However the ISO 9002 and 9003 standards were integrated and one single certifiable standard was created under ISO 9001:2000. Since December 2003, ISO 9002 and 9003 standards are not valid, and the organizations previously holding these standards need to do a transition from the old to the new standards. The ISO 9004:2000 document gives guidelines for performance improvement over and above the basic standard (i.e. ISO 9001:2000).

The Quality Management System standards created by ISO are meant to certify the processes and the system of an organization and not the product or service itself. ISO 9000 standards do not certify the quality of the product or service.

Recently the International Organization released a new standard, ISO 22000, meant for the food industry. This standard covers the values and principles of ISO 9000 and the HACCP standards. It gives one single integrated standard for the food industry and is expected to become more popular in the coming years in such industry.

The most elaborated and accepted concept of quality management is the model of the EFQM Excellence Model.

SKILLS MANAGEMENT

Skills Management is the practice of understanding, developing and deploying people and their skills. Well-implemented skills management should identify the skills that job roles require, the skills of individual employees, and any gap between the two.

An Overview

The skills involved can be defined by the organization concerned, or by third party institutions. They are usually defined in terms of a skills framework, also known as a competency framework or skills matrix. This consists of a list of skills, and a grading system, with a definition of what it means to be at particular level for a given skill. (For an example of a mature skills framework, see the Skills Framework for the Information Age,, a technical IT skills framework owned by a British not-for-profit organization.)

To be most useful, skills management needs to be conducted as an ongoing process, with individuals assessing and updating their recorded skill sets regularly. These updates should occur at least as frequently as employees' regular line manager reviews, and certainly when their skill sets have changed.

Skills management systems record the results of this process in a database, and allow analysis of the data.

Employees who Benefit

Skills management provides a structured approach to developing individual and collective skills, and gives a common vocabulary for discussing skills. As well as this general benefit, three groups of employees receive specific benefits from skills management.

Individual Employees

As a result of skills management, employees should be aware of the skills their job requires, and any skills gaps that they have. Depending on their employer, it may also result in a personal development plan (PDP) of training to bridge some or all of those skills gaps over a given period.

Line Managers: Skills management enables managers to know the skill strengths and weaknesses of employees reporting to them. It can also enable them to search for employees with particular skill sets (e.g. to fill a role on a particular project).

Organization Executives: A rolled-up view of skills and skills gaps across an organization can enable its executives to see areas of skill strength and weakness. This enables them to plan for the future against the current and future abilities of staff, as well as to prioritise areas for skills development.

Talent Manager

A talent manager, also known as a personal manager, is one who guides the career of artists in the entertainment business. The responsibility of the talent manager is to oversee the day to day business affairs of an artist; to advise and counsel talent about professional matters and personal decisions which may affect their career.

The roles and responsibilities of a manager vary slightly from industry to industry, as do the commissions to which the manager is entitled. Music managers duties differ from those who advise actors, writers, directors, etc.

Music Managers

Music managers can manage Bands, singers and DJs. The role of a music manager is extensive, often tasks are divided among personal managers, business managers, tour managers, agents, bookers, and promoters.

Starting off: Early on in an artist's career, the different facets of management and marketing falls upon either the band itself or, if they have one, the manager. Because the band or artist is relatively unknown, promotion, booking, and touring are minimal. When starting off, a new music manager should establish a clear understanding of what the artist(s) want. This can be done through a written or verbal contract. A music managers' first task should be focused around a CD launch.

Compensation: Rates should be clearly stated initially. A good manager should understand the artist's perspective. A new manager has no experience or clout. In a band of six members, each member might receive less than the manager (who normally gets 15-20%). A tentative agreement, which can be renegotiated at a later date is often best. Managers who insist on a number that the band does not agree with can expect to be let go at the first convenient opportunity.

Gigs: It is important for a band to have experience in front of crowds. Fundraisers and talent shows are good experience and do not require a lot of commitment (in terms of fan pull) on the part of the artist. If the artist wants a gig in a pub or bar, expect there to be conditions. The following is a list of questions asked by bar owners/managers (in order of importance).

- What kind of music?
- How many people can you bring?

That's all. In some cases they may ask for a demo (a recording of four of the artists' best songs). The main objective for the bar owner is to fill their floor on any given night. They don't care if you're terrible they just want to see numbers. Under 75 people is generally frowned upon and will result in a minimum fee. A minimum fee could be upwards of $100. Some bar owners will waive or reduce their $100, $200, or $300 charge if the artist can pull in a significant number of people (predetermined during negotiations-usually a handshake).

Photography: While the artist is recording, a photographer should be searched. Pictures of the artist can be used for websites, CD labels/jackets, posters, and press kit. Cost for high quality rolls of film and their processing could be upwards of $200 for 150 pictures (labour not included). Finding a photographer friend is helpful but don't expect him or her to cover material cost. Have the photographs taken before your CD designs or artwork go into production.

CD Launch Venue

Once a production date is given you can safely go out searching venues. CD launches are more attractive to bar owners because it nearly guarantees an audience. Consequently CD launch venues are relatively easy to land. Try to book a place where the crowd will feel good walking into and out of. Presentation is everything. The crowd should be talking about the artist on arrival; not the crappy conditions of the neighbourhood or bar. The size of the venue should be relative to your means. If the place is too big, the artist will look unimportant. A small place can be a good thing. Just make sure the stage can fit the band's gear.

Press Kit: Once a CD launch date is established a press kit should be prepared. The press kit is used to contact the press to promote the band. By this stage in the artist's career they should have a good grasp of their level of talent. A press kit consists of:

- Pamphlet with artist(s) biography, career highlights and pictures.
- A written article about the artist that the press can easily edit and submit in their paper (less work for them).
- A demo CD (in some cases the entire CD should be sent so the magazine/newspaper/radio station can review the entire CD.
- Two tickets to the CD launch (if there is one)

It is important for the press kit to be flashy and attractive. It does not have to be expensive.

Typical large artist management companies include Gremlin UK, Triskele and Wise Buddah.

Lecturers' Managers: Since the mid 80's Lecturers have Personal Managers, similar to their colleagues in the Music industry, the Lecturer's Managers are representing the lecturer's interests and marketing their lectures.

TIME MANAGEMENT

Time management includes tools or techniques for planning and scheduling time, usually with the aim to increase the effectiveness and/or efficiency of personal and corporate time use. These are embodied in a number of books, seminars and courses, which may offer conflicting advice. The common denominators of these strategies are a to-do-list, setting priorities and goal management. Some of the best known examples of time management strategies are tied to specific lines of time management products.

Time management for personal use is a type of self-management. In a corporate setting, time management software can satisfy the need to control employees, make it easier to coordinate work and increases accountability of individual employees. Planning time and writing to-do-lists also consumes time and needs to be scheduled. This is one of the major criticisms of time management.

An Overview

Time management strategies are usually associated with the recommendation to set goals. These goals are written down and broken down into a project, an action plan or a simple to-do-list. Deadlines are set and priorities are assigned to the individual items on the to-do-list. This process results in a daily plan with a to-do-list. Some authors recommend a weekly instead of a daily perspective.

The Task List

A task list (also to-do list) is a list of tasks to be completed, such as chores or steps toward completing a project. It is an inventory tool that serves as an alternative to memory.

Task lists are used in self-management, grocery lists, business management, project management, and software development. It may involve more than one list.

When you accomplish one of the items on a task list, you check it off or cross it off. The traditional method is to write these on a piece of paper with a pen or pencil, usually on a note pad or clip-board. Numerous software equivalents are now available, and many popular e-mail clients include task list applications, as do most PDAs. There are also several web-based task list applications, many of which are free.

Task List Organization

Task lists are often tiered. The simplest tiered system includes a general to-do list (or task-holding file) to record all the tasks the person needs to accomplish, and a daily to-do list which is created each day by transferring tasks from the general to-do list. Task lists are often prioritized:

- One method of organizing a general to-do list is the ABC method. With this approach, the list is divided into three sections, labelled A, B, and C, containg tasks that need to be done within a day, a week, and a month, respectively.
- To prioritize a daily task list, one either records the tasks in the order of highest priority, or assigns them a number after they are listed ("1" for highest priority, "2" for second highest priority, etc.) which indicates in which order to execute the tasks. The latter method is generally faster, allowing the tasks to be recorded more quickly.

Software Applications

Modern task list applications may have built-in task hierarchy (tasks are composed of subtasks which again may contain subtasks), may support multiple methods of filtering and ordering the list of tasks, and may allow to associate arbitrarily long notes for each task.

Task list applications may be thought as lightweight personal information manager or project management software.

Task list is also a synonym for process list i.e. the list of program instances (processes) the computer is currently executing.

Dwelling on the Lists

- According to Sandberg, task lists "aren't the key to productivity [that] they're cracked up to be". He reports an estimated "30% of listers spend more time managing their lists than [they do] completing what's on them".

- This could be caused by procrastination: by prolonging the planning activity, the individual avoids the tasks he should be doing by creating the illusion that he's still necessarily preparing for them. This is akin to analysis paralysis. As with any activity, there's a point of diminishing returns. For a task system to be efficient and effective, the user must recognize this, conquer his or her procrastination, and focus on completing the tasks.

Rigid Adherence

- Hendrickson asserts that rigid adherence to task lists can create a "tyranny of the to-do list" that forces one to "waste time on unimportant activities".
- Again, the point of diminishing returns applies here too, but toward the size of the task. Some level of detail must be taken for granted for a task system to work. Rather than put "clean the kitchen", "clean the bedroom", and "clean the bathroom", it is more efficient to put "housekeeping" and save time spent writing and reduce the system's administrative load (each task entered into the system generates a cost in time and effort to manage it, aside from the execution of the task).
- Listing routine tasks wastes time. If you are in the habit of brushing your teeth every day, then there is no reason to put it down on the task list. The same goes for getting out of bed, fixing meals, etc. If you need to track routine tasks, then a standard list or chart may be useful, to avoid the procedure of manually listing these items over and over.
- To remain flexible, a task system must allow adaptation, in the form of rescheduling in the face of unexpected problems and opportunities, to save time spent on irrelevant or less than optimal tasks.
- To avoid getting stuck in a wasteful pattern, the task system should also include regular (monthly, semi-

annual, and annual) planning and system-evaluation sessions, to weed out inefficiencies and ensure the user is headed in the direction he or she truly desires.

- If some time is not regularly spent on achieving long-range goals, the individual may get stuck in a perpetual holding pattern on short-term plans, like staying at a particular job much longer than originally planned.

THE FOUR GENERATIONS OF TIME MANAGEMENT

Stephen R. Covey offers a categorization scheme for the hundreds of time management approaches that are on the market today.

First Generation: Reminders

Aficionados of this approach limit their time management efforts to keeping lists and notes. They see these papers as reminders. Items that are not done by the end of the day are transferred to the next day's list in the evening. Covey also calls this type of style the "Far Eastern, Go with the Flow".

Second Generation: Planning and Preparation

People in the second generation use calendars and appointment books. They will note where meetings are held and identify deadlines; this is sometimes even done on a computer. As opposed to the first generation, the second generation plans and prepares, schedules future appointments, and sets goals. This in turn saves their time.

Third Generation: Planning, Prioritizing, Controlling

Third generation time managers prioritize their activities on a daily basis. They tend to use detailed forms of daily planning on a computer or on a paper-based organizer. This approach implies spending some time in clarifying values and priorities.

Fourth Generation: being Efficient and Proactive

Stephen R. Covey, in First Things First, refers to his approach as the 4th generation time management, and emphasizes the difference between urgency and importance in planning. For example: some people may go their entire lives completely missing out on important things (like spending time with their children before they have grown up) because it was never "urgent." The point is not to ignore urgent things, but to embrace important things without waiting for them to become urgent.

Urgency can be deceptive. It can make some unimportant things appear to be important. Also, making time for important things may require spending less time on unimportant things, regardless of their urgency.

TECHNIQUES FOR SETTING PRIORITIES

ABC Analysis: A technique that has been used in business management for a long time is the categorization of large data into groups. These groups are often marked A, B, and C-hence the name. Activities that are perceived as having highest priority are assigned an A, those with lowest priority are labeled C. ABC analysis can incorporate more than three groups. ABC analysis is frequently combined with Pareto analysis.

Pareto Analysis: This is the idea that 80% of tasks can be completed in 20% of the disposable time. The remaining 20% of tasks will take up 80% of the time. This principle is used to sort tasks into two parts. According to this form of Pareto analysis it is recommended that tasks that fall into the first category be assigned a higher priority.

The 80-20-rule can also be applied to increase productivity: it is assumed that 80% of the productivity can be achieved by doing 20% of the tasks. If productivity is the aim of time management, then these tasks should be prioritized higher.

MANAGEMENT PROCESS

Management process is a process of planning and controlling the performance or execution of any type of activity, such as:

- a project (project management process) or
- a process (process management process, sometimes referred to as the process performance measurement and management system).

Organization's top management is responsible for carrying out its management process.

PROJECT PLANNING

Project planning is part of project management, which relates to the use of schedules such as Gantt charts to plan and subsequently report progress within the project environment.

Initially, the project scope is defined and the appropriate methods for completing the project are determined. Following this step, the durations for the various tasks necessary to complete the work are listed and grouped into a work breakdown structure. The logical dependencies between tasks are defined using an activity network diagram that enables identification of the critical path. Float or slack time in the schedule can be calculated using project management software. Then the necessary resources can be estimated and costs for each activity can be allocated to each resource, giving the total project cost. At this stage, the project plan may be optimized to achieve the appropriate balance between resource usage and project duration to comply with the project objectives. Once established and agreed, the plan becomes what is known as the baseline. Progress will be measured against the baseline throughout the life of the project. Analyzing progress compared to the baseline is known as earned value management.

10

Strategic Management

Strategic management is that set of managerial decisions and actions that determines the long-run performance of a corporation. It includes environmental scanning, strategy formulation, strategy implementation and evaluation and control.

OVERVIEW

An organization's strategy must be appropriate for its resources, environmental circumstances, and core objectives, The process involves matching the company's [internal resources (eg IT) and capabilities (eg quality management)] to the external business environment the organization faces. Strategy formulation involves:

- Doing a situation analysis: both internal and external; both micro-environmental and macro-environmental.
- Concurrent with this assessment, objectives are set. This involves crafting vision statements (long term view of a possible future), mission statements (the role that the organization gives itself in society), overall corporate objectives (both financial and strategic), strategic business unit objectives (both financial and strategic), and tactical objectives.
- These objectives should, in the light of the situation analysis, suggest a strategic plan. The plan provides the details of how to achieve these objectives.

This three-step strategy formulation process is sometimes referred to as determining where you are now, determining where you want to go, and then determining how to get there. These three questions are the essence of strategic planning. SWOT Analysis: I/O Economics for the external factors and RBV for the internal factors.

Strategy implementation involves:

- Allocation of sufficient resources (financial, personnel, time, technology support)
- Establishing a chain of command or some alternative structure (such as cross functional teams)
- Assigning responsibility of specific tasks or processes to specific individuals or groups
- It also involves managing the process. This includes monitoring results, comparing to benchmarks and best practices, evaluating the efficacy and efficiency of the process, controlling for variances, and making adjustments to the process as necessary.
- When implementing specific programs, this involves acquiring the requisite resources, developing the process, training, process testing, documentation, and integration with (and/or conversion from) legacy processes.

Strategy formulation and implementation is an on-going, never-ending, integrated process requiring continuous reassessment and reformation. Strategic management is dynamic; see Strategy dynamics. It involves a complex pattern of actions and reactions. It is partially planned and partially unplanned. Strategy is both planned and emergent, dynamic, and interactive. Some people (such as Andy Grove at Intel) feel that there are critical points at which a strategy must take a new direction in order to be in step with a changing business environment. These critical points of change are called strategic inflection points.

TIME SCALES

Strategic management operates on several time scales. Short term strategies involve planning and managing for the present. Long term strategies involve preparing for and preempting the future. Marketing strategist Derek Abell (1993), has suggested that understanding this dual nature of strategic management is the least understood part of the process. He claims that balancing the temporal aspects of strategic planning requires the use of dual strategies simultaneously.

Strategic Management is actually a solid foundation or a framework within which all the functionning managerial operations are bundled together. This is the highest level corporate activity that sets the terms and goals for a company that it should follow for prosperity.

GENERAL APPROACHES

In general terms, there are two main approaches to strategic management which are opposite but complement each other in some ways:

- The Industrial Organization Approach
    - o based on economic theory-deals with issues like competitive rivalry, resource allocation, economies of scale
    - o assumptions-rationality, self discipline behaviour, profit maximization
- The Sociological Approach
    - o deals primarily with human interactions
    - o assumptions-bounded rationality, satisficing behaviour, profit sub-optimality. An example of a company that currently operates this way is Google

Strategic management techniques can be viewed as bottom-up, top-down, or collaborative processes. In the bottom-up approach, employees submit proposals to their managers who, in turn, funnel the best ideas further up the organization. This is often accomplished by a capital budgeting process. Proposals are assessed using financial criteria such as return on investment or cost-benefit analysis. The proposals that are approved form the substance of a new strategy, all of which is done without a grand strategic design or a strategic architect. The top-down approach is the most common by far. In it, the CEO, possibly with the assistance of a strategic planning team, decides on the overall direction the company should take. Some organizations are starting to experiment with collaborative strategic planning techniques that recognize the emergent nature of strategic decisions.

THE STRATEGY OF HIERARCHY

In most (large) corporations there are several levels of strategy. Strategic management is the highest in the sense that it is the broadest, applying to all parts of the firm. It gives direction to corporate values, corporate culture, corporate goals, and corporate missions. Under this broad corporate strategy there are often functional or business unit strategies.

Functional strategies include marketing strategies, new product development strategies, human resource strategies, financial strategies, legal strategies, and information technology management strategies. The emphasis is on short and medium term plans and is limited to the domain of each department's functional responsibility. Each functional department attempts to do its part in meeting overall corporate objectives, and hence to some extent their strategies are derived from broader corporate strategies.

Many companies feel that a functional organizational structure is not an efficient way to organize activities so they have reengineered according to processes or Strategic business units (SBUs). A strategic business unit is a semi-autonomous unit within an organization. It is usually responsible for its own budgeting, new product decisions, hiring decisions, and price setting. An SBU is treated as an internal profit centre by corporate headquarters. Each SBU is responsible for developing its business strategies, strategies that must be in tune with broader corporate strategies.

The "lowest" level of strategy is Operational strategy. It is very narrow in focus and deals with day-to-day operational activities such as scheduling criteria. It must operate within a budget but is not at liberty to adjust or create that budget. Operational strategy was encouraged by Peter Drucker in his theory of Management by objectives (MBO). Operational level strategies are informed by business level strategies which, in turn, are informed by corporate level strategies. Business strategy, which refers to the aggregated operational strategies of single business firm or that of an SBU in a diversified corporation refers to the way in which a firm competes in its chosen arenas.

Corporate strategy, then, refers to the overarching strategy of the diversified firm. Such corporate strategy answers the questions of "in which businesses should we compete?" and "how does being in one business add to the competitive advantage of another portfolio firm, as well as the competitive advantage of the corporation as a whole?"

Since the turn of the millennium, there has been a tendency in some firms to revert to a simpler strategic structure. This is being driven by information technology. It is felt that knowledge management systems should be used to share information and create common goals. Strategic divisions are thought to hamper this process. Most recently, this notion of strategy has been captured under the rubric of dynamic strategy, popularized by the strategic management textbook authored by Carpenter and Sanders This work builds on that of Brown and Eisenhart as well as Christensen and portrays firm strategy, both business and corporate, as necessarily embracing ongoing strategic change, and the seamless integration of strategy formulation and implementation. Such change and implementation are usually built into the strategy through the staging and pacing facets.

11

Corporate Governance

Corporate governance is the set of processes, customs, policies, laws and institutions affecting the way a corporation is directed, administered or controlled. Corporate governance also includes the relationships among the many players involved (the stakeholders) and the goals for which the corporation is governed. The principal players are the shareholders, management and the board of directors. Other stakeholders include employees, suppliers, customers, banks and other lenders, regulators, the environment and the community at large.

Corporate governance is a multi-faceted subject. An important theme of corporate governance deals with issues of accountability and fiduciary duty, essentially advocating the implementation of guidelines and mechanisms to ensure good behaviour and protect shareholders. Another key focus is the economic efficiency view, through which the corporate governance system should aim to optimize economic results, with a strong emphasis on shareholders welfare. There are yet other sides to the corporate governance subject, such as the stakeholder view, which calls for more attention and accountability to players other than the shareholders (e.g.: the employees or the environment).

Recently there has been considerable interest in the corporate governance practices of modern corporations, particularly since the high-profile collapses of large US firms such as Enron Corporation and Worldcom.

Definition: The term corporate governance has come to mean two things.

- the processes by which companies are directed and controlled.
- a field in economics, which studies the many issues arising from the separation of ownership and control.

Relevant rules include applicable laws of the land as well as internal rules of a corporation. Relationships include those between all related parties, the most important of which are the owners, managers, directors of the board, regulatory authorities and to a lesser extent employees and the community at large. Systems and processes deal with matters such as delegation of authority.

The corporate governance structure spells out the rules and procedures for making decisions on corporate affairs. It also provides the structure through which the company objectives are set, as well as the means of attaining and monitoring the performance of those objectives.

Corporate governance is used to monitor whether outcomes are in accordance with plans and to motivate the organisation to be more fully informed in order to maintain or alter organisational activity. Corporate governance is the mechanism by which individuals are motivated to align their actual behaviours with the overall participants.

History: In the 19th century, state corporation law enhanced the rights of corporate boards to govern without unanimous consent of shareholders in exchange for statutory benefits like appraisal rights, in order to make corporate governance more efficient. Since that time, and because most large publicly traded corporations in America are incorporated under corporate administration friendly Delaware law, and because America's wealth has been increasingly securitized into various corporate entities and institutions, the rights of individual owners and shareholders have become increasingly derivative and dissipated. The concerns of shareholders over administration pay and stock losses periodically has led to more frequent calls for Corporate Governance reforms.

In the 20th century in the immediate aftermath of the Wall Street Crash of 1929 legal scholars such as Adolf Augustus Berle, Edwin Dodd, and Gardiner C. Means pondered on the changing role of the modern corporation in society. Berle and Means' monograph "The Modern Corporation and Private Property" (1932, Macmillan) continues to have a profound influence on the conception of corporate governance in scholarly debates today.

From the Chicago school of economics, Ronald Coase's "Nature of the Firm" (1937) introduced the notion of transaction costs into the understanding of why firms are founded and how they continue to behave. Fifty years later, Eugene Fama and Michael Jensen's "The Separation of Ownership and Control" (1983, Journal of Law and Economics) firmly established agency theory as a way of understanding corporate governance: the firm is seen as a series of contracts. Agency theory's dominance was highlighted in a 1989 article by Kathleen Eisenhardt (Academy of Management Review).

American expansion after World War II through the emergence of multinational corporations saw the establishment of the managerial class. Accordingly, the following Harvard Business School management professors published influential monographs studying their prominence: Myles Mace (entrepreneurship), Alfred D. Chandler, Jr. (business history), Jay Lorsch (organizational behavior) and Elizabeth MacIver (organizational behavior). According to Lorsch and MacIver "many large corporations have dominant control over business affairs without sufficient accountability or monitoring by their board of directors."

Current preoccupation with corporate governance can be pinpointed at two events: The East Asian Crisis of 1997 saw the economies of Thailand, Indonesia, South Korea, Malaysia and The Philippines severely affected by the exit of foreign capital after property assets collapsed.

The lack of corporate governance mechanisms in these countries highlighted the weaknesses of the institutions in their economies. The second event was the American corporate crises of 2001-2002 which saw the collapse of two big corporations: Enron and WorldCom, and the ensuing scandals and collapses in other corporations such as Arthur Andersen, Global Crossing and Tyco.

ROLE OF INSTITUTIONAL INVESTORS

Many years ago, worldwide, buyers and sellers of corporation stocks were individual investors, such as wealthy businessmen. Over time, markets have become more institutionalized; buyers and sellers are largely institutions (e.g., pension funds, insurance companies, mutual funds, hedge funds, investor groups, and banks). The rise of the institutional investor has brought with it some increase of professional diligence which has tended to improve regulation of the stock market (but not necessarily in the interest of the small investor or even of the naïve institutions, of which there are many). Note that this process occurred simultaneously with the direct growth of individuals investing in the market (for example individuals have twice as much money in mutual funds as they do in bank accounts). However this growth occurred primarily in individuals turning over their funds to professionals to manage, such as in mutual funds. In this way, the majority of investment now is described as "institutional investment" even though the vast majority of the funds are for the benefit of individual investors.

Unfortunately, there has been a concurrent lapse in the oversight of large corporations, which are now almost all owned by large institutions. The Board of Directors of large corporations used to be chosen by the principal shareholders, who usually had an emotional as well as monetary investment in the company (think Ford), and the Board diligently kept an eye on the company and its principal executives (they usually hired and fired the President, or Chief executive officer-CEO). Nowadays, if the owning institutions don't like what the President/CEO is doing and they feel that firing him will be costly (think "golden handshake") and/or time consuming, they will simply sell out their interest. Also, nowadays, the Board is mostly chosen by the President/CEO, and may be made up primarily of his cronies (or, at least, officers of the corporation, who owe their jobs to him, or fellow CEOs from other corporations). Since the (institutional) shareholders rarely object, the President/CEO generally takes the Chairman of the Board position for himself (which makes it much more difficult for the institutional owners to "fire" him). Finally, the largest pools of invested money (such as the mutual fund 'Vanguard 500', or the largest investment management firm for corporations, State Street) are designed simply to invest in a very large number of companies with sufficient liquidity, based on the idea that this strategy will largely eliminate individual company or financial risk and, therefore, these investors have even less interest in what a particular company is doing.

Since the marked rise in the use of Internet transactions in the 1990s, both individual and professional stock investors around the world have emerged as a potential new kind of major (short term) force in the ownership of corporations and in the markets: the casual participant. Even as the purchase of individual shares in any one corporation by individual investors diminishes, the sale of derivatives (e.g., exchange-traded funds (ETFs), Stock market index options, etc.) has soared. So, the interests of most investors are now increasingly rarely tied to the fortunes of individual corporations.

But, the ownership of stocks in markets around the world varies; for example, the majority of the shares in the Japanese market are held by financial companies and industrial corporations (there is a large amount of cross-holding among Japanese keiretsu corporations and within S. Korean chaebol 'groups'), whereas stock in the USA or the UK and Europe are much more broadly owned, often still by large individual investors.

In the latter half of the 1990s, during the Asian financial crisis, a lot of the attention fell upon the corporate governance systems of the developing world, which tend to be heavily into cronyism and nepotism.

In the first half of the 1990s, the issue of corporate governance in the U.S. received considerable press attention due to the wave of (belated?) CEO dismissals (e.g.: IBM, Kodak, Honeywell) by their boards. CALPERS led a wave of institutional shareholder activism (something only very rarely seen before), as a way of ensuring that corporate value would not be destroyed by the now traditionally cozy relationships between the CEO and the board of directors. In the early 2000s, the massive bankruptcies (and criminal malfeasance) of Enron and Worldcom, as well as lesser corporate debacles, such as Adelphia Communications, AOL, Arthur Andersen, Global Crossing, Tyco, and, more recently, Freddie Mac and led to increased shareholder and governmental interest in corporate governance, culminating in the passage of the Sarbanes-Oxley Act of 2002. Since then, the stock market has greatly recovered, and shareholder zeal has waned accordingly.

PARTIES TO CORPORATE GOVERNANCE

Parties involved in corporate governance include the regulatory body (e.g. the Chief Executive Officer, the board of directors, management and shareholders. Other stakeholders who take part include suppliers, employees, creditors, customers and the community at large.

In corporations, the shareholder delegates decision rights to the manager to act in the principal's best interests. This separation of ownership from control implies a loss of effective control by shareholders over managerial decisions. Partly as a result of this separation between the two parties, a system of corporate governance controls is implemented to assist in aligning the incentives of managers with those of shareholders. With the significant increase in equity holdings of investors, there has been an opportunity for a reversal of the separation of ownership and control problems because ownership is not so diffuse.

A board of directors often plays a key role in corporate governance. It is their responsibility to endorse the organisation's strategy, develop directional policy, appoint, supervise and remunerate senior executives and to ensure accountability of the organisation to its owners and authorities.

All parties to corporate governance have an interest, whether direct or indirect, in the effective performance of the organisation. Directors, workers and management receive salaries, benefits and reputation, while shareholders receive capital return. Customers receive goods and services; suppliers receive compensation for their goods or services. In return these individuals provide value in the form of natural, human, social and other forms of capital.

A key factor in an individual's decision to participate in an organisation e.g. through providing financial capital and trust that they will receive a fair share of the organisational returns. If some parties are receiving more than their fair return then participants may choose to not continue participating leading to organisational collapse.

BASIC PRINCIPLES

Key elements of good corporate governance principles include honesty, trust and integrity, openness, performance orientation, responsibility and accountability, mutual respect, and commitment to the organisation.

Of importance is how directors and management develop a model of governance that aligns the values of the corporate participants and then evaluate this model periodically for its effectiveness. In particular, senior executives should conduct themselves honestly and ethically, especially concerning actual or apparent conflicts of interest, and disclosure in financial reports.

Commonly accepted principles of corporate governance include:

- *Rights and Equitable Treatment of Shareholders:* Organisations should respect the rights of shareholders and help shareholders to exercise those rights. They can help shareholders exercise their rights by effectively communicating information that is understandable and accessible and encouraging shareholders to participate in general meetings.
- *Interests of other Stakeholders:* Organisations should recognise that they have legal and other obligations to all legitimate stakeholders.
- *Role and Responsibilities of the Board:* The board needs a range of skills and understanding to be able to deal with various business issues and have the ability to review and challenge management performance. It needs to be of sufficient size and have an appropriate level of commitment to fulfill its responsibilities and duties. There are issues about the appropriate mix of executive and non-executive directors. The key roles of chairperson and CEO should not be held by the same person.

- *Integrity and Ethical Behaviour:* Organisations should develop a code of conduct for their directors and executives that promotes ethical and responsible decision making. It is important to understand, though, that systemic reliance on integrity and ethics is bound to eventual failure. Because of this, many organizations establish Compliance and Ethics Programs to minimize the risk that the firm steps outside of ethical and legal boundaries.
- *Disclosure and Transparency:* Organisations should clarify and make publicly known the roles and responsibilities of board and management to provide shareholders with a level of accountability. They should also implement procedures to independently verify and safeguard the integrity of the company's financial reporting. Disclosure of material matters concerning the organisation should be timely and balanced to ensure that all investors have access to clear, factual information.

Issues involving corporate governance principles include:

- oversight of the preparation of the entity's financial statements
- internal controls and the independence of the entity's auditors
- review of the compensation arrangements for the chief executive officer and other senior executives
- the way in which individuals are nominated for positions on the board
- the resources made available to directors in carrying out their duties
- oversight and management of risk
- dividend policy

MECHANISMS AND CONTROLS

Corporate governance mechanisms and controls are designed to reduce the inefficiencies that arise from moral hazard and adverse selection. For example, to monitor managers' behaviour, an independent third party (the auditor) attests the accuracy of information provided by management to investors. An ideal control system should regulate both motivation and ability.

Internal Corporate Governance Controls

Internal corporate governance controls monitor activities and then take corrective action to accomplish organisational goals. Examples include:

- *Monitoring by the Board of Directors:* The board of directors, with its legal authority to hire, fire and compensate top management, safeguards invested capital. Regular board meetings allow potential problems to be identified, discussed and avoided. Whilst non-executive directors are thought to be more independent, they may not always result in more effective corporate governance and may not increase performance. Different board structures are optimal for different firms. Moreover, the ability of the board to monitor the firm's executives is a function of its access to information. Executive directors possess superior knowledge of the decision-making process and therefore evaluate top management on the basis of the quality of its decisions that lead to financial performance outcomes, ex ante. It could be argued, therefore, that executive directors look beyond the financial criteria.
- *Remuneration:* Performance-based remuneration is designed to relate some proportion of salary to individual performance. It may be in the form of cash or non-cash payments such as shares and share options, superannuation or other benefits. Such incentive schemes, however, are reactive in the sense that they provide no mechanism for preventing mistakes or opportunistic behaviour, and can elicit myopic behaviour.
- Audit committees.

External Corporate Governance Controls

External corporate governance controls encompass the controls external stakeholders exercise over the organisation. Examples include:

- debt covenants
- external auditors
- government regulations
- media pressure
- takeovers
- competition
- managerial labour market

SYSTEMIC PROBLEMS OF CORPORATE GOVERNANCE

- *Supply of Accounting Information:* Financial accounts form a crucial link in enabling providers of finance to monitor directors. Imperfections in the financial reporting process will cause imperfections in the effectiveness of corporate governance. This should, ideally, be corrected by the working of the external auditing process.
- *Demand for Information:* A barrier to shareholders using good information is the cost of processing it, especially to a small shareholder. The traditional answer to this problem is the efficient market hypothesis (in finance, the efficient market hypothesis (EMH) asserts that financial markets are efficient), which suggests that the shareholder will free ride on the judgements of larger professional investors.
- *Monitoring Costs:* In order to influence the directors, the shareholders must combine with others to form a significant voting group which can pose a real threat of carrying resolutions or appointing directors at a general meeting.

ROLE OF THE ACCOUNTANT

Financial reporting is a crucial element necessary for the corporate governance system to function effectively. Accountants and auditors are the primary providers of information to capital market participants. The directors of the company should be entitled to expect that management prepare the financial information in compliance with statutory and ethical obligations, and rely on auditors' competence. Current accounting practice allows a degree of choice of method in determining the method of measurement, criteria for recognition, and even the definition of the accounting entity. The exercise of this choice to improve apparent performance (popularly known as creative accounting) imposes extra information costs on users. In the extreme, it can involve non-disclosure of information.

One area of concern is whether the accounting firm acts as both independent auditor and management consultant to the firm they are auditing. This may result in a conflict of interest which places the integrity of financial reports in doubt due to client pressure to appease management. The power of the corporate client to initiate and terminate management consulting services and, more fundamentally, to select and dismiss accounting firms contradicts the concept of an independent auditor. Changes enacted in the United States in the form of the Sarbanes-Oxley Act (in response to the Enron situation as noted below) prohibit accounting firms from providing both auditing and management consulting services.

The Enron collapse is an example of misleading financial reporting. Enron concealed huge losses by creating illusions that a third party was contractually obliged to pay the amount of any losses. However, the third party was an entity in which Enron had a substantial economic stake. In discussions of accounting practices with Arthur Andersen, the partner in charge of auditing, views inevitably led to the client prevailing.

However, good financial reporting is not a sufficient condition for the effectiveness of corporate governance if users don't process it, or if the informed user is unable to exercise a monitoring role due to high costs.

REGULATION

Rules versus Principles

Rules are typically thought to be simpler to follow than principles, demarcating a clear line between acceptable and unacceptable behaviour. Rules also reduce discretion on the part of individual managers or auditors. In practice rules can be more complex than principles. They may be ill-equipped to deal with new types of transactions not covered by the code. Moreover, even if clear rules are followed, one can still find a way to circumvent their underlying purpose-this is harder to achieve if one is bound by a broader principle.

Enforcement: Enforcement can affect the overall credibility of a regulatory system. They both deter bad actors and level the competitive playing field. Nevertheless, greater enforcement is not always better, for taken too far it can dampen valuable risk-taking. In practice, however, this is largely a theoretical, as opposed to a real, risk.

CORPORATE GOVERNANCE MODELS

Anglo-American Model

There are many different models of corporate governance around the world. These differ according to the variety of capitalism in which they are embedded. The liberal model that is common in Anglo-American countries tends to give priority to the interests of shareholders. The coordinated model that one finds in Continental Europe and Japan also recognizes the interests of workers, managers, suppliers, customers, and the community. Both models have distinct competitive advantages, but in different ways. The liberal model of corporate governance encourages radical innovation and cost competition, whereas the coordinated model of corporate governance facilitates incremental innovation and quality competition.

In the United States, a corporation is governed by a board of directors, which has the power to choose an executive officer, usually known as the chief executive officer. The CEO has broad power to manage the corporation on a daily basis, but needs to get board approval for certain major actions, such as hiring his/her immediate subordinates, raising money, acquiring another company, major capital expansions, or other expensive projects. Other duties of the board may include policy setting, decision making, monitoring management's performance, or corporate control.

The board of directors is nominally selected by and responsible to the shareholders, but the bylaws of many companies make it difficult for all but the largest shareholders to have any influence over the makeup of the board; normally, individual shareholders are not offered a choice of board nominees among which to choose, but are merely asked to rubberstamp the nominees of the sitting board. Perverse incentives have pervaded many corporate boards in the developed world, with board members beholden to the chief executive whose actions they are intended to oversee. Frequently, members of the boards of directors are CEOs of other corporations, which some see as a conflict of interest.

Non Anglo-American Model

In East Asian countries, family-owned companies dominate. A study by Claessens, Djankov and Lang (2000) investigated the top 15 families in East Asian countries and found that they dominated listed corporate assets. In countries such as Pakistan, Indonesia and the Philippines, the top 15 families controlled over 50% of publicly owned corporations through a system of family cross-holdings, thus dominating the capital markets. Family-owned companies also dominate the Latin model of corporate governance, that is companies in Italy, Spain, France (to a certain extent), Brazil, Mexico and other countries in South America.

CODES AND GUIDELINES

Corporate governance principles and codes have been developed in different countries and issued from stock exchanges, corporations, institutional investors, or associations (institutes) of directors and managers with the support of governments and international organizations. As a rule, compliance with these governance recommendations is not mandated by law, although the codes linked to stock exchange listing requirements may have a coercive effect.

For example, companies quoted on the London and Toronto Stock Exchanges formally need not follow the recommendations of their respective national codes. However, they must disclose whether they follow the recommendations in those documents and, where not, they should provide explanations concerning divergent practices. Such disclosure requirements exert a significant pressure on listed companies for compliance.

In the United States, companies are primarily regulated by the state in which they incorporate though they are also regulated by the federal government and, if they are public, by their stock exchange. The highest number of companies are incorporated in Delaware, including more than half of the Fortune 500. This is due to Delaware's generally business-friendly corporate legal environment and the existence of a state court dedicated solely to business issues (Delaware Court of Chancery). Most states' corporate law generally follow the American Bar Association's Model Business Corporation Act. While Delaware does not follow the Act, it still considers its provisions and several prominent Delaware justices, including former Delaware Supreme Court Chief Justice E. Norman Veasey, participate on ABA committees.

One issue that has been raised since the Disney decision in 2005 is the degree to which companies manage their governance responsibilities; in other words, do they merely try to supersede the legal threashold or should they create governance guidelines that ascend to the level of best practice. For example, the guidelines issued by associations of directors, corporate managers and individual companies tend to be wholly voluntary. For example, The GM Board Guidelines reflect the company's efforts to improve its own governance capacity. Such documents, however, may have a wider multiplying effect prompting other companies to adopt similar documents and standards of best practice.

One of the most influential guidelines has been the 1999 OECD Principles of Corporate Governance. This was revised in 2004. The OECD remains a proponent of corporate governance principles throughout the world.

The World Business Council for Sustainable Development WBCSD has also done substantial work on corporate governance, particularly on accountability and reporting, and in 2004 created an Issue Management Tool: Strategic challenges for business in the use of corporate responsibility codes, standards, and frameworks. This document aims to provide general information, a "snap-shot" of the landscape and a perspective from a think-tank/professional association on a few key codes, standards and frameworks relevant to the sustainability agenda.

Corporate Governance and Firm Performance

In its 'Global Investor Opinion Survey' of over 200 institutional investors first undertaken in 2000 and updated in 2002, McKinsey found that 80% of the respondents would pay a premium for well-governed companies. They defined a well-governed company as one that had mostly out-side directors, who had no management ties, undertook formal evaluation of its directors, and was responsive to investors' requests for information on governance issues. The size of the premium varied by market, from 11% for Canadian companies to around 40% for companies where the regulatory backdrop was least certain (those in Morocco, Egypt and Russia).

Other studies have linked broad perceptions of the quality of companies to superior share price performance. In a study of five year cumulative returns of Fortune Magazine's survey of 'most admired firms', Antunovich et al found that those "most admired" had an average return of 125%, whilst the 'least admired' firms returned 80%. In a separate study Business Week enlisted institutional investors and 'experts' to assist in differentiating between boards with good and bad governance and found that companies with the highest rankings had the highest financial returns. On the other hand, research into the relationship between specific corporate governance controls and firm performance has been mixed and often weak. The following examples are illustrative.

Board Composition

Some researchers have found support for the relationship between frequency of meetings and profitability. Others have found a negative relationship between the proportion of external directors and firm performance, while others found no relationship between external board membership and performance. In a recent paper Bagahat and Black found that companies with more independent boards do not perform better than other companies. It is unlikely that board composition has a direct impact on firm performance.

Remuneration/Compensation

The results of previous research on the relationship between firm performance and executive compensation have failed to find consistent and significant relationships between executives' remuneration and firm performance. Low average levels of pay-performance alignment do not necessarily imply that this form of governance control is inefficient. Not all firms experience the same levels of agency conflict, and external and internal monitoring devices may be more effective for some than for others.

Some researchers have found that the largest CEO performance incentives came from ownership of the firm's shares, while other researchers found that the relationship between share ownership and firm performance was dependent on the level of ownership. The results suggest that increases in ownership above 20% cause management to become more entrenched, and less interested in the welfare of their shareholders.

Some argue that firm performance is positively associated with share option plans and that these plans direct managers' energies and extend their decision horizons toward the long-term, rather than the short-term, performance of the company. However, that point of view came under substantial criticism circa 2005-2006 in the wake of various security scandals including mutual fund timing episodes and, in particular, the backdating of option grants as documented by University of Iowa academician Erik Lie and reported by James Blander and Charles Forelle of the Wall Street Journal.

Even before the negative influence on public opinion caused by the 2006 backdating scandal, use of options faced various criticisms. A particularly forceful and long running argument concerned the interaction of executive options with corporate stock repurchase programs. Numerous authorities (including U.S. Federal Reserve Board economist Weisbenner) determined options may be employed in concert with stock buybacks in a manner contrary to shareholder interests.

These authors argued that, in part, corporate stock buybacks for U.S. Standard & Poors 500 companies surged to a $500 billion annual rate in late 2006 because of the impact of options. A compendium of academic works on the option/buyback issue is included in the study Scandalby author M. Gumport issued in 2006.

A combination of accounting changes and governance issues led options to become a less popular means of remuneration as 2006 progressed, and various alternative implementations of buybacks surfaced to challenge the dominance of "open market" cash buybacks as the preferred means of implementing a share repurchase plan.

ATTENTION TO CORPORATE GOVERNANCE

Corporate governance issues are receiving greater attention in both developed and developing countries as a result of the increasing recognition that a firm's corporate governance affects both its economic performance and its ability to access long-term, low-cost investment capital. In response to calls by OECD ministers, a revised version of its "Principles of Corporate Governance" was produced in 2004.

Numerous high-profile cases of corporate governance failure have focused the minds of governments, companies and the general public on the threat posed to the integrity of financial markets, although it is not clear that any system will or should prevent business failures, or that it is possible to provide a guarantee against fraud.

Corporate Governance concerns have been widely studied. For the United States, an analysis of these concerns has been published by the New York Society of Securities Analysts in their 2003 Corporate Governance Handbook. What constitutes good and bad corporate governance is an on-going debate in politics, civil society, and academia. For an international survey of the scientific literature see Becht, Bolton and Roell 2002.

The OECD publishes an annual paper on corporate governance. First issued in 1999, this paper has provided the framework for regional corporate governance roundtables in cooperation with the World Bank around the world. It has been endorsed as one of the Financial Stability Forum's 12 key standards, and form the basis for the World Bank's Review of Observance of Standards and Codes.

12

World Trade Organization

The World Trade Organization (WTO, French: Organisation mondiale du commerce, German: Welthandelsorganisation, Spanish: Organización Mundial del Comercio) is an international organization that establishes rules for international trade through consensus among its member states. It also resolves disputes between the members, which are all signatories to its set of trade agreements.

The organization's headquarters are located in Geneva, Switzerland. There are 150 member states in the organization, the latest to join being Vietnam on January 11, 2007. Pascal Lamy is the current Director-General of the World Trade Organization. Since its inception in 1995, the WTO has been a major focus for protests by civil society groups in many countries.

HISTORY

The Bretton Woods Conference of 1944 proposed the creation of an International Trade Organization (ITO) to establish rules and regulations for trade between countries. Members of the UN Conference on Trade and Employment in Havana agreed to the ITO charter in March 1948, but ratification was blocked by the U.S. Senate (WTO, 2004b).

Some historians have argued that the failure may have resulted from fears within the American business community that the International Trade Organization could be used to regulate big business (Lisa Wilkins, 1997; Helen Milner 1993). Only one element of the ITO survived: the General Agreement on Tariffs and Trade (GATT). Seven rounds of negotiations occurred under the GATT before the eighth round-known as the Uruguay Round-which began in 1986 and concluded in 1995 with the establishment of the WTO. The GATT principles and agreements were adopted by the WTO, which was charged with administering and extending them and approximately 30 other agreements and resolving trade disputes between member countries. Unlike the GATT, the WTO has a substantial institutional structure.

AIMS AND OBJECTIVES

The WTO states that its aims are to increase international trade by promoting lower trade barriers and providing a platform for the negotiation of trade and to their business.

Principles of the Trading System

The WTO discussions should follow these fundamental principles of trading.

1. A trading system should be free of discrimination in the sense that one country cannot privilege a particular trading partner above others within the system, nor can it discriminate against foreign products and services.
2. A trading system should tend toward more freedom, that is, toward fewer trade barriers (tariffs and non-tariff barriers).
3. A trading system should be predictable, with foreign companies and governments reassured that trade barriers will not be raised arbitrarily and that markets will remain open.
4. A trading system should tend toward greater competition.
5. A trading system should be more accommodating for less developed countries, giving them more time to adjust, greater flexibility, and more privileges.

FORMAL STRUCTURE

According to WTO rules, all WTO members may participate in all councils, committees, etc., except Appellate Body, Dispute

Settlement panels, and plurilateral committees. In practice, most of the WTO's decisions are made in informal meetings, often called "Green Room" meetings, to which most members are not invited.

Highest Level: Ministerial Conference

The topmost decision-making body of the WTO is the Ministerial Conference, which has to meet at least every two years. It brings together all members of the WTO, all of which are countries or separate customs territories. The Ministerial Conference can make decisions on all matters under any of the multilateral trade agreements.

Second Level: General Council

The daily work of the ministerial conference is handled by three groups: the General Council, the Dispute Settlement Body, and the Trade Policy Review Body. All three consist of the same membership-representatives of all WTO members-but each meets under different rules.

1. The General Council-is the WTO's highest-level decision-making body in Geneva, meeting regularly to carry out the functions of the WTO. It has representatives (usually ambassadors or equivalent) from all member governments and has the authority to act on behalf of the ministerial conference which only meets about every two years. The council acts on behalf on the Ministerial Council on all of the WTO affairs. The current chairman is Amb. Eirik Glenne (Norway).
2. The Dispute Settlement Body-Made up of all member governments, usually represented by ambassadors or equivalent. The current chairperson is H.E. Mr. Muhamad Noor Yacob (Malaysia).
3. The Trade Policy Review Body (TPRB)-the WTO General Council meets as the Trade Policy Review Body to undertake trade policy reviews of Members under the TRPM. The TPRB is thus open to all WTO Members. The current chairperson is H.E. Ms. Claudia Uribe (Colombia).

Third Level: Councils for Trade

The Councils for Trade work under the General Council. There are three councils-Council for Trade in Goods, Council for Trade-Related Aspects of Intellectual Property Rights, and Council for Trade in Services-each council works in different fields. Apart from these three councils, six other bodies report to the General Council reporting on issues such as trade and development, the environment, regional trading arrangements and administrative issues.

1. Council for Trade in Goods-The workings of the General Agreement on Tariffs and Trade (GATT) which covers international trade in goods, are the responsibility of the Council for Trade in Goods. It is made up of representatives from all WTO member countries. The current chairperson is Amb. Yonov Frederick Agah (Nigeria).
2. Council for Trade-Related Aspects of Intellectual Property Rights-Information on intellectual property in the WTO, news and official records of the activities of the TRIPS Council, and details of the WTO's work with other international organizations in the field.
3. Council for Trade in Services-The Council for Trade in Services operates under the guidance of the General Council and is responsible for overseeing the functioning of the General Agreement on Trade in Services (GATS). It's open to all WTO members, and can create subsidiary bodies as required.

Fourth Level: Subsidiary Bodies

There are subsidiary bodies under each of the three councils.

1. The Goods Council-subsidiary under the Council for Trade in Goods. It has 11 committees consisting of all member countries, dealing with specific subjects such as agriculture, market access, subsidies, anti-dumping measures and so on. Committees include the following:
   - Information Technology Agreement (ITA) Committee
   - State Trading Enterprises

- Textiles Monitoring Body-Consists of a chairman and 10 members acting under it.
- Groups dealing with notifications-process by which governments inform the WTO about new policies and measures in their countries.

2. The Services Council-subsidiary under the Council for Trade in Services which deals with financial services, domestic regulations and other specific commitments.
3. Dispute Settlement panels and Appellate Body-subsidiary under the Dispute Settlement Body to resolve disputes and the Appellate Body to deal with appeals.

Other committees:

- Committees on
  - o Trade and Environment
  - o Trade and Development (Subcommittee on Least-Developed Countries)
  - o Regional Trade Agreements
  - o Balance of Payments Restrictions
  - o Budget, Finance and Administration
- Working parties on
  - o Accession
  - • Working groups on
  - o Trade, debt and finance
  - o Trade and technology transfer

TRADE NEGOTIATIONS

While most international organizations operate on a one country, one vote or even a weighted voting basis, many WTO decisions, such as adopting agreements (and revisions to them) are officially determined by consensus of all members. The advantage of consensus decision-making is that it encourages efforts to find the most widely acceptable decision. Main disadvantages include large time requirements and many rounds of negotiation to develop a consensus decision, and the tendency for final agreements to use ambiguous language on contentious points that makes future interpretation of treaties difficult.

In reality, WTO negotiations proceed not by consensus of all members, but by a process of informal negotiations between small groups of countries. Such negotiations are often called "Green Room" negotiations (after the colour of the WTO Director-General's Office in Geneva), or "Mini-Ministerials", when they occur in other countries. These processes have been regularly criticized by many of the WTO's developing country members which are often totally excluded from the negotiations.

Richard Steinberg (2002) argues that although the WTO's consensus governance model provides law-based initial bargaining, trading rounds close through power-based bargaining favouring Europe and the United States, and may not lead to Pareto improvement.

Doha Round

The WTO began the current round of negotiations, the Doha round, at the Fourth Ministerial Conference in Doha, Qatar in November 2001. The talks have been highly contentious and agreement has not been reached, despite continuing talks at Fifth Ministerial Conference in Cancún in 2003 and at the Sixth Ministerial Conference in Hong Kong on December 13-December 18, 2005 and Seventh Ministerial Conference in Geneva-July 2006.

DISPUTE RESOLUTION

Apart from hosting negotiations on trade rules, one of the principal functions of the WTO is to act as an arbiter of disputes between member countries. Countries can bring disputes to the WTO's Dispute Settlement Body (DSB) if they believe another member has breached WTO rules. The DSB is the WTO General Council acting in a specialized role under a separate chair. It administers the Understanding on Rules and Procedures Governing Settlement of Disputes (DSU), which regulates dispute settlement under all covered WTO agreements.

Disputes are heard by a Dispute Settlement Panel, usually made up of three trade officials. The panels meet in secret and are not required to alert national parliaments that their laws have been challenged by another country.

Either side can appeal a panel's ruling. Appeals have to be based on points of law such as legal interpretation-they cannot reexamine existing evidence or examine new issues. Each appeal is heard by three members of a permanent seven-member Appellate Body set up by the Dispute Settlement Body and broadly representing the range of WTO membership.

Members of the Appellate Body have four-year terms. They have to be individuals with recognized standing in the field of law and international trade, not affiliated with any government. The appeal can uphold, modify or reverse the panel's legal findings and conclusions.

Normally appeals should not last more than 60 days, with an absolute maximum of 90 days. The Dispute Settlement Body has to accept or reject the appeals report within 30 days-and rejection is only possible by consensus.

Unlike most other international organizations, the WTO has significant power to enforce its decisions through the authorization of trade sanctions against members which fail to comply with its decisions.

The WTO dispute settlement system has been quite active since the founding of the organization. Proceedings have produced a huge corpus of what is sometimes called WTO law.

If decisions of the Dispute Settlement Body are not complied with, it may authorize "retaliatory measures"-trade sanctions-in favour of the member(s) which brought the dispute. While such measures are a strong mechanism when applied by economically powerful countries like the United States or the European Union, when applied by economically weak countries against stronger ones, they can often be ignored. This has been the case, for example, with the March 2005 Appellate Body ruling in case DS 267, which declared US cotton subsidies illegal.

In order to assist developing countries overcome their limited expertise in WTO law and assist them in the management of complex trade disputes, an Advisory Centre on WTO Law was established in 2001. The aim is to level the playing field for these countries and customs territories in the WTO system by enabling them to have a full understanding of their rights and obligations under the WTO Agreement.

MEMBERSHIP

The WTO has 150 members (almost all of the 123 nations participating in the Uruguay Round signed on at its foundation, and the rest had to get membership). The 27 states of the European Union are represented also as the European Communities. Some non-sovereign autonomous entities of member states are included as separate members.

The Kingdom of Tonga was admitted on 15 December 2005 during the ministerial conference. However, Tonga has yet to finalize ratification of this admittance, and is not expected to do so until July 2007. A current list of members can be found here.

The shortest accession negotiation was that of the Kyrgyz Republic, lasting 2 years and 10 months. The longest was that of the People's Republic of China, lasting 15 years and 5 months. Russia, having first applied to join GATT in 1993, is still in negotiations for membership. Recently, it has made much bigger strides by securing a bilateral trade agreement with the US. It is expected to form trade agreements with Moldova and Georgia, the remaining two nations that Russia must make agreements with, very soon despite minor trade issues. Russia is expected to join the WTO in mid 2007.

A number of non-members have been observers (31) at the WTO and are currently negotiating their membership: Algeria, Andorra, Azerbaijan, Bahamas (process frozen in 2001), Belarus, Bhutan, Bosnia and Herzegovina, Cape Verde, Equatorial Guinea (expected to start membership negotiations until 4 April 2007), Ethiopia, Holy See (Vatican; special exception from the rules allows it to remain observer without starting negotiations), Iran 1, Iraq, Kazakhstan, Lao People's Democratic Republic, Lebanon, Libya, Montenegro, Russian Federation, Samoa, Sao Tome and Principe, Serbia, Seychelles (negotiations frozen since 1998), Sudan, Tajikistan, Ukraine, Uzbekistan,

Vanuatu (accession agreed in 2001, but not ratified by Vanuatu itself), and Yemen.

Syria first applied to join the WTO in October 2001, then again in January 2004 and September 2005. Its application for membership is currently still pending, waiting for WTO General Council approval to start negotiations.

The following states (15) and territories (2) so far have no official interaction with the WTO: the states of Eritrea, Somalia, Liberia, Turkmenistan, North Korea, Monaco, San Marino, East Timor, Comoros, Nauru, Tuvalu, Palau, Kiribati, Micronesia, Marshall Islands and the territories of Western Sahara, Palestine.

AGREEMENTS

The WTO oversees about 60 different agreements which have the status of international legal texts. Member countries must sign and ratify all WTO agreements on accession. A list of WTO agreements can be found here A discussion of some of the most important agreements follows.

Agreement on Agriculture (AoA)

The AoA came into effect with the establishment of the WTO at the beginning of 1995. The AoA has three central concepts, or "pillars": domestic support, market access and export subsidies.

Domestic Support: The first pillar of the AoA is "domestic support". The AoA structures domestic support (subsidies) into three categories or "boxes": a Green Box, an Amber Box and a Blue Box. The Green Box contains fixed payments to producers for environmental programmes, so long as the payments are "decoupled" from current production levels.

The Amber Box contains domestic subsidies that governments have agreed to reduce but not eliminate. The Blue Box contains subsidies which can be increased without limit, so long as payments are linked to production-limiting programmes.

The AoA's domestic support system currently allows Europe and the USA to spend $380 billion annually on agricultural subsidies alone. "It is often still argued that subsidies are needed to protect small farmers but, according to the World Bank, more than half of EU support goes to 1% of producers while in the US 70% of subsidies go to 10% of producers, mainly agri-businesses.".

The effect of these subsidies is to flood global markets with below-cost commodities, depressing prices and undercutting producers in poor countries-a practice known as dumping.

Market Access: "Market access" is the second pillar of the AoA, and refers to the reduction of tariff (or non-tariff) barriers to trade by WTO members. The 1995 AoA required tariff reductions of:

- 36% average reduction by developed countries, with a minimum per tariff line reduction of 15% over five years.
- 24% average reduction by developing countries with a minimum per tariff line reduction of 10% over nine years.

Least Developed Countries (LDCs) were exempted from tariff reductions, but either had to convert non-tariff barriers to tariffs-a process called tariffication-or "bind" their tariffs, creating a "ceiling" which could not be increased in future.

Export Subsidies: "Export subsidies" is the third pillar of the AoA. The 1995 AoA required developed countries to reduce export subsidies by at least 35% (by value) or by at least 21% (by volume) over the five years to 2000.

Criticism: The AoA is criticized for reducing tariff protections for small farmers-a key source of income for developing countries-while allowing rich countries to continue to pay their farmers massive subsidies which developing countries cannot afford.

General Agreement on Trade in Services (GATS)

The Agreement on the Application of Sanitary and Phytosanitary Measures-also known as the SPS Agreement was negotiated during the Uruguay Round of the General Agreement on Tariffs and Trade, and entered into force with the establishment of the WTO at the beginning of 1995. Under the SPS agreement, the WTO sets constraints on members' policies relating to food safety (bacterial contaminants, pesticides, inspection and labelling) as well as animal and plant health (imported pests and diseases).

SPS and Genetically Modified Organisms (GMOs)

In 2003, the USA challenged a number of EU laws restricting the importation of Genetically Modified Organisms (GMOs), arguing they are "unjustifiable" and illegal under SPS agreement. In May 2006, the WTO's dispute resolution panel issued a complex ruling which took issue with some aspects of the EU's regulation of GMOs, but dismissed many of the claims made by the USA. A summary of the decision can be found here

Criticism: Quarantine policies plays an important role in ensuring the protection of human, animal and plant health. Yet under the SPS agreement, quarantine barriers can be a 'technical trade barrier' used to keep out foreign competitors.

The SPS agreement gives the WTO the power to override a country's use of the precautionary principle-a principle which allows them to act on the side of caution if there is no scientific certainty about potential threats to human health and the environment. Under SPS rules, the burden of proof is on countries to demonstrate scientifically that something is dangerous before it can be regulated, even though scientists agree that it is impossible to predict all forms of damage posed by insects or pest plants.

Agreement on Technical Barriers to Trade (TBT)

The Agreement on Technical Barriers to Trade-also known as the TBT Agreement is an international treaty of the World Trade Organization. It was negotiated during the Uruguay Round of the General Agreement on Tariffs and Trade, and entered into force with the establishment of the WTO at the end of 1994.

The object of the TBT Agreement is to "to ensure that technical negotiations and standards, as well as testing and certification procedures, do not create unnecessary obstacles to trade"

Chronology

- 1986-1994-Uruguay Round of GATT negotiations culminating in the Marrakech Agreement that established the WTO.
- January 1, 1995-The WTO came into existence.
- May 1, 1995-Renato Ruggiero became director-general for a 4-year term.
- December 9-December 13, 1996-The inaugural ministerial conference in Singapore. Disagreements between largely developed and developing economies emerged during this conference over four issues initiated by this conference, which led to them being collectively referred to as the "Singapore issues".
- May 18-May 20, 1998-2nd ministerial conference in Geneva, Switzerland.
- September 1, 1999-Mike Moore became director-general. The post had been fiercely contested; eventually a compromise was reached with Mike Moore and Supachai Panitchpakdi taking half each of a six-year term.
- November 30-December 3, 1999-3rd ministerial conference in Seattle, Washington, USA. The conference itself ended in failure, with massive demonstrations and riots drawing worldwide attention.
- November 9-November 13, 2001-4th ministerial conference in Doha, Qatar begins the Doha round. Issuance of the Doha Declaration.
- December 11, 2001-The People's Republic of China joined the WTO after 15 years of negotiations (the longest in GATT history).
- January 1, 2002-Taiwan joined under the name "Separate Customs Territory of Taiwan, Penghu, Kinmen and Matsu".
- September 1, 2002-Supachai Panitchpakdi became director-general.
- September 10-September 14, 2003-5th ministerial conference in Cancún, Mexico aims at forging agreement

on the Doha round. An alliance of 22 southern states, the G20 (led by India, People's Republic of China and Brazil), resisted demands from the North for agreements on the so-called "Singapore issues" and called for an end to agricultural subsidies within the EU and the US. The talks broke down without progress, although trade facilitation, one of the Singapore issues, re-emerged with the support from both developed and developing countries in later Doha trade round discussion.

- August 2004-Geneva talks achieve a framework agreement on the Doha round. Developed countries will lower agricultural subsidies, and in exchange the developing countries will lower tariff barriers to manufactured goods.
- May 2005-Paris talks aimed at finalizing issues for agreement before the December 2005 ministerial conference in Hong Kong are hung over technical issues. The group of five (U.S., Australia, the EU, Brazil and India) fail to agree over chicken, beef and rice. France continues to protest restrictions on subsidies to farmers. Oxfam accuses the EU of delaying tactics which threaten to scupper the Doha round.
- November 11-WTO General Council successfully adopts Saudi Arabia's terms of Accession
- December 13-December 18, 2005-6th ministerial conference in Hong Kong.
- July 24, 2006-The Doha Development Agenda negotiations were suspended, because gaps between key players remained too wide.

Criticism: The stated aim of the WTO is to promote free trade and stimulate economic growth. Many people argue that free trade does not make ordinary people's lives more prosperous but only results in the rich (both people and countries) becoming richer.

WTO treaties have also been accused of a partial and unfair bias toward multinational corporations and wealthy nations. Critics contend that small countries in the WTO wield little influence, and despite the WTO aim of helping the developing countries, the influential nations in the WTO focus on their own commercial interests.

They also claim that the issues of health, safety and environment are steadfastly ignored.

Martin Khor argues that the WTO does not manage the global economy impartially, but in its operation has a systematic bias toward rich countries and multinational corporations, harming smaller countries which have less negotiation power. Some examples of this bias are:

- Rich countries are able to maintain high import duties and quotas in certain products, blocking imports from developing countries (e.g. clothing);
- The increase in non-tariff barriers such as anti-dumping measures allowed against developing countries;
- The maintenance of high protection of agriculture in developed countries while developing ones are pressed to open their markets;
- Many developing countries do not have the capacity to follow the negotiations and participate actively in the Uruguay Round; and
- The TRIPs agreement which limits developing countries from utilizing some technology that originates from abroad in their local systems (including medicines and agricultural products).

Jagdish Bhagwati, although pro-free trade and pro-globalization, has strongly criticized the introduction of TRIPs (forum shifting) into the WTO/GATT framework. His fear is that other non-trade agendas might overwhelm the organization's function.

Many non-governmental organizations, such as the World Federalist Movement, are calling for the creation of a WTO parliamentary assembly to allow for more democratic participation in WTO decision making.

Dr Caroline Lucas recommended that such an assembly "have a more prominent role to play in the form of parliamentary scrutiny, and also in the wider efforts to reform the WTO processes, and its rules". However, Dr Raoul Marc Jennar argues that a consultative parliamentary assembly would be ineffective for the following reasons:

- It does not resolve the problem of "informal meetings" whereby industrialized countries negotiate the most important decisions;
- It does not reduce the de facto inequality which exists between countries with regards to an effective and efficient participation to all activities within all WTO bodies;
- It does not rectify the multiple violations of the general principles of law which affect the dispute settlement mechanism.

MINISTERIAL CONFERENCES

First Ministerial Conference: The inaugural ministerial conference was held in Singapore in 1996. Disagreements between largely developed and developing economies emerged during this conference over four issues initiated by this conference, which led to them being collectively referred to as the "Singapore issues".

Second Ministerial Conference: Was held in Geneva in Switzerland.

Third Ministerial Conference: The third conference in Seattle, Washington ended in failure, with massive demonstrations and police and National Guard crowd control efforts drawing worldwide attention.

Fourth Ministerial Conference: Was held in Doha.

Fifth Ministerial Conference: The ministerial conference was held in Cancún, Mexico, aiming at forging agreement on the Doha round. An alliance of 22 southern states, the G20 (led by India, People's Republic of China and Brazil), resisted demands from the North for agreements on the so-called "Singapore issues" and called for an end to agricultural subsidies within the EU and the US. The talks broke down without progress.

Sixth Ministerial Conference: The sixth WTO Conference Ministerial was held in Hong Kong from December 13-December 18, 2005. It was considered vital if the four-year-old Doha Development Agenda negotiations were to move forward sufficiently to conclude the round in 2006.

In this meeting, countries agreed to phase out all their agricultural export subsidies by the end of 2013, and terminate any cotton export subsidies by the end of 2006. Further concessions to developing countries included an agreement to introduce duty free, tariff free access for goods from the Least Developed Countries, following the Everything But Arms initiative of the European Union-but with up 3% of tariff lines exempted. Other major issues were left for further negotiation to be completed by the end of 2006.

13

International Development

International development is a concept that lacks a universally accepted definition, but it is most used in a holistic and multi-disciplinary context of human development-the development of livelihoods and greater quality of life for humans. It therefore encompasses governance, healthcare, education, disaster preparedness, infrastructure, economics, human rights, environment and issues associated with these.

International development is by definition a process undertaken by countries and communities with assistance from other nations' governments and communities, from international Non-Governmental Organisations (such as charities) or from intergovernmental organisations (such as the United Nations, the International Monetary Fund and the World Bank). As such it is distinct from development which would take place anyway, without international involvement.

International development is also distinct from, though conceptually related to, disaster relief and humanitarian aid. While these two forms of international support seek to alleviate some of the problems associated with a lack of development, they are most often short term fixes-they are not necesarily sustainable solutions.

International development, on the other hand, seeks to implement long-term solutions to problems by helping developing countries create the necessary capacity needed to provide such sustainable solutions to their problems. A truly sustainable development project is one which will be able to carry on indefinitely with no further international involvement or support, whether it be financial or otherwise.

International development projects may consist of a single, transformative project to address a specific problem or a series of projects targeted at several aspects of society.

HISTORICAL PERSPECTIVE

International development has existed as long as nations have existed. In history this has consisted of nations co-operating for mutual benefit, or alternatively with nations being conquered and acquiring 'developments' as a result.

For example, the trade of goods and ideas has throughout history furthered the development of countries, while the Roman Empire covered much of Europe and spread knowledge and technological advancement with it.

As the human race has become more mobile and more able to communicate, so international development has changed. Migration has throughout history also led to significant international development. As people move, their culture, knowledge, skills and technologies move with them. Migrants' ties with their past homes and communities lead to international relationships and further flows of goods, capital and knowledge. The value of remittances sent home by migrants in modern times is much greater than the total in international aid given.

DEVELOPMENTAL ERA

The second half of the 20th century has been called the 'era of development'. The origins of this era have been attributed to:

- the need for reconstruction in the immediate aftermath of World War II;
- the collapse of colonialism and the establishment of new relationships between so-called 'developed' and 'underdeveloped' nations;
- the start of the Cold War and the desire of the United States and its allies to prevent the Third World from drifting towards communism.

It has been argued that this era was launched on January 20th, 1949, when Harry S. Truman made the following remarks in his inaugural address: "We must embark on a bold new program for making the benefits of our scientific advances and industrial progress available for the improvement and growth of underdeveloped areas. The old imperialism-exploitation for foreign profit-has no place in our plans. What we envisage is a program of development based on the concept of democratic fair dealing."

Before this date, however, the United States had taken a leading role in the creation of the International Bank for Reconstruction and Development (now part of the World Bank Group) and the International Monetary Fund (IMF), both established in 1944, and in the United Nations in 1945.

The launch of the Marshall Plan in 1947 heralded a new role of international development aid-it came with political strings attached. This new approach which used aid to promote a Western, primarily U.S., agenda, was given conceptual support during the 1950s in the form of modernization theory espoused by Walt Rostow and other American economists. The changes in the 'developed' world's approach to international development were further necessitated by the gradual collapse of Western Europe's empires over the next decades; now independent ex-colonies no longer received support in return for their subjugation.

By the late 1960s, the critics of modernization were advancing a dependency theory to explain the evolving relationship between the West and the Third World. In the 1970s and early 80's, the modernists at the World Bank and IMF adopted the neoliberal ideas of Milton Friedman, which were implemented in the form of structural adjustment programs, while their opponents were promoting various 'bottom up' approaches, ranging from civil disobedience and conscientization to appropriate technology and Rapid Rural Appraisal.

By the 1990s, development theory had reached an impasse and some academics were imagining a postdevelopment era. The Cold War had ended, capitalism had become the dominant mode of social organization, and UN statistics showed that living standards around the world had improved over the past 40 years. Nevertheless, a large portion of the world's population were still living in poverty, their governments were crippled by debt and concerns about the environmental impact of globalization were rising.

In response to the impasse, the rhetoric of development is now focussing on the issue of poverty, with the metanarrative of modernization being replaced by shorter term vision embodied by the Millenium Development Goals. At the same time, some development agencies are exploring opportunities for public-private partnerships and promoting the idea of Corporate social responsibility with the apparent aim of integrating international development with the process of economic globalization.

The critics have suggested that this integration has always been part of the underlying agenda of development. They argue that poverty can be equated with powerlessness, and that the way to overcome poverty is through emancipatory social movements and civil society, not paternalistic aid programmes or corporate charity.

While some critics have been debating the end of development other have predicted a development revival as part of the War on Terror. To date, however, there is limited evidence to support the notion that aid budgets are being used to counter islamic fundamentalism in the same way that they were used 40 years ago to counter communism.

DEVELOPMENTAL THEORIES

Modernization Theory: Modernization Theory is a theory of development which states that the development can be achieved through following the processes of development that were used by the currently developed countries. Scholars such as Walt Rostow and A.F.K. Organski developed stages of development through which every country develops. Samuel Huntington determined development to be a linear process which every country must go through. Modernization Theory was built upon Classical Liberalism and the belief in individuality, free trade and the market fundamentalism. Technology played a key role in this development theory because it was believed that as technology was developed and introduced to lesser developed countries it would spur growth. One key factor in Modernization Theory is the belief that development requires the assistance of developed countries to aid developing countries to learn from their development. In addition, it was believed that the lesser developed countries would develop and grow faster than developed countries. Thus, this theory is built upon the theory that it is possible for equal development to be reached between the developed and lesser developed countries.

Dependency Theory

In response, came the rise of Dependency Theory which was critical of Modernization Theory. Dependency Theory is founded on the concept that the effects of colonialism on lesser developed countries must be considered when creating future development. Dependency Theory grew out of Latin America and scholars such as Raul Prebisch, due to observation that Modernization Theory was failing to address the consequences of colonialism such as trade inequities in which the colonial trade patterns of exporting raw materials and agriculture and importing the processed and manufactured goods continued to persist. Scholars such as Andre Gunder Frank and Fernando Enrique Cardoso have furthered the theory attributing the Modernization Theory to be a development process through which the developing countries only became further entrenched and dependent upon the developed countries. In addition, Dependency Theory divided countries into two different categories of development, periphery and center. The center was determined to be the developed and colonizing countries and the periphery consists of the developing and colonized countries. The relationship is outlined as one of exploitation in which the center exploits the periphery and it is through this colonial and post-colonial exploitation that the center countries were able to develop. This approach aims to discredit Modernization Theory's development process by stating that since exploitation allowed the center to develop it is impossible for the same process to lead to the development of the previously exploited countries.

Some criticisms of Dependency Theory are that it provides no feasible development solution, it does not acknowledge distinctions within the periphery or vulonerability in the center and does not outline any means of observing change within development.

World Systems Theory

In response to some of the criticisms of Dependency Theory came World Systems Theory, which the division of periphery and center was further divided into a trimodal system consisting of the core, semi-periphery and periphery. In this system, the semi-periphery lies between the core and periphery and is exploited by the core and exploits the periphery. This division aims to explain the industrilization within lesser developed countries. World Systems Theory was initiated by Immanuel Wallerstein and focuses on inequality as a seperate entity from growth in development and examines change in the global capitalist system. One distinguishing feature of this theory is a distrust for the state and a view in which the state is seen as a group of elites and that industrialization cannot be equated with development. Out of this theory stem anti-systemic movements which attempt to reverse the terms of the system's inequality through social democratic and labor movements.

State Theory

In response to the distrust of the state in World Systems Thoery, is State Theory. State Theory is based upon the view that the economy is intertwined with politics and therefore the take-off period in development is unique to each country. State Theory emphasized the effects of class relations and the strength and autonomy of the state on historical outcomes. Thus, development involves interactions between the state and social relations because class relations and the nature of the state impact the ability of the state to function. Development is dependent upon state stability and influence externally as well as internally. State Theorists believe that a developmentalist state is required for development by taking control of the development process within one state.

Millennium Development Goals

In the year 2000, United Nations made the United Nations Millennium Declaration. This represented the first time that a holistic strategy to meet the development needs of the world has been established, with measurable targets and defined indicators.

Because the MDGs are a multilateral United Nations programme, they are more removed from (but by no means independent of) individual national interests than unilateral development programmes, which are consistently subject to claims that they are used to further national economic interests or ideology, often with considerable justification.

The first seven Millennium Development Goals present measurable goals, while the eighth lists a number of 'stepping stone' goals-ways in which progress towards the first six goals could be made. The MDGs have catalysed a significant amount of action, including new initiatives such as Millennium Promise. Most of these initiatives however work in small scale interventions which do not reach the millions of people required by the MDGs.

Recent critiscism has been that it will be impossible to meet the first seven goals without meeting the eighth by forming a Global Partnership for Development. No current organisation has the capacity to solve the enormous problems of the developing world alone-especially in cities, where an increasing number of poor people live-as demonstrated by the almost non-exist progress on the goal of improving the lives of at least 100 Million slum dwellers.

The Institution of Civil Engineers recent Engineers Without Frontiers panel and its recommendations, and the recent Brunel Lecture by the ICE's next president Paul Jowitt, are representative of a change of approach in the UK at least to start drawing together the huge capacity available to western governments, industry, academia and charity to develop such a partnership.

DEVELOPMENT CONCEPTS

During recent decades, development thinking has shifted from modernization and structural adjustment programs to poverty reduction. Under the former system, poor countries were encouraged to undergo social and economical structural transformations as part of their development, creating industrialization and intentional industrial policy. Poverty reduction rejects this notion, consisting instead of direct budget support for social welfare programs that create macroeconomic stability leading to an increase in economic growth.

Poverty

The concept of poverty can apply to different circumstances depending on context. In general, it applies to a lack and need of material wealth and social inclusion-often manifested in a lack of dignity.

Dignity: Modern poverty reduction and development programmes often have dignity as a central theme. Dignity is also a central theme of the Universal Declaration of Human Rights, the very first article of which starts with: "All human beings are born free and equal in dignity and rights."

The concept of dignity in development has been extensively explored by many, and related to all of the development sectors. For example, in Development with Dignity Amit Bhaduri argues that full employment with dignity for all is both important and possible in India, while the UN Millinnium Project's task force on Water and Sanitation links the sector directly to dignity in the report Health, Dignity and Development: What will it take?..

The Asian Human Rights Commission on July 27, 2006, released a statement claiming that "Human dignity is the true measure of human development.".

Participation: The concept of participation is concerned with ensuring that the intended beneficiaries of development projects and programmes are themselves involved in the planning and execution of those projects and programmes. This is considered important as it empowers the recipients of development projects to influence and manage their own development-thereby removing any culture of dependency. It is widely considered to be one of the most important concepts in modern development theory, with. The 'UN System Network on Rural Development and Food Security' describes participation as one of the ends as well as one of the means of development.

APPROPRIATE DEVELOPMENT

The concept of something being appropriate is concerned with ensuring that a development project or programme is of the correct scale and technical level, and is culturally and socially suitable for its beneficiaries. This should not be confused with ensuring something is low-tech, cheap or basic-a project is appropriate if it is acceptable to its recipients and owners, ecomomically affordable and sustainable in the context in which it is executed.

For example, in a rural sub-Saharan community it may not be appropriate to provide a chlorinated water system because it cannot be maintained or controlled adequately-simple handpumps may be better; while in a big city in the same country it would be inappropriate to provide water with handpumps, and the chlorinated system would be the correct response.

The economist E. F. Schumacher championed the cause of appropriate technology and founded the organisation ITDG (Intermediate Technology Design Group), which develops and provides appropriate technologies for development (ITDG has now been renamed Practical Action.

Sustainability

A sustainable approach to development is one which takes account of economic, social and environmental factors to produce projects and programmes which will have results which are not dependent on finite resources. Something which is sustainable will not use more natural resources than the local environment can supply, more financial resources than the local community and markets can sustain and will have the necessary support from the community, government and other stakeholders to carry on indefinitely.

It is on of the key concepts in international development, and is critical in removing dependency.

Capacity Building

Capacity building is concerned with increasing the ability of the recipients of development projects do continue their future development alone, without external support. It is a parallel concept to sustainability, as it furthers the ability of society to function independently in its own microcosm.

DEVELOPMENT IN PRACTICE

Measuring Development: The judging of how developed a country or a community is is highly subjective, often highly controversial, and very important in judging what further development is necessary or desirable.

There are many different measures of human development, many of them related to the different sectors above. Some of them are:

- National GDP
- Literacy rates
- Life expectancy
- Human Development Index
- Gini coefficient
- Per capita income
- Maternal survival rate
- HIV infection rates
- Number of doctors per capita

MAJOR SECTORS

International development and disaster relief are both often grouped into sectors, which correlate with the major themes of international development (and with the Millennium Development Goals-which are included in the descriptions below). There is no clearly defined list of sectors, but some of the more established and universally accepted sectors are further explored here. The sectors are highly interlinked, illustrating the complexity of the problems they seek to deal with.

Water and Sanitation

In development, this is the provision of drinking water and sanitary provision (toilets, bathing facilities, a healthy environment) of sufficient quantity and quality to supply an acceptable standard of living. This is different to a relief response, where it is the provision of water and sanitation in sufficient quantity and quality to maintain life.

The provision of water and sanitation is primarily an engineering challenge, but also often includes an education element and is closely connected with shelter, politics and human rights.

The seventh Millennium Development Goal is to Ensure environmental sustainability, including reducing by half the proportion of people without sustainable access to safe drinking water and achieving significant improvement in lives of at least 100 million slum dwellers, by 2020

Examples of organisations specialising in Water & Sanitation are:

- OXFAM
- WaterAid

Health: This is provision of access to healthcare to the population. The standard and level of provision that is acceptable or appropriate depends on many factors and is highly specific to country and location. For example, in large city (whether in a 'developing' country or not), it is appropriate and often practical to provide a high standard hospital which can offer a full range of treatments; in a remote rural community it may be more appropriate and practical to provide a visiting healthworker on a periodic basis, possibly with a rural clinic serving several different communities.

The provision of access to healthcare is both an engineering challenge as it requires infrastructure such as hospitals and transport systems and an education challenge as it requires qualified healthworkers.

The fourth Millennium Development Goal is to reduce by two thirds the mortality rate among children under five.

The fifth Millennium Development Goal is to reduce by three quarters the maternal mortality ratio.

The sixth Millennium Development Goal is to halt and begin to reverse the spread of HIV/AIDS and to halt and begin to reverse the incidence of malaria and other major diseases.

Education: The provision of education often focusses on providing free primary level education, but also covers secondary and further education. A lack of access to education is one of the primary limits on human development, and is related closely to every one of the other sectors. Almost every development project includes an aspect of education as development by its very nature requires a change in the way people live.

The second Millennium Development Goal is to Provide universal primary education.

The provision of education is itself an education challenge, as it requires qualified teachers.

Shelter: The provision of appropriate shelter is concerned with providing suitable housing for families and communities. It is highly specific to context of culture, location, climate and other factors. In development, it is concerned with providing housing of an appropriate quality and type to accommodate people in the long-term. This is distinct from shelter in relief, which is concerned with providing sufficient shelter to maintain life.

Examples of organisations specialising in shelter are:

- UN-HABITAT (development)
- UNHCR (relief)
- Shelter Centre (mainly relief)

Human Rights: The provision of human rights is concerned with ensuring that all people everywhere receive the rights conferred on them by International human rights instruments. There are many of these, but the most important are:

- The Universal Declaration of Human Rights
- The Declaration of the Rights of the Child
- The Geneva Conventions (this is of more relevance to relief than development)

Human rights covers a huge range of topics. Some of those more relevant to international development projects include rights associated with gender equality, justice, employment, social welfare and culture.

The third Millennium Development Goal is to promote gender equality and empower women by eliminating gender disparity in primary and secondary education preferaably by 2005, and at all levels by 2015

Livelihoods: This is concerned with ensuring that all people are able to make a living for themselves and provide themselves with an adequate standard of living, without compromising their human rights and while maintaining dignity.

The first Millennium Development Goal is to reduce by half the proportion of people living on less than a dollar a day and reduce by half the proportion of people who suffer from hunger.

Finance: Several organisations and initiatives exist which are concerned with providing financial systems and frameworks which allow people to organise or purchase services, items or projects for their own development.

The 2006 Nobel Peace Prize was awarded jointly to Muhammad Yunus and the Grameen Bank, which he founded, for their work in providing microcredit to the poor.

CONCERNS ABOUT DEVELOPMENT

However, even the terms "developed" and "developing" (or "underdeveloped"), have proven problematic in forming policy as they ignore issues of wealth distribution and the lingering effects of colonialism. Some theorists see development efforts as fundamentally neo-colonial, in which a wealthier nation forces its industrial and economic structure on a poorer nation, which will then become a consumer of the developed nation's goods and services. Post-developmentalists, for example, see development as a form of Western cultural imperialism that hurts the people of poor countries and endangers the environment to such an extent that they suggest rejection of development altogether.

CRITICISMS OF DEVELOPMENT

Trade is a key factor in economic development. A successful use of trade can boost a country's development. On the other hand, opening up markets to international trade may leave local producers swamped by more competitive foreign producers. The current consensus is that trade, development, and poverty reduction are intimately linked. Sustained strong growth over longer periods is strongly associated with poverty reduction, while trade and growth are strongly linked. Countries that develop invariably increase their integration with the global economy, while export-led growth has been a key part of many countries' successful development strategies.

Continents, countries and sectors that have not developed and remain largely poor have comparative advantage in three main areas:

- natural resource exploitation, i.e. running down of natural capital such as rain forest timber;
- low-education labor-intensive manufacturing, due to high population densities and little suitable land per person;
- agriculture, due to low population densities and relatively large areas of suitable land per person.

Crucially for poverty reduction, the latter two at least are labor-intensive, helping to ensure that growth in these sectors will be poverty-reducing. However, low value-added, price instability and unsustainability in these commodity sectors means they should be used only temporarily as stepping stones in the path to economic development.

Agriculture: In many developing countries, agriculture employs a large proportion of the labor force, whilst food consumption accounts for a large share of household income. UNCTAD notes that this means that "even small changes in agricultural employment opportunities, or prices, can have major socio-economic effects in developing countries".

Thus whatever the development strategy a particular country adopts, the role of agriculture will often be crucial. In 1994, the agricultural sector employed over 70 % of the labor force in low-income countries, 30 % in middle-income countries, and only 4 % in high-income countries (UNCTAD 1999).

In poor countries with low population densities and enough suitable land area, which includes most countries in Africa and Latin America, agriculture is central to the economy. In poor regions and rural areas within middle-income developing countries, the concentration of poverty in rural areas of otherwise better-off developing countries makes the development of agriculture vital there. Finally, in Net Food Importing Developing Countries (NFIDCs), there is a positive link between growing agricultural exports and increases in local food production, which makes agricultural development if anything even more important, as food security and the financial stability of the government are also at stake.

In Vietnam in the 1990s, increases in production and export of coffee of 15% a year contributed to a nearly 50% rise in food production in the same period. As agricultural GDP grew 4.6% per year, rural poverty fell from 66% in 1993 to 45% in 1998 (Global Economic Prospects 2002:40).

Anderson et al (1999) estimate annual welfare losses of $19.8 billion for developing countries from agricultural tariffs-even after Uruguay Round reforms. This is three times the loss from OECD import restrictions on textiles and clothing. A combination of better market access, and domestic reforms and foreign aid to enhance the ability of developing countries to take advantage of it, could have a significant impact on poverty reduction, and help to meet the Millennium Development Goals.

The largest beneficiaries of agricultural liberalization would be OECD countries themselves: welfare losses of $62.9bn a year are estimated as resulting from the distortionary policies (Binswanger and Ernst 1999:5). Nor is the traditional objective of OECD agricultural subsidy (supporting small farmers) achieved by this system in a manner that could be characterised as efficient: most of the producer support incomes goes to better-off farmers, with the poorest 40% receiving just 8% of the support spent.

MARKET ACCESS

Market Access to Developed Countries: The issue of market access to high-income countries is a thorny but crucial one. The issues fall into three main groups: first, those relating to deliberately imposed barriers to trade, such as tariffs, quotas, and tariff escalation. Second, barriers to trade resulting from domestic and external producer support, primarily in the form of subsidies, but also including, for example, export credits.

Third, those relating to indirect barriers to trade resulting from developing countries' lack of institutional capacity to engage in the global economy and in multilateral institutions (eg the World Trade Organization) on equal terms.

Barriers to Trade

- High tariffs are imposed on agriculture: in high-income countries, the average tariff rate on agriculture is almost double the tariff for manufactures. And more than one third of the European Union's agricultural tariff lines, for instance, carry duties above 15% Trade Organization. Tariff peaks within agriculture occur most frequently on processed products and temperate commodities, rather than the major export crops of least developed countries (unprocessed fruits and vegetables and tropical commodities). However, many developing countries in temperate zones have the potential of competing as lower-cost producers in temperate commodities. Thus liberalization could open up new development-through-trade possibilities.
- Strong tariff escalation is typically imposed on agricultural and food products by high-income countries. This strongly discourages the development of high value added exports, and hinders diversification in particular as well as development in general. In high-income countries, tariffs on agricultural products escalate steeply, especially in the EU and Japan.
- Complex tariffs make it more difficult for developing country exporters to access industrialised-country markets because of the disadvantages developing countries face in accessing, and in their capacity to process, information. Not only are price signals distorted, they are often unclear, subject to change (for example seasonally) and difficult to interpret.
- Tariff quotas (TRQs), introduced by the Uruguay Round with the aim of securing a minimum level of market access, have performed poorly. Average fill rates have been low and declining, from 67% in 1995 to 63% in 1998, with about a quarter of TRQs filled to less than

20%. The low fill rate may reflect high in-quota rates. Overall, the UR tariffication process which produced them has not resulted in the increased market access developing countries hoped for.

Producer Support

- Support to agricultural producers remains sizable, at about five times the level of international development assistance-$245 billion in 2000. Total support to agriculture, as defined by the OECD, reaches $327 billion-1.3% of OECD countries' GDP. To some extent these can be justified by "multifunctionality" arguments, but it remains a priority to find means of support which effectively meet the primary objectives without the negative developmental and environmental consequences that have been seen in the past.
- The dumping of unwanted production surpluses onto the world market through export subsidies has depressed prices for many temperate agricultural commodities, with EU surpluses of exportable wheat a prime example. (Despite several CAP reforms, domestic support for wheat-as measured by OECD producer support estimates-declined only marginally from an average 52% of gross farm receipts in 1986-88, to around 48% in 1998-2000.) The URAA has been relatively unsuccessful in disciplining export subsidies, with the proportion of subsidised exports in total exports increasing in many products of export interest for developing countries: for example for wheat, from 7% in 1995 to 25% in 1998. The cost to developing country production and exports is considerable, and only partially offset by the lower food prices available to NFIDC consumers. This form of transfer from high-income country taxpayers to low-income consumers is in any case rather inefficient, and the lower prices may harm production for local consumption even in NFIDCs. Agricultural reform as a whole, including the removal of export subsidies, would only result in quite small price rises for developing-country consumers.

- The counter-cyclical nature of producer support is also harmful to developing-country producers. High-income farmers are insulated from changes in world prices, making production less responsive to swings in demand. As a result, world commodity prices are more volatile, and the burden of adjustment falls disproportionately on developing-country producers.

LACK OF CAPACITY

This includes non-tariff barriers such as food regulations and standards, which developing countries are often not (or not effectively) involved in setting, and which may be deliberately used to reduce competition from developing countries. In any case, the lack of capacity to meet implement regulations and ensure compliance with standards constitutes a barrier to trade, and must be met by increasing that capacity.

Market Access to Developing Countries

- Average applied tariffs in agriculture are higher in developing countries (although most of the very high rates, over 100%, are found in developed countries). With an increasing share of agricultural exports directed toward other developing countries, high levels of tariff protection in the South may impede prospects for export-led growth. This may be particularly true for the export opportunities of low-income countries, which have increased export market share in agriculture.
- "Open regionalism" holds the potential to stimulate global trade and improve the efficiency of regional producers. But regional arrangements can also become a vehicle for protection, trade diversion, and unintended inefficiency. Agreements in particular between richer and poorer developing countries risk generating trade losses for the poorer ones when their imports are diverted toward the richer members whose firms are not internationally competitive. However, where regional arrangements lead to the reduction of non-tariff barriers, trade creation is likely, and the dynamic benefits of

effective regional integration in terms of improved governance and regional stability are likely to outweigh diversion concerns. The World Bank suggests that key conditions to benefit from expanded trade and investment include lowering common external trade barriers, stimulating competition, reducing transaction costs, and reinforcing nondiscriminatory investment and services policies. It should be noted that the greater structural differences between North and South economies mean that North-South arrangements hold the greatest promise for economic convergence and trade creation, including in agricultural products, underlining the importance of links between South-South arrangements and northern economies.

- Trade liberalization. According to the World Bank, "most analyses suggest that unilateral reduction in barriers can produce the greatest and the quickest gains." Some countries, such as Chile, China and Costa Rica, have undertaken domestic policy reforms. Caution must however be employed: as the case of Haiti shows, liberalization when institutions and the economy are not strong enough to face risks and opportunities can be harmful (Rodrik 2001). And while reforms may be beneficial in the long run, for example by reducing possibilities for customs corruption, in the short run they create both winners and losers. Low-income consumers, unskilled workers in sheltered industries, and previously-shielded producers may suffer in the transition period as the economy adapts to changed incentive structures. Temporary safety nets can help cushion the blow and ensure trade-led growth is pro-poor. Specific assistance to meet costs of adaptation-for example of switching to a different crop-may be appropriate.
- Some middle-income countries, such as South Korea, also have high producer subsidies. High-income countries will be in a better position to persuade middle-income countries to relinquish protection if they lead by example.

MARKET ACCESSIBILITY

It is important to recognise that the issues facing LDCs and middle-income developing countries differ significantly. For the middle-income countries, the primary issue is market access. Many of the world's poor live in these countries, and so market access alone can have significant poverty-reducing effects in these countries. However, for the least-developed countries, the principal problem is not market access, but lack of production capacity to achieve new trading opportunities. This is recognised by paragraph 42 of the Doha Development Agenda:

"We recognize that the integration of the LDCs into the multilateral trading system requires meaningful market access, support for the diversification of their production and export base, and trade-related technical assistance and capacity building."

So whilst the further development of middle-income countries, and in particular the tackling of rural poverty in these countries, can be achieved most importantly through increased market access in agriculture, lower-income countries need additional help, not only to take advantage of new opportunities, but to be able to adapt to changing conditions due to the loss of preferences. This additional help must take three main forms: support for developing-country agricultural production; support for participation in trade; and support for good policies and good governance.

Support for Agricultural Production

- Support for agricultural modernization and development-investment in productive capacity in agriculture and food processing.
- Support for agricultural-related development institutions which are not trade-distorting, eg research; eg risk-management of agricultural product price fluctuations; eg diversification.

SUPPORT FOR PARTICIPATION IN TRADE

Cases such as Haiti's post-1986 liberalization show that the opportunities thereby created will not be taken advantage of if macroeconomic policies, institutions, and the investment climate are not favorable. This includes

- trade-related infrastructure: the cost of exporting must be low enough to ensure competitiveness in rapidly-expanding high-value agricultural markets where competition is stiff-such as fruits and vegetables.
- It also includes related issues that are part of the general investment climate but can be particularly important for exports, such as a weak financial sector. Here, export finance "is often a major constraint inhibiting exports in many low-income countries."
- Other issues are more specific to exports: developing countries and their exporters may have difficulty with both the implementation of, and showing compliance with, international product standards and other multilateral agreements. Low-income developing countries need both technical and financial assistance in this area.
- Technical Assistance for negotiations is also needed to further developing-country interests in multilateral and bilateral arenas and ensure the success of future negotiations and agreements.
- Marketing of exports is also a challenge for low-income countries: product and country brands need to be built, and quality concerns met.

Given the importance of agriculture for poverty reduction, additional policies and institutional capacity are needed to ensure an effective supply response to market incentives provide by better market access. Rural infrastructure is particularly important in enabling agricultural exports in developing countries. Sufficient credit at competitive conditions is important for private sector investment in storage, transportation and marketing of agricultural products. Investment in skills and education in rural areas is needed to bolster agricultural productivity. Trade policy reforms must address any remaining anti-export bias. Efficient land policies and land tenure institutions are needed to ensure the functioning of land markets, property rights, and efficient farm structures.

14

Investment Management

Investment management, the professional management of various securities (shares, bonds etc) and other assets (e.g. real estate), to meet specified investment goals for the benefit of the investors. Investors may be institutions (insurance companies, pension funds, corporations etc.) or private investors (both directly via investment contracts and more commonly via collective investment schemes eg. mutual funds).

The term asset management is often used to refer to the investment management of collective investments, whilst the more generic fund management may refer to all forms of institutional investment as well as investment management for private investors. Investment managers who specialize in advisory or discretionary management on behalf of (normally wealthy) private investors may often refer to their services as wealth management or portfolio management often within the context of so-called "private banking".

The provision of 'investment management services' includes elements of financial analysis, asset selection, stock selection, plan implementation and ongoing monitoring of investments.

Investment management is a large and important global industry in its own right responsible for caretaking of trillions of dollars, euros, pounds and yen. Coming under the remit of financial services many of the worlds largest companies are at least in part investment managers and employ millions of staff and create billions in revenue. Fund manager (or investment advisor in the U.S.) refers to both a firm that provides investment management services and an individual(s) who directs 'fund management' decisions.

INDUSTRY SCOPE

The business of investment management has several facets, including the employment of professional fund managers, research (of individual assets and asset classes), dealing, settlement, marketing, internal auditing, and the preparation of reports for clients. The largest financial fund managers are firms that exhibit all the complexity their size demands. Apart from the people who bring in the money (marketers) and the people who direct investment (the fund managers), there are compliance staff (to ensure accord with legislative and regulatory constraints), internal auditors of various kinds (to examine internal systems and controls), financial controllers (to account for the institutions' own money and costs), computer experts, and "back office" employees (to track and record transactions and fund valuations for up to thousands of clients per institution).

KEY PROBLEMS OF RUNNING BUSINESSES

Key problems include:

- revenue is directly linked to market valuations, so a major fall in asset prices causes a precipitous decline in revenues relative to costs;
- above-average fund performance is difficult to sustain, and clients may not be patient during times of poor performance;
- successful fund managers are expensive and may be headhunted by competitors;
- above-average fund performance appears to be dependent on the unique skills of the fund manager; however, clients are loath to stake their investments on the ability of one or two men or women-they would rather see firm-wide success, attributable to a single philosophy and internal discipline;
- evidence suggests that size of an investment firm correlates inversely with fund performance, i.e., the smaller the firm the better the chance of good performance;

- analysts who generate above-average returns often become sufficiently wealthy that they eschew corporate employment in favor of managing their personal portfolios.

The most successful investment firms in the world have probably been those that have been separated physically and psychologically from banks and insurance companies. That is, the best performance and also the most dynamic business strategies (in this field) have generally come from independent investment management firms.

Representing the Owners of Shares

Institutions often control huge shareholdings. In most cases they are acting as agents (intermediaries between owners of the shares and the companies owned) rather than principals (direct owners). The owners of shares theoretically have great power to alter the companies they own...via the voting rights the shares carry and the consequent ability to pressure managements, and if necessary out-vote them at annual and other meetings.

In practice, the ultimate owners of shares often do not exercise the power they collectively hold (because the owners are many, each with small holdings); financial institutions (as agents) sometimes do. There is a general belief that shareholders-in this case, the institutions acting as agents-could and should exercise more active influence over the companies in which they hold shares (e.g., to hold managers to account, to ensure Boards effective functioning). Such action would add a pressure group to those (the regulators and the Board) overseeing management.

Some institutions have been more vocal and active in pursuing such matters; for instance, some firms believe that there are investment advantages to accumulating substantial minority shareholdings (i.e., 10% or more) and putting pressure on management to implement significant changes in the business. In some cases, institutions with minority holdings work together to force management change. Perhaps more frequent is the sustained pressure that large institutions bring to bear on management teams through persuasive discourse and PR. On the other hand, some of the largest investment managers-such as Barclays Global Investors and Vanguard-advocate simply owning every company, reducing the incentive to influence management teams.

The national context in which shareholder representation considerations are set is variable and important. The USA is a litigious society and shareholders use the law as a lever to pressure management teams.

In Japan it is traditional for shareholders to be low in the 'pecking order,' which often allows management and labor to ignore the rights of the ultimate owners. Whereas US firms generally cater to shareholders, Japanese businesses generally exhibit a stakeholder mentality, in which they seek consensus amongst all interested parties (against a background of strong unions and labour legislation).

SIZE OF THE GLOBAL FUND MANAGEMENT INDUSTRY

Assets of the global fund management industry increased for the third year running in 2006 to reach a record $55.0 trillion. This was up 10% on the previous year and 54% on 2002. Growth during the past three years has been due to an increase in capital inflows and strong performance of equity markets.

Pension assets totalled $20.6 trillion in 2005, with a further $16.6 trillion invested in insurance funds and $17.8 trillion in mutual funds. Merrill Lynch also estimates the value of private wealth at $33.3 trillion of which about a third was incorporated in other forms of conventional investment management.

The US was by far the largest source of funds under management in 2005 with 48% of the world total. It was followed by Japan with 11% and the UK with 7%. The Asia-Pacific region has shown the strongest growth in recent years. Countries such as China and India offer huge potential and many companies are showing an increased focus in this region.

Ten Largest Asset Management Firms

Global Investor's 2005 top 10 asset managers by assets under management.

Rank	Company	Assets under management (US$million)	Country
1.	Barclays Global Investors	1,400,491	UK
2.	State Street Global Advisors	1,367,269	US
3.	Fidelity Investments	1,299,400	US
4.	Capital Group Companies	1,050,435	US
5.	Legg Mason	891,400	US
6.	The Vanguard Group	852,000	US
7.	Allianz Global Investors	790,513	Germany
8.	JPMorgan Asset Management	782,646	US
9.	Mellon Financial Corporation	738,294	US
10.	Deutsche Asset Management	723,366	Germany

THE CONCEPT OF THREE P'S

The 3-P's (Philosophy, Process and People) are often used to describe the reasons why the manager is able to produce above average results.

- Philosophy refers to the over-arching beliefs of the investment organisation. For example, does the manager buy growth or value shares (and why), does he believe in market timing (and on what evidence), does he rely on external research or does he employ a team of researchers. It is helpful if any and all of such fundamental beliefs are supported by proof-statements.
- Process refers to the way in which the overall philosophy is implemented. For example, which universe of assets is explored before particular assets are chosen as suitable investments; how does the manager decide what to buy and when; how does the manager decide what to sell and when; who takes the decisions and are they taken by committee; what controls are in place to ensure that a rogue fund (one very different from others and from what is intended) cannot arise;
- People refers to the staff, especially the fund managers. The question is who are they, how are they selected,

how old are they, who reports to whom, how deep is the team (and do all the members understand the philosophy and process they are supposed to be using), and most important of all how long has the team been working together. This last question is vital because whatever performance record was presented at the outset of the relationship with the client may or may not relate to (have been produced by) a team that is still in place. If the team has changed greatly (high staff turnover), then arguably the performance record is completely unrelated to the existing team (of fund managers).

INVESTMENT MANAGERS AND PORTFOLIO STRUCTURES

At the heart of the investment management industry are the managers who invest and divest client investments.

A certified company investment advisor should conduct an assessment of each client's individual needs and risk profile. The advisor then recommends appropriate investments.

Asset Allocation

The different asset classes are stocks, bonds, real-estate, derivatives, and commodities. The exercise of allocating funds among these assets (and among individual securities within each asset class) is for what investment management firms are paid. Asset classes exhibit different market dynamics, and different interaction effects; thus, the allocation of monies among asset classes will have a significant effect on the performance of the fund. Some research suggests that allocation among asset classes has more predictive power than the choice of individual holdings in determining portfolio return. Arguably, the skill of a successful investment manager resides in constructing the asset allocation, and separately the individual holdings, so as to outperform certain benchmarks (e.g., the peer group of competing funds, bond and stock indices).

Long-term Returns

It is important to look at the evidence on the long-term returns to different assets, and to holding period returns (the returns that accrue on average over different lengths of investment). For example, over very long holding periods (eg. 10+ years) in most countries, equities have generated higher returns than bonds, and bonds have generated higher returns than cash. According to financial theory, this is because equities are riskier (more volatile) than bonds which are themselves more risky than cash.

Diversification

Against the background of the asset allocation, fund managers consider the degree of diversification that makes sense for a given client (given its risk preferences) and construct a list of planned holdings accordingly. The list will indicate what percentage of the fund should be invested in each particular stock or bond. The theory of portfolio diversification was originated by Markowitz and effective diversification requires management of the correlation between the asset returns and the liability returns, issues internal to the portfolio (individual holdings volatility), and cross-correlations between the returns.

Investment Styles

There are a range of different styles of fund management that the institution can implement. For example, growth, value, market neutral, small capitalisation, indexed, etc. Each of these approaches has its distinctive features, adherents and, in any particular financial environment, distinctive risk characteristics.

For example, there is evidence that growth styles (buying rapidly growing earnings) are especially effective when the companies able to generate such growth are scarce; conversely, when such growth is plentiful, then there is evidence that value styles tend to outperform the indices particularly successfully.

PERFORMANCE MEASUREMENT

Fund performance is the acid test of fund management, and in the institutional context accurate measurement is a necessity. For that purpose, institutions measure the performance of each fund (and usually for internal purposes components of each fund) under their management, and performance is also measured by external firms that specialise in performance measurement. The leading performance measurement firms (e.g. Frank Russell in the USA) compile aggregate industry data e.g showing how funds in general performed against given indices and peer groups over various time periods.

In a typical case (let us say an equity fund), then the calculation would be made (as far as the client is concerned) every quarter and would show a percentage change compared with the prior quarter (e.g. +4.6% total return in US dollars). This figure would be compared with other similar funds managed within the institution (for purposes of monitoring internal controls), with performance data for peer group funds, and with relevant indices (where available) or tailor-made performance benchmarks where appropriate.

The specialist performance measurement firms calculate quartile and decile data and close attention would be paid to the (percentile) ranking of any fund.

Generally speaking it is probably appropriate for an investment firm to persuade its clients to assess performance over a longer periods (e.g. 3 to 5 years) to smooth out very short term fluctuations in performance and the influence of the business cycle. This can be difficult however and, industrywide, there is a serious pre-occupation with short-term numbers and the effect on the relationship with clients (and resultant business risks for the institutions).

Absolute versus Relative Performance

In the USA and the UK, two of the world's most sophisticated fund management markets, the tradition is for institutions to manage client money relative to benchmarks. For example, an institution believes it has done well if it has generated a return of 5% when the average manager has achieved 4%.

In other markets however, e.g. Switzerland, the mentality is different and clients and fund managers focus on absolute return management, i.e. returns relative to cash (e.g. Swiss franc or Yen cash) where (performance) fees are payable only if the return exceeds some absolute figure (e.g. 10% per annum).

EDUCATION OR CERTIFICATION

Increasingly, international business schools are incorporating the subject into their course outlines and some have formulated the title of 'Investment Management' conferred as specialist bachelors degrees. (i.e. Cass Business School, London).

Due to global cross-recognition agreements with the 2 major accrediting agencies AACSB and ACBSP which accredit over 560 of the best business school programs, the Certification of MFP Master Financial Planner Professional from the American Academy of Financial Management is available to AACSB and ACBSP business school graduates with finance or financial services related concentrations.

15

Finance and Funding

SECURITIES

A security is a fungible, negotiable interest representing financial value. Securities are broadly categorized into debt and equity securities. The company or other entity issuing the security is called the issuer. Securities may be represented by a certificate or, more typically, by an electronic book entry interest. Certificates may be bearer, meaning they entitle the holder to rights under the security merely by holding the security, or registered, meaning they entitle the holder to rights only if he or she appears on a security register maintained by the issuer or an intermediary. They include shares of corporate stock or mutual funds, bonds issued by corporations or governmental agencies, stock options or other options, limited partnership units, and various other formal investment instruments that are negotiable and fungible.

THE CLASSIFICATION

Securities may be classified according to the following categories:

- Issuer
- Currency of denomination
- Ownership rights
- Term to maturity
- Degree of liquidity
- Income payments
- Tax treatment

By Type of Issuer

Issuers of securities include commercial companies, government agencies, local authorities and international and supranational organizations (such as the World Bank). Debt securities issued by a government (called government bonds or sovereign bonds) generally carry a lower interest rate than corporate debt issued by commercial companies. Interests in an asset--for example, the flow of royalty payments from intellectual property--may also be turned into securities. These repackaged securities resulting from a securitization are usually issued by a company established for the purpose of the repackaging-called a special purpose vehicle (SPV). New capital: Commercial enterprises have traditionally used securities as a means of raising new capital. Securities may be an attractive option relative to bank loans depending on their pricing and market demand for particular characteristics. Another disadvantage of bank loans as a source of financing is that the bank may seek a measure of protection against default by the borrower via extensive financial covenants. Through securities, capital is provided by investors who purchase the securities upon their initial issuance. In a similar way, governments may raise capital through the issuance of securities.

Repackaging: In recent decades securities have been issued to repackage existing assets. In a traditional securitisation, a financial institution may wish to remove assets from its balance sheet in order to achieve regulatory capital efficiencies or to accelerate its receipt of cash flow from the original assets. Alternatively, an intermediary may wish to make a profit by acquiring financial assets and repackaging them in a way which makes them more attractive to investors.

By Type of Holder

Investors in securities may be retail, i.e. members of the public investing other than by way of business. The greatest part in terms of volume of investment is wholesale, i.e. by financial institutions acting on their own account, or on behalf of clients. Important institutional investors include investment banks, insurance companies, pension funds and other managed funds.

Investment: The traditional economic function of the purchase of securities is investment, with the view to receiving income and/or achieving capital gain. Debt securities generally offer a higher rate of interest than bank deposits, and equities may offer the prospect of capital growth. Equity investment may also offer control of the business of the issuer. Debt holdings may also offer some measure of control to the investor if the company is a fledgling start-up or an old giant undergoing 'restructuring'. In these cases, if interest payments are missed, the creditors may take control of the company and liquidate it to recover some of their investment.

Collateral: The last decade has seen an enormous growth in the use of securities as collateral. Purchasing securities with borrowed money secured by other securities is called "buying on margin." Where A is owed a debt or other obligation by B, A may require B to deliver property rights in securities to A. These property rights enable A to satisfy its claims in the event that B becomes insolvent. Collateral arrangements are divided into two broad categories, namely security interests and outright collateral transfers. Commonly, commercial banks, investment banks and government agencies are significant collateral takers.

DEBT AND EQUITY

Securities are traditionally divided into debt securities and equities.

Debt: Debt securities may be called debentures, bonds, notes or commercial paper depending on their maturity and certain other characteristics. The holder of a debt security is typically entitled to the payment of principal and interest, together with other contractual rights under the terms of the issue, such as the right to receive certain information. Debt securities are generally issued for a fixed term and redeemable by the issuer at the end of that term. Debt securities may be protected by collateral or may be unsecured, and if they are unsecured. may be contractually "senior" to other unsecured debt meaning their holders would have a priority in a bankruptcy of the issuer. Debt that is not senior is "subordinated".

Corporate bonds represent the debt of commercial or industrial entities. Debentures have a long maturity, typically at least ten years, whereas notes have a shorter maturity. Commercial paper is a simple form of debt security that essentially represents a post-dated check with a maturity of not more than 270 days.

Money market instruments are short term debt instruments that may have characteristics of deposit accounts, such as certificates of deposit, and certain bills of exchange. They are highly liquid and are sometimes referred to as "near cash". Commercial paper is also often highly liquid.

Euro debt securities are securities issued internationally outside their domestic market in a denomination different from that of the issuer's domicile. They include eurobonds and euronotes. Eurobonds are characteristically underwritten, and not secured, and interest is paid gross. A euronote may take the form of euro-commercial paper (ECP) or euro-certificates of deposit.

Government bonds are medium or long term debt securities issued by sovereign governments or their agencies. Typically they carry a lower rate of interest than corporate bonds. In addition to serving as a source of finance for governments. U.S. federal government bonds are called treasuries. Because of their liquidity and perceived low risk, treasuries are used to manage the money supply in the open market operations of non-US central banks.

Sub-sovereign government bonds, known in the U.S. as municipal bonds, represent the debt of state, provincial, territorial, municipal or other governmental units other than sovereign governments.

Supranational bonds represent the debt of international organizations such as the World Bank, the International Monetary Fund, regional multilateral development banks and others.

Equity: An equity security is a share in the capital stock of a company (typically common stock, although preferred equity is also a form of capital stock). The holder of an equity is a shareholder, owning a share, or fractional part of the issuer. Unlike debt securities, which typically require regular payments (interest) to the holder, equity securities are not entitled to any payment. In bankruptcy, they share only in the residual interest of the issuer after all obligations have been paid out to creditors. However, equity generally entitles the holder to a pro rata portion of control of the company, meaning that a holder of a majority of the equity is usually entitled to control the isssuer. Equity also enjoys the right to profits and capital gain, whereas holders of debt securities receive only interest and repayment of principal regardless of how well the issuer performs financially. Furthermore, debt securities do not have voting rights outside of bankruptcy. In other words, equity holders are entitled to the "upside" of the business and to control the business.

Hybrid: Hybrid securities combine some of the characteristics of both debt and equity securities.

Preference shares form an intermediate class of security between equities and debt. If the issuer is liquidated, they carry the right to receive interest and/or a return of capital in priority to ordinary shareholders. However, from a legal perspective, they are capital stock and therefore may entitle holders to some degree of control depending on whether they contain voting rights.

Convertibles are bonds or preferred stock which can be converted, at the election of the holder of the convertibles, into the common stock of the issuing company. The convertibility, however, may be forced if the convertible is a callable bond, and the issuer calls the bond. The bondholder has about 1 month to convert it, or the company will call the bond by giving the holder the call price, which may be less than the value of the converted stock. This is referred to as a forced conversion.

Equity warrants are options issued by the company that allows the holder of the warrant to purchase a specific number of shares at a specified price within a specified time. They are often issued together with bonds or existing equities, and are, sometimes, detachable from them and separately tradable. When the holder of the warrant exercises it, he pays the money directly to the company, and the company issues new shares to holder.

Warrants, like other convertible securities, increases the number of shares outstanding, and are always accounted for in financial reports as fully diluted earnings per share, which assumes that all warrants and convertibles will be exercised.

THE SECURITIES MARKET

Primary and Secondary Market

The public securities markets can be divided into primary and secondary markets. The distinguishing difference between the two markets is that in the primary market, the money for the securities is received by the issuer of those securities from investors, whereas in the secondary market, the money goes from one investor to the other. When a company issues public stock for the first time, this is called an Initial Public Offering (IPO). A company can later issue more new shares, or issue shares that have been previously registered in a shelf registration. These later new issues are also sold in the primary market, but they are not considered to be an IPO. Issuers usually retain investment banks to assist them in administering the IPO, getting SEC approval, and selling the new issue. When the investment bank buys the entire new issue from the issuer at a discount to resell it at a markup, it is called an underwriting, or firm commitment. However, if the investment bank considers the risk too great for an underwriting, it may only assent to a best effort agreement, where the investment bank will simply do its best to sell the new issue.

In order for the primary market to thrive, there must be a secondary market, or aftermarket, where holders of securities can sell them to other investors for cash, hopefully at a profit. Otherwise, few people would purchase primary issues, and, thus, companies and governments would be unable to raise money for their operations. Organized exchanges constitute the main secondary markets. Many smaller issues and most debt securities trade in the decentralized, dealer-based over-the-counter markets.

In Europe, the principal trade organization for securities dealers is the International Capital Market Association. In the U.S., the principal organization for securities dealers is the Securities Industry Association. The Bond Market Association represents bond dealers globally.

In the primary markets, securities may be offered to the public in a public offer. Alternatively, they may be offered privately to a limited number of qualified persons in a private placement. Often a combination of the two is used. The distinction between the two is important to securities regulation and company law. Privately placed securities are often not publicly tradable and may only be bought and sold by sophisticated qualified investors. As a result, the secondary market is not as liquid.

Another category, sovereign debt, is generally sold by auction to a specialised class of dealers.

Listing and OTC Dealing

Securities are often listed in a stock exchange, an organised and officially recognised market on which securities can be bought and sold. Issuers may seek listings for their securities in order to attract investors, by ensuring that there is a liquid and regulated market in which investors will be able to buy and sell securities.

Growth in informal electronic trading systems has challenged the traditional business of stock exchanges. Large volumes of securities are also bought and sold "over the counter" (OTC). OTC dealing involves buyers and sellers dealing with each other by telephone or electronically on the basis of prices that are displayed electronically, usually by commercial information vendors such as Reuters and Bloomberg.

There are also eurosecurities, which are securities that are issued outside their domestic market into more than one jurisdiction. They are generally listed on the Luxembourg Stock Exchange or admitted to listing in London. The reasons for listing eurobonds include regulatory and tax considerations, as well as the investment restrictions.

International Debt Market

London is the centre of the eurosecurities markets. There was a huge rise in the eurosecurities market in London in the early 1980s. Settlement of trades in eurosecurities is currently effected through two European computerised systems called

Euroclear (in Belgium) and Clearstream (formerly Cedelbank in Luxembourg). The main market for Eurobonds is the EuroMTS, owned by Borsa Italiana and Euronext.

PHYSICAL NATURE OF SECURITIES

Certificated Securities

Securities that are represented by certificates are called certificated securities. They may be bearer or registered.

Bearer Securities

Bearer securities are completely negotiable and entitle the holder to the rights, e.g. to payment if it is a debt security and voting if it is a debt security, under the security. They are transferred by delivering the instrument from person to person. In some cases, transfer is by endorsement, or signing the back of the instrument, and delivery.

Regulatory and fiscal authorities sometimes regard bearer securities negatively, as they may be used to facilitate the evasion of regulatory restrictions and tax. In the United Kingdom, for example, the issue of bearer securities was heavily restricted firstly by the Exchange Control Act 1947 until 1963. Bearer securities are very rare in the United States because of the negative tax implications they may have to the issuer and holder.

Registered Securities

In the case of registered securities, certificates bearing the name of the holder are issued, but these merely represent the securities. A person does not automatically acquire legal ownership by having possession of the certificate. Instead, the issuer (or its appointed agent) maintains a register in which details of the holder of the securities are entered and updated as appropriate. A transfer of registered securities is effected by amending the register.

Uncertificated Securities and Global Certificates

Modern practice has developed to eliminate both the need for certificates and maintenance of a complete security register by the issuer. There are two general ways this has been accomplished.

Uncertificated Securities

In some jurisdictions, such as France, it is possible for issuers of that jurisdiction to maintain a legal record of their securities electronically.

Global Certificates and Book Entry Interests

In the United States, the corporation laws typically do not permit securities to be issued without being represented by one or more registered certificates. In order to facilitate the electronic transfer of interests in securities, a system has developed whereby issuers deposit a single global certificate representing all the outstanding securities of a class or series with a universal depository. This depository is called the Depository Trust Corporation, or DTC. DTC is a non-profit cooperative owned by approximately thirty of the largest Wall Street players that typically act as brokers or dealers in securities. These thirty banks are called the DTC participants. DTC, through a legal nominee, owns each of the global securities on behalf of all the DTC participants.

All securities traded through DTC are in fact held, in electronic form, on the books of various intermediaries between the ultimate owner, e.g. a retail investor, and the DTC participants. For example, Mr. Smith may hold 100 shares of Coca Cola, Inc. in his brokerage account at local broker Jones & Co. brokers. In turn, Jones & Co. may hold 1000 shares of Coca Cola on behalf of Mr. Smith and nine other customers. These 1000 shares are held by Jones & Co. in an account with Goldman Sachs, a DTC participant, or in an account at another DTC participant. Goldman Sachs in turn may hold millions of Coca Cola shares on its books on behalf of hundreds of brokers similar to Jones & Co. Each day, the DTC participants settle their accounts with the other DTC participants and adjust the number of shares held on their books for the benefit of customers like Jones & Co. Ownership of securities in this fashion is called beneficial ownership. Each intermediary holds on behalf of someone beneath him in the chain. The ultimate owner is called the beneficial owner. This is also referred to as owning in "Street name".

Other Depositories: Euroclear and Clearstream

Besides DTC, two other large securities depositories exist, both in Europe: Euroclear and Clearstream.

Divided and Undivided Security

The terms "divided" and "undivided" relate to the proprietary nature of a security.

Each divided security constitutes a separate asset, which is legally distinct from each other security in the same issue. Pre-electronic bearer securities were divided. Each instrument constitutes the separate covenant of the issuer and is a separate debt.

With undivided securities, the entire issue makes up one single asset, with each of the securities being a fractional part of this undivided whole. Shares in the secondary markets are always undivided.

The issuer owes only one set of obligations to shareholders under its memorandum, articles of association and company law. A share represents an undivided fractional part of the issuing company. Registered debt securities also have this undivided nature.

Fungible and Non-fungible Security

The terms "fungible" and "non-fungible" relate to the way in which securities are held.

If an asset is fungible, this means that when such an asset is lent, or placed with a custodian, it is customary for the borrower or custodian to be obliged at the end of the loan or custody arrangement to return assets equivalent to the original asset, rather than the identical asset. In other words, the redelivery of fungibles is equivalent and not in specie (identical).

Undivided securities are always fungible by logical necessity. Divided securities may or may not be fungible, depending on market practice. The clear trend is towards fungible arrangements.

REGULATION

In the offer and sale of securities is either registered pursuant to a registration statement that is filed with the U.S. Securities and Exchange Commission (SEC) or are offered and sold pursuant to an exemption therefrom. Dealing in securities is heavily regulated by both the federal authorities (SEC) and state authorities. In addition the industry is heavily self policed by Self Regulatory Organizations (SROs), such as the NASD or the MSRB.

Due to the difficulty of creating a general definition that covers all securities, the SEC attempts to define "securities" exhaustively (and not very precisely) as: "any note, stock, treasury stock, security future, bond, debenture, certificate of interest or participation in any profit-sharing agreement or in any oil, gas, or other mineral royalty or lease, any collateral-trust certificate, preorganization certificate or subscription, transferable share, investment contract, voting-trust certificate, certificate of deposit for a security, any put, call, straddle, option, or privilege on any security, certificate of deposit, or group or index of securities (including any interest therein or based on the value thereof), or any put, call, straddle, option, or privilege entered into on a national securities exchange relating to foreign currency, or in general, any instrument commonly known as a 'security'; or any certificate of interest or participation in, temporary or interim certificate for, receipt for, or warrant or right to subscribe to or purchase, any of the foregoing; but shall not include currency or any note, draft, bill of exchange, or bankers' acceptance which has a maturity at the time of issuance of not exceeding nine months, exclusive of days of grace, or any renewal thereof the maturity of which is likewise limited."-Section 3a item 10 of the 1934 Act.

The US Courts have developed a broad definition for securities that must then be registered with the SEC. There is an investment of money, a common enterprise and expectation of profits to come primarily from the efforts of others.

BONDS

In finance, a bond is a debt security, in which the issuer owes the holders a debt and is obliged to repay the principal and interest (the coupon) at a later date, termed maturity. Other stipulations may also be attached to the bond issue, such as the obligation for the issuer to provide certain information to the bond holder, or limitations on the behavior of the issuer.

Bonds are generally issued for a fixed term (the maturity) longer than ten years. U.S Treasury securities issued debt with life of ten years or more is a bond. New debt between one year and ten years is a note, and new debt less than a year is a bill.

A bond is simply a loan, but in the form of a security, although terminology used is rather different. The issuer is equivalent to the borrower, the bond holder to the lender, and the coupon to the interest. Bonds enable the issuer to finance long-term investments with external funds. Debt securities with a maturity shorter than one year are typically bills. Certificates of deposit (CDs) or commercial paper are considered money market instruments.

Traditionally, the U.S. Treasury uses the word bond only for their issues with a maturity longer than ten years, and calls issues between one and ten year notes. Elsewhere in the market this distinction has disappeared, and both bonds and notes are used irrespective of the maturity. Market participants normally use bonds for large issues offered to a wide public, and notes for smaller issues originally sold to a limited number of investors. There are no clear demarcations. There are also "bills" which usually denote fixed income securities with three years or less, from the issue date, to maturity. Bonds have the highest risk, notes are the second highest risk, and bills have the least risk. This is due to a statistical measure called duration, where lower durations have less risk, and are associated with shorter term obligations.

Bonds and stocks are both securities, but the difference is that stock holders own a part of the issuing company (have an equity stake), whereas bond holders are in essence lenders to the issuer. Also bonds usually have a defined term, or maturity, after which the bond is redeemed whereas stocks may be outstanding indefinitely. An exception is a consol bond, which is a perpetuity, a bond with no maturity.

Issuers

The range of issuers of bonds is very large. Almost any organization could issue bonds, but the underwriting and legal costs can be prohibitive. Regulations to issue bonds are very strict. Issuers are often classified as follows:

- Supranational agencies, such as the European Investment Bank or the Asian Development Bank issue supranational bonds.
- National Governments issue government bonds in their own currency. They also issue sovereign bonds in foreign currencies.
- Sub-sovereign, provincial, state or local authorities (municipalities). In the U.S. state and local government bonds are known as municipal bonds.
- Government sponsored entities. In the U.S., examples include the Federal Home Loan Mortgage Corporation (Freddie Mac), the Federal National Mortgage Association (Fannie Mae), and the Federal Home Loan Banks. The bonds of these entities are known as agency bonds, or agencies.
- Companies (corporates) issue corporate bonds.
- Special purpose vehicles are companies set up for the sole purpose of containing assets against which bonds are issued, often called asset-backed securities.

Issuing Bonds

Bonds are issued by public authorities, credit institutions, companies and supranational institutions in the primary markets. The most common process of issuing bonds is through underwriting. In underwriting, one or more securities firms or banks, forming a syndicate, buy an entire issue of bonds from an issuer and re-sell them to investors. Government bonds are typically auctioned.

The pictured bond was issued for the construction of the building now known as New York City Center. The elaborate engraving is typical of certificated bonds, in this case using the fraternal organization's logo, rather than neoclassical human figures, idealized versions of the corporation's business, or architectural elements, all common decorations on bonds. Coupons from this bond can be seen under Coupon. The bond and the coupons have no economic value today because the corporation became insolvent within a few years of the Wall Street Crash of 1929. The bond was purchased from a dealer of worthless securities, sometimes called wallpaper.

Features of Bonds

The most important features of a bond are:

- nominal, principal or face amount-the amount over which the issuer pays interest, and which has to be repaid at the end.
- issue price-the price at which investors buy the bonds when they are first issued. The net proceeds that the issuer receives are calculated as the issue price, less issuance fees, times the nominal amount.
- maturity date-the date on which the issuer has to repay the nominal amount. As long as all payments have been made, the issuer has no more obligations to the bond holders after the maturity date. The length of time until the maturity date is often referred to as the term or maturity of a bond. The maturity can be any length of time, although debt securities with a term of less than one year are generally designated money market instruments rather than bonds. Most bonds have a term of up to thirty years. Some bonds have been issued with maturities of up to one hundred years, and some even do not mature at all. In early 2005, a market developed in euros for bonds with a maturity of fifty years. In the market for U.S. Treasury securities, there are three groups of bond maturities:
    - o short term (bills): maturities up to one year;
    - o medium term (notes): maturities between one and ten years;
    - o long term (bonds): maturities greater than ten years.
- coupon-the interest rate that the issuer pays to the bond holders. Usually this rate is fixed throughout the life

of the bond. It can also vary with a money market index, such as LIBOR, or it can be even more exotic. The name coupon originates from the fact that in the past, physical bonds were issued which had coupons attached to them. On coupon dates the bond holder would give the coupon to a bank in exchange for the interest payment.

- coupon dates-the dates on which the issuer pays the coupon to the bond holders. In the U.S., most bonds are semi-annual, which means that they pay a coupon every six months. In Europe, most bonds are annual and pay only one coupon a year.
- indenture or covenants-a document specifying the rights of bond holders. In the U.S., federal and state securities and commercial laws apply to the enforcement of those documents, which are construed by courts as contracts. The terms may be changed only with great difficulty while the bonds are outstanding, with amendments to the governing document generally requiring approval by a majority (or super-majority) vote of the bond holders.
- Optionality: a bond may contain an embedded option; that is, it grants option like features to the buyer or issuer:
  - o callability-Some bonds give the issuer the right to repay the bond before the maturity date on the call dates; see call option. These bonds are referred to as callable bonds. Most callable bonds allow the issuer to repay the bond at par. With some bonds, the issuer has to pay a premium, the so called call premium. This is mainly the case for high-yield bonds. These have very strict covenants, restricting the issuer in its operations. To be free from these covenants, the issuer can repay the bonds early, but only at a high cost.
  - o puttability-Some bonds give the bond holder the right to force the issuer to repay the bond before the maturity date on the put dates; see put option.
  - o call dates and put dates-the dates on which callable and puttable bonds can be redeemed early. There are four main categories.

* A Bermudan callable has several call dates, usually coinciding with coupon dates.
* A European callable has only one call date. This is a special case of a Bermudan callable.
* An American callable can be called at any time until the maturity date.
* A death put is an optional redemption feature on a debt instrument allowing the beneficiary of the estate of the deceased to put (sell) the bond (back to the issuer) in the event of the beneficiary's death or legal incapacitation. Also known as a "survivor's option".
* An IMRU callable can only be purchased by buyers of the highest quality (in financial terms) and remains the highest quality and hardest to obtain bond on the market. Originally conceived by financial guru M. Last with the help of A. Thein and T. Gardner.

- sinking fund provision of the corporate bond indenture requires a certain portion of the issue to be retired periodically. The entire bond issue can be liquidated by the maturity date. If that is not the case, then the remainder is called balloon maturity. Issuers may either pay to trustees, which in turn call randomly selected bonds in the issue, or, alternatively, purchase bonds in open market, then return them to trustees.
- convertible bond lets a bondholder exchange a bond to a number of shares of the issuer's common stock.
- exchangeable bond allows for exchange to shares of a corporation other than the issuer.

TYPES OF BOND

- Fixed rate bonds have a coupon that remains constant throughout the life of the bond.
- Floating rate notes (FRN's) have a coupon that is linked to a money market index, such as LIBOR or Euribor, for example three months USD LIBOR +0.20%. The

coupon is then reset periodically, normally every three months.

- High yield bonds are bonds that are rated below investment grade by the credit rating agencies. As these bonds are relatively risky, investors expect to earn a higher yield. These bonds are also called junk bonds.
- Zero coupon bonds do not pay any interest. They trade at a substantial discount from par value. The bond holder receives the full principal amount as well as value that has accrued on the redemption date. An example of zero coupon bonds are Series E savings bonds issued by the U.S. government. Zero coupon bonds may be created from fixed rate bonds by financial institutions by "stripping off" the coupons. In other words, the coupons are separated from the final principal payment of the bond and traded independently.
- Inflation linked bonds, in which the principal amount is indexed to inflation. The interest rate is lower than for fixed rate bonds with a comparable maturity. However, as the principal amount grows, the payments increase with inflation. The government of the United Kingdom was the first to issue inflation linked Gilts in the 1980s. Treasury Inflation-Protected Securities (TIPS) and I-bonds are examples of inflation linked bonds issued by the U.S. government.
- Other indexed bonds, for example Equity Linked Notes and bonds indexed on a business indicator (income, added value) or on a country GDP...
- Asset-backed securities are bonds whose interest and principal payments are backed by underlying cash flows from other assets. Examples of asset-backed securities are mortgage-backed securities (MBS's), collateralized mortgage obligations (CMOs) and collateralized debt obligations (CDOs).
- Subordinated bonds are those that have a lower priority than other bonds of the issuer in case of liquidation. In case of bankruptcy, there is a hierarchy of creditors. First the liquidator is paid, then government taxes, etc.

The first bond holders in line to be paid are those holding what is called senior bonds. After they have been paid, the subordinated bond holders are paid. As a result, the risk is higher. Therefore, subordinated bonds usually have a lower credit rating than senior bonds. The main examples of subordinated bonds can be found in bonds issued by banks, and asset-backed securities. The latter are often issued in tranches. The senior tranches get paid back first, the subordinated tranches later.

- Perpetual bonds are also often called perpetuities. They have no maturity date. The most famous of these are the UK Consols, which are also known as Treasury Annuities or Undated Treasuries. Some of these were issued back in 1888 and still trade today. Some ultra long-term bonds (sometimes a bond can last centuries: West Shore Railroad issued a bond which matures in 2361 (i.e. 24th century)) are sometimes viewed as perpetuities from a financial point of view, with the current value of principal near zero.
- Bearer bond is an official certificate issued without a named holder. In other words, the person who has the paper certificate can claim the value of the bond. Often they are registered by a number to prevent counterfeiting, but may be traded like cash. Bearer bonds are very risky because they can be lost or stolen. Especially after federal income tax began in the United States, bearer bonds were seen as an opportunity to conceal income or assets. U.S. corporations stopped issuing bearer bonds in the 1960s, the U.S. Treasury stopped in 1982, and state and local tax-exempt bearer bonds were prohibited in 1983.
- Registered bond is a bond whose ownership (and any subsequent purchaser) is recorded by the issuer, or by a transfer agent. It is the alternative to a Bearer bond. Interest payments, and the principal upon maturity, are sent to the registered owner.
- Municipal bond is a bond issued by a state, U.S. Territory, city, local government, or their agencies. Interest income

received by holders of municipal bonds is often exempt from the federal income tax and from the income tax of the state in which they are issued, although municipal bonds issued for certain purposes may not be tax exempt.

- Book-entry bond is a bond that does not have a paper certificate. As physically processing paper bonds and interest coupons became more expensive, issuers (and banks that used to collect coupon interest for depositors) have tried to discourage their use. Some book-entry bond issues do not offer the option of a paper certificate, even to investors who prefer them.
- Lottery bond is a bond issued by a state, usually a European state. Interest is paid like a traditional fixed rate bond, but the issuer will redeem randomly selected individual bonds within the issue according to a schedule. Some of these redenptions will be for a higher value than the face value of the bond.

Bonds Issued by Foreign Entities

Some companies, banks, governments, and other soverign entities may decide to issue bonds in foreign currencies as it may appear to be more stable and predictable than their domestic currency. Some foreign issuer bonds are called by their nicknames, such as the "Samurai bond", but this is ironic in that the issuer is neither a samurai nor even Japanese.

- Eurodollar bond is a bond issued by a non-European entity in the European market in Euro-dollar denominations.
- Samurai bond is a bond issued by a non-Japanese entity in the Japanese market in Japanese Yen denominations.
- Yankee bond is a bond issued by a non-US entity in the US market in US Dollar denominations.

TRADING AND VALUING BONDS

The interest rate that the issuer of a bond must pay is influenced by a variety of factors, such as current market interest rates, the length of the term and the credit worthiness of the issuer.

These factors are likely to change over time, so the market value of a bond can vary after it is issued. Because of these differences in market value, bonds are priced in terms of percentage of par value. Bonds are not necessarily issued at par (100% of face value, corresponding to a price of 100), but all bond prices converge to par at the moment before they reach maturity. At other times, prices can either rise (bond is priced at greater than 100), which is called trading at a premium, or fall (bond is priced at less than 100), which is called trading at a discount. Most government bonds are denominated in units of $1000, if in the United States, or in units of £100, if in the United Kingdom. Hence, a deep discount US bond, selling at a price of 75.26, indicates a selling price of $752.60 per bond sold. (Often, bond prices are quoted in points and thirty-seconds of a point, rather than in decimal form.) Some short-term bonds, such as the U.S. T-Bill, are always issued at a discount, and pay par amount at maturity rather than paying coupons. This is called a discount bond.

The market price of a bond is the present value of all future interest and principal payments of the bond discounted at the bond's yield, or rate of return. The yield represents the current market interest rate for bonds with similar characteristics. The yield and price of a bond are inversely related so that when market interest rates rise, bond prices generally fall and vice versa.

The market price of a bond may include the accrued interest since the last coupon date. (Some bond markets include accrued interest in the trading price and others add it on explicitly after trading.) The price including accrued interest is known as the "flat" or "dirty price". The price excluding accrued interest is sometimes known as the Clean price.

The interest rate adjusted for the current price of the bond is called the "current yield" or "earnings yield" (this is the nominal yield multiplied by the par value and divided by the price).

Taking into account the expected capital gain or loss (the difference between the current price and the redemption value) gives the "redemption yield": roughly the current yield plus the capital gain (negative for loss) per year until redemption.

The relationship between yield and maturity for otherwise identical bonds is called a yield curve.

Bonds markets, unlike stock or share markets, often do not have a centralized exchange or trading system. Rather, in most developed bond markets such as the U.S., Japan and western Europe, bonds trade in decentralized, dealer-based over-the-counter markets. In such a market, market liquidity is provided by dealers and other market participants committing risk capital to trading activity. In the bond market, when an investor buys or sells a bond, the counterparty to the trade is almost always a bank or securities firm acting as a dealer. In some cases, when a dealer buys a bond from an investor, the dealer carries the bond "in inventory." The dealer's position is then subject to risks of price fluctuation. In other cases, the dealer immediately resells the bond to another investor.

Bond markets also differ from stock markets in that investors generally do not pay brokerage commissions to dealers with whom they buy or sell bonds. Rather, dealers earn revenue for trading with their investor customers by means of the spread, or difference, between the price at which the dealer buys a bond from one investor--the "bid" price--and the price at which he or she sells the same bond to another investor--the "ask" or "offer" price. The bid/offer spread represents the total transaction cost associated with transferring a bond from one investor to another.

Investing in Bonds

Bonds are bought and traded mostly by institutions like pension funds, insurance companies and banks. Most individuals who want to own bonds do so through bond funds. Still, in the U.S., nearly ten percent of all bonds outstanding are held directly by households.

As a rule, bond markets rise (while yields fall) when stock markets fall. Thus bonds are generally viewed as safer investments than stocks, but this perception is only partially correct. Bonds do suffer from less day-to-day volatility than stocks, and bonds' interest payments are higher than dividend payments that the same company would generally choose to pay to its stockholders. Bonds are liquid-it is fairly easy to sell one's bond investments, though not nearly as easy as it is to sell stocks-and the certainty of a fixed interest payment twice per year is attractive. Bondholders also enjoy a measure of legal protection: under the law of most countries, if a company goes bankrupt, its bondholders will often receive some money back, whereas the company's stock often ends up valueless. However, bonds can be risky:

- Fixed rate bonds are subject to interest rate risk, meaning their market price will decrease in value when the generally prevailing interest rate rises. Since the payments are fixed, a decrease in the market price of the bond means an increase in its yield. When the market's interest rates rise, then the market price for bonds will fall, reflecting investors' improved ability to get a good interest rate for their money elsewhere-perhaps by purchasing a newly issued bond that already features the newly higher interest rate. This drop in the bond's market price does not affect the interest payments to the bondholder at all, so long-term investors need not worry about price swings in their bonds.

However, price changes in a bond immediately affect mutual funds that hold these bonds. Many institutional investors have to "mark to market" their trading books at the end of every day. If the value of the bonds held in a trading portfolio has fallen over the day, the "mark to market" value of the portfolio may also have fallen. This can be damaging for professional investors such as banks, insurance companies, pension funds and asset managers. If there is any chance a holder of individual bonds may need to sell his bonds and "cash out" for some reason, interest rate risk could become a real problem. (Conversely, bonds' market prices would increase if the prevailing interest rate were to drop, as it did from 2001 through 2003.) One way to quantify the interest rate risk on a bond is in terms of its duration. Efforts to control this risk are called immunization or hedging.

- Bond prices can become volatile if one of the credit rating agencies like Standard & Poor's or Moody's upgrades or downgrades the credit rating of the issuer. A downgrade can cause the market price of the bond to fall. As with interest rate risk, this risk does not affect the bond's interest payments, but puts at risk the market price, which affects mutual funds holding these bonds, and holders of individual bonds who may have to sell them.

- A company's bondholders may lose much or all their money if the company goes bankrupt. Under the laws of the United States and many other countries, bondholders are in line to receive the proceeds of the sale of the assets of a liquidated company ahead of some other creditors. Bank lenders, deposit holders (in the case of a deposit taking institution such as a bank) and trade creditors may take precedence.

There is no guarantee of how much money will remain to repay bondholders. As an example, after an accounting scandal and a Chapter 11 bankruptcy at the giant telecommunications company Worldcom, in 2004 its bondholders ended up being paid 35.7 cents on the dollar. In a bankruptcy involving reorganization or recapitalization, as opposed to liquidation, bondholders may end up having the value of their bonds reduced, often through an exchange for a smaller number of newly issued bonds.

- Some bonds are callable, meaning that even though the company has agreed to make payments plus interest towards the debt for a certain period of time, the company can choose to pay off the bond early. This creates reinvestment risk, meaning the investor is forced to find a new place for his money, and the investor might not be able to find as good a deal, especially because this usually happens when interest rates are falling.

Bond Indices

A number of bond indices exist for the purposes of managing portfolios and measuring performance, similar to the S&P 500 or Russell Indexes for stocks. The most common American benchmarks are the Lehman Aggregate, Citigroup BIG and Merrill Lynch Domestic Master. Most indices are parts of families of broader indices that can be used to measure global bond portfolios, or may be further subdivided by maturity and/or sector for managing specialized portfolios.

BRADY BONDS

Brady bonds were created in March 1989 in order to convert bonds issued by mostly Latin American countries into a variety or "menu" of new bonds after many of those countries defaulted on their debt in the 1980's. At that time, the market for sovereign debt was small and illiquid, and the standardization of emerging-market debt facilitated risk-spreading and trading. In exchange for commercial bank loans, the countries issued new bonds for the principal and, in some cases, unpaid interest. Because they were tradeable and came with some guarantees, in some cases they were more valuable to the creditors than the original bonds.

The key innovation behind the introduction of Brady Bonds was to allow the commercial banks to exchange their claims on developing countries into tradeable instruments, allowing them to get the debt off their balance sheets. This reduced the concentration risk to these banks.

The plan included two rounds. In the first round, creditors bargained with debtors over the terms of these new claims. Loosely interpreted, the options contained different mixes of "exit" and "new money" options. The exit options were designed for creditors who wanted to reduce their exposure to a debtor country. These options allowed creditors to reduce their exposure to debtor nations, albeit at a discount. The new money options reflected the belief that those creditors who chose not to exit would experience a capital gain from the transaction, since the nominal outstanding debt obligation of the debtor would be reduced, and with it the probability of future default. These options allowed creditors to retain their exposure, but required additional credit extension designed to "tax" the expected capital gains. The principal of many instruments was collateralized, as were "rolling interest guarantees," which guaranteed payment for fixed short periods. The first round negotiations thus involved the determination of the effective magnitude of discount on the exit options together with the amount of new lending called for under the new money options.

In the second round, creditors converted their existing claims into their choice among the "menu" of options agreed upon in the first round. The penalties for creditors failing to comply with the terms of the deal were never made explicit. Nevertheless, compliance was not an important problem under the Brady Plan. Banks wishing to cease their foreign lending activities tended to choose the exit option under the auspices of the deal.

By offering a "menu" of options, the Brady Plan permitted credit restructurings to be tailored to the heterogeneous preferences of creditors. The terms achieved under these deals indicate that debtors used the menu approach to reduce the cost of debt reduction. Furthermore, it reduced the holdout problem where certain shareholders have an incentive to not participate in the restructuring in hopes of getting a better deal.

The principal amount is usually but not always collateralized by specially issued U.S. Treasury 30-year zero-coupon bonds purchased by the debtor country using a combination of International Monetary Fund, World Bank, and the country's own foreign currency reserves. Interest payments on Brady bonds, in some cases, are guaranteed by securities of at least double-A-rated credit quality held with the Federal Reserve Bank of New York.

Countries that participated in the initial round of Brady bond issuance were Argentina, Brazil, Bulgaria, Costa Rica, Dominican Republic, Ecuador, Mexico, Morocco, Nigeria, Philippines, Poland, Uruguay.

Types of Brady Bonds

There are two main types of Brady bonds:

- Par bonds were issued to the same value as the original loan, but the coupon on the bonds is below market rate, principal and interest payments are usually guaranteed.
- Discount bonds were issued at a discount to the original value of the loan, but the coupon is at market rate, principal and interest payments are usually guaranteed.

Other, less common, types include front-loaded interest-reduction bonds (FLIRB), new-money bonds, debt-conversion bonds (DCB), and past-due interest bonds (PDI). Brady Bond negotiations generally involved some form of "haircut"-meaning that the value of the Bonds resulting from the restructurings was less than the face value of the claims before the restructurings. For Par Bonds, creditors kept the same face value, but received a below-market interest rate, while for Discount bonds, investors received a market interest rate on a lower bond face value.

Guarantees attached to Brady bonds include collateral to guarantee the principal, rolling interest guarantees, and value recovery rights. Not all Brady bonds will necessary have all of these forms of guarantee and the specifics will vary from issuance to issuance.

Current Status

Although the Brady Bond process ended during the 1990s, many of the innovations introduced in these restructurings (call options embedded in the bonds, "stepped" coupons, Pars and Discounts) were retained in the later sovereign restructurings in, for example, Russia and Ecuador. Ecuador, in 1999, became the first country to default on its Brady bonds. In 2003, Mexico became the first country to retire its Brady debt.

DEBT

Debt is that which is owed; usually referencing assets owed, but the term can cover other obligations. In the case of assets, debt is a means of using future purchasing power in the present before a summation has been earned. Some companies and corporations use debt as a part of their overall corporate finance strategy.

A debt is created when a creditor agrees to loan a sum of assets to a debtor. In modern society, debt is usually granted with expected repayment; in many cases, plus interest. Historically, debt was responsible for the creation of indentured servants.

Payment

Before a debt can be had, both the debtor and the creditor must agree on the manner in which the debt will be repaid, known as the standard of deferred payment. This payment is usually denominated as a sum of money in units of currency, but can sometimes be denominated in terms of goods. Payment can be made in increments over a period of time, or all at once at the end of the loan agreement.

Types of Debt

There are numerous types of debt, including basic loans, syndicated loans, bonds, and promissory notes. Debt, especially large sums of debt, can also be secured through a mortgage or other security interest over some of the debtor's property, in which case the creditor will have some rights over that property in the event that the debtor becomes unable to repay the debt and defaults on the loan. A basic loan is the simplest form of debt. It consists of an agreement to lend a principal sum for a fixed period of time, to be repaid by a certain date. In commercial loans interest, calculated as a percentage of the principal sum per annum, will also have to be paid by that date.

A syndicated loan is a loan that is granted to companies that wish to borrow more money than any single lender is prepared to risk in a single loan, usually many millions of dollars. In such a case, a syndicate of banks can each agree to put forward a portion of the principal sum.

A bond is a debt security issued by certain institutions such as companies and governments. A bond entitles the holder to repayment of the principal sum, plus interest. Bonds are issued to investors in a marketplace when an institution wishes to borrow money. Bonds have a fixed lifetime, usually a number of years; with long-term bonds, lasting over 30 years, being less common. At the end of the bond's life the money should be repaid in full. Interest may be added to the end payment, or can be paid in regular instalments (known as coupons) during the life of the bond. Bonds may be traded in the bond markets, and are widely used as relatively safe investments in comparison to stocks.

Accounting Debt

In national accounting debts are added according to those who are indebted. Household debt is the debt held by households. "National" or Public debt is the debt held by the various governmental institutions (federal government, states, cities...).

Business debt is the debt held by businesses. Financial debt is the debt held by the financial sector (from one financial institution to another). Total debt is the sum of all those debts, excluding financial debt to prevent double accounting. These various types of debt can be computed in debt/GDP ratios. Those ratios help to assess the speed of variations in the indebtness and the size of the debt due. For example the USA have a high consumer debt and a low public debt, while in European countries the opposite tends to be true.

There are differences in the accounting of debt for private and public agents. If a private agent promises to pay something later, it has a debt, and this debt is enforceable by public agents. If a public body passes a law stating that it'll pay something later (a kind of promise), it keeps the right to change the law later (and not to pay). This is why for instance the money governments promised to pay for retirements does not show up in the public debt assessment, whereas the money private companies promised to pay for retirements do.

Securitization

Securitization occurs when a company groups together assets or receivables and sells them in units to the market through a trust. Any asset with a cashflow can be securitized. The cash flows from these receivables are used to pay the holders of these units. Companies often do this in order to remove these assets from their balance sheets and monetize an asset. Although these assets are "removed" from the balance sheet and are supposed to be the responsibility of the trust, that does not end the company's involvement. Often the company maintains a special interest in the trust which is called an "interest only strip" or "first loss piece". Any payments from the trust must be made to regular investors in precedence to this interest. This protects investors from a degree of risk, making the securitization more attractive. The aforementioned brings into question whether the assets are truly off balance sheet given the company's exposure to losses on this interest.

Debt, Inflation and the Exchange Rate

As noted above, debt is normally denominated in a particular monetary currency, and so changes in the valuation of that currency can change the effective size of the debt. This can happen due to inflation or deflation, so it can happen even though the borrower and the lender are using the same currency. Thus it is important to agree on standards of deferred payment in advance, so that a degree of fluctuation will also be agreed as acceptable. It is for instance common to agree to "US dollar denominated" debt.

The form of debt involved in banking accounts for a large proportion of the money in most industrialised nations. There is therefore a complex relationship between inflation, deflation, the money supply, and debt. The store of value represented by the entire economy of the industrialized nation itself, and the state's ability to levy tax on it, acts to the foreign holder of debt as a guarantee of repayment, since industrial goods are in high demand in many places worldwide.

Inflation Indexed Debt

Borrowing and repayment arrangements linked to inflation-indexed units of account are possible and are used in some countries. For example, the US government issues two types of inflation-indexed bonds, Treasury Inflation-Protected Securities (TIPS) and I-bonds. These are one of the safest forms of investment available, since the only major source of risk-that of inflation-is eliminated. A number of other governments issue similar bonds, and some did so for many years before the US government.

In countries with consistently high inflation, ordinary borrowings at banks may also be inflation indexed.

Risk-free Interest Rate

Lendings to stable financial entities such as large companies or governments are often termed "risk free" or "low risk" and made at a so-called "risk-free interest rate". This is because the debt and interest are highly unlikely to be defaulted. A good example of such risk-free interest is a US Treasury security-it yields the minimum return available in economics, but investors have the comfort of the (almost) certain expectation that the US Treasury will not default on its debt instruments. A risk-free rate is also commonly used in setting floating interest rates, which are usually calculated as the risk-free interest rate plus a bonus to the creditor based on the creditworthiness of the debtor (in other words, the risk of him defaulting and the creditor losing the debt). In reality, no lending is truly risk free, but borrowers at the "risk free" rate are considered the least likely to default.

However, if the real value of a currency changes during the term of the debt, the purchasing power of the money repaid may vary considerably from that which was expected at the commencement of the loan. So from a practical investment point of view, there is still considerable risk attached to "risk free" or "low risk" lendings. The real value of the money may have changed due to inflation, or, in the case of a foreign investment, due to exchange rate fluctuations.

The Bank for International Settlements is an organisation of central banks that sets rules to define how much capital banks have to hold against the loans they give out.

Ratings and Creditworthiness

Specific bond debts owed by both governments and private corporations is rated by rating agencies, such as Moody's, A.M. Best and Standard & Poor's. The government or company itself will also be given its own separate rating. These agencies assess the ability of the debtor to honor his obligations and accordingly give him a credit rating. Moody's uses the letters Aaa Aa A Baa Ba B Caa Ca C, where ratings Aa-Caa are qualified by numbers 1-3. Munich Re, for example, currently is rated Aa3 (as of 2004). S&P and other rating agencies have slightly different systems using capital letters and +/-qualifiers.

A change in ratings can strongly affect a company, since its cost of refinancing depends on its creditworthiness. Bonds below Baa/BBB (Moody's/S&P) are considered junk-or high risk bonds. Their high risk of default (approximately 1.6% for Ba) is compensated by higher interest payments. Bad Debt is a loan that can not (partially or fully) be repaid by the debtor. The debtor is said to default on his debt. These types of debt are frequently repackaged and sold below face value. Buying junk bonds is seen as a risky but potentially profitable form of investment.

Cancellation

Short of bankruptcy, it is rare that debts are wholly or partially forgiven. Traditions in some cultures demand that this be done on a regular (often annual) basis, in order to prevent systemic inequities between groups in society, or anyone becoming a specialist in holding debt and coercing repayment. Under English law, when the creditor is deceived into forgoing payment. International Third World debt has reached the scale that many economists are convinced that debt cancellation is the only way to restore global equity in relations with the developing nations.

Effects of Debt

Debt allows people and organizations to do things that they otherwise wouldn't be able or allowed to. Commonly, people in industrialised nations use it to purchase houses, cars and many other things too expensive to buy with cash on hand. Companies also use debt in many ways to leverage the investment made in their private equity. This leverage, the proportion of debt to equity, is considered important in determining the riskiness of an investment; the more debt per equity, the riskier.

Debt as a whole is a sign that a society is optimistic, that it believes in its future earnings capacity, arguably that it lacks a strong work ethic (though the money must be repaid), and perhaps that it is postponing the solution to present problems (for example, it may compensate a fall in revenues that is perceived as short term by an increase in debt).

Excesses in debt accumulation have been blamed for exacerbating economic problems. For example, prior to the beginning of the Great Depression debt/GDP ratio was very high. Economic agents were heavily indebted. This excess in debt, equivalent to excessive expectations on future returns, accompanied asset bubbles on the stock markets. When expectations corrected, deflation and credit crunch followed. Deflation effectively made debt more expansive and, as Fisher explained, this reinforced deflation again, because, in order to reduce their debt level, economic agents reduced their consumption and investment. The reduction in demand reduced business activity and caused further unemployment. In a more direct sense, more bankruptcies also occurred due both to increased debt cost caused by deflation and to the reduced demand.

It is possible for some organizations to enter into alternative types of borrowing and repayment arrangements which will not result in bankruptcy. For example, companies can sometimes convert debt that they owe into equity in themselves. In this case, the creditor hopes to regain something equivalent to the debt and interest in the form of dividends and capital gains of the borrower. The "repayments" are therefore proportional to what the borrower earns and so can not in themselves cause bankruptcy. Once debt is converted in this way, it is no longer known as debt.

Arguments Against Debt

Some argue against debt as an instrument and institution, on a personal, family, social, corporate and governmental level. Economics criticism focuses on debt fostering inequality. Islam forbids lending with interest, as the Catholic church long did, and the Torah states that all debts should be erased every 7 years and every 50 years. Debt from a religious view point is condemned because, by tying past and future, it cuts from the present where God is to be found.

Feminism concentrates on the perceived coercive nature of debt contracts. Environmental critics point out the disparity between the material use of resources from economic growth and the limited resources of natural production. Examples would be the low ecological yield of natural resources and the limited usable energy from the sun.

Debt will increase through time if it is not repaid faster than it grows through interest. In some systems of economics this effect is termed usury, in others, the term "usury" refers only to an excessive rate of interest, in excess of a reasonable profit for the risk accepted.

DEBT RELIEF

Debt relief is the partial or total forgiveness of debt, or the slowing or stopping of debt growth, owed by individuals, corporations, or nations. It concerns in particular the Third World debt, which started exploding with the Latin American debt crisis (Mexico 1982, etc.).

Debt relief for heavily indebted and underdeveloped developing countries was the subject in the 1990s of a campaign by a broad coalition of development NGOs, Christian organisations and others, under the banner of Jubilee 2000. This campaign, involving, for example, demonstrations at the 1998 G8 meeting in Birmingham, was successful in pushing debt relief onto the agenda of Western governments and international organisations such as the International Monetary Fund and World Bank. Ultimately the Heavily Indebted Poor Countries (HIPC) initiative was launched to provide systematic debt relief for the poorest countries, whilst trying to ensure the money would be spent on poverty reduction. Thailand now owes 1 trillion dollars in debt back to many different countries around the world.

The HIPC programme has been subject to conditionalities similar to those often attached to IMF and World Bank loans, requiring structural adjustment reforms, sometimes including the privatisation of public utilities, including water and electricity. To qualify for irrevocable debt relief, countries must also maintain macroeconomic stability and implement a Poverty Reduction Strategy satisfactorily for at least one year. Under the goal of reducing inflation, some countries have been pressured to reduce spending in the health and education sectors.

The Multilateral Debt Relief Initiative (MDRI) is an extension of HIPC. The MDRI was agreed following the G8's Gleneagles meeting in July 2005. It offers 100% cancellation of multilateral debts owed by HIPC countries to the World Bank, IMF and African Development Bank.

Arguments against Debt Relief

Opponents of debt relief argue that it is a blank cheque to governments, and fear savings will not reach the poor in countries plagued by corruption. Others argue that countries will go out and contract further debts, under the belief that these debts will also be forgiven in some future date. They use the money to enhance the wealth and spending ability of the rich, many of whom will spend or invest this money in the rich countries, thus not even creating a trickle-down effect. They argue that the money would be far better spent in specific aid projects which actually help the poor. They further argue that it would be unfair to third-world countries that managed their credit successfully, or don't go into debt in the first place, that is, it actively encourages third world governments to overspend in order to receive debt relief in the future. Others argue against the conditionalities attached to debt relief. These conditions of structural adjustment have a history, especially in Latin America, of widening the gap between the rich and the poor, as well as increasing economic dependence on the global North.

Personal Debt Relief

Personal debt has become an increasingly large problem in recent years. For instance, it is estimated that the average US household has $19,000 in non-mortgage debt. With such large debt loads, many individuals have difficulty making repayments on debts and are in need of help.

There are many companies who offer debt consolidation services. However, such services may not always be in the best interests of the person involved and may involve taking out a loan secured on a person's home. Marketing materials are designed to persuade customers to take up the company's offer rather than offering a personal best solution for reducing debt. Where debt has become a problem, it is often best to turn to an independent consumer's association for advice before calling debt consolidation companies as they often have great experience with such problems and may be able to advise the most effective avenues for debt relief.

16

Anti-globalization

Anti-globalization is a term most commonly ascribed to the political stance of people and groups who oppose certain aspects of globalization in its current form.

"Anti-globalization" is considered by many to be a social movement, while others consider it to be an umbrella term that encompasses a number of separate social movements. In either case, participants are united in opposition to the political power of large corporations, as exercised in trade agreements and elsewhere, which they say undermines the environment, labor rights, national sovereignty, the third world, and other concerns.

Most people who are labelled "anti-globalization" reject the term, preferring instead to describe themselves as the Global Justice Movement, the Movement of Movements (a popular term in Italy), the "alter-globalization" movement (popular in France), and a number of other terms.

IDEOLOGY AND CAUSES WITHIN THE MOVEMENT

The groups and individuals that would come to be known as the "anti-globalization movement" developed in the late twentieth century to combat the globalization of corporate economic activity and the free trade with developing nations that might result from such activity.

Members of the anti-globalization movement generally advocate anarchist, nationalist, socialist, social democratic or Eco-socialist alternatives to liberal economics, and seek to protect the world's population and ecosystem from what they believe to be the damaging effects of globalization. Support for human rights NGOs is another cornerstone of the anti-globalization movement's platform. They advocate for labor rights, environmentalism, feminism, freedom of migration, preservation of the cultures of indigenous peoples, biodiversity, cultural diversity, food safety, and ending or reforming capitalism. Many of the protesters are veterans of single-issue campaigns, including anti-logging activism, living wage, labor union organizing, and anti-sweatshop campaigns. Although most movement members see most or all of the aforementioned goals as complementary to one another, the number of different issues has fueled a leading criticism that the movement lacks a consistent, coherent, or realistic cause.

By contrast, certain paleo-conservative American opponents of globalization, such as Patrick Buchanan, argue against globalization from a point of view of economic nationalism. Against outsourcing, such paleo-conservative opponents of globalization phrase their opposition in nativist and xenophobic terms. The industrialized world must protect itself against the Global South, Buchanan argues, because what he calls the "Third World" is racked with disease and the peoples there lack a Western culture. Economic globalization, therefore, will result in the "Death of the West".

Although adherents of the movement often work together, the movement itself is heterogeneous. It includes diverse and sometimes opposing understandings of the globalization process, and incorporates alternative visions, strategies and tactics. Many of the groups and organizations that are considered part of the movement were not founded as antiglobalist, but have their roots in various pre-existing social and political movements (with the possible exception of ATTAC). The anti-globalization movement has its precursors in such movements as the 1968 movement in Europe and the protest against the Vietnam War in the United States. The anti-globalization movement as it is now known stems from the convergence of these different political experiences when their members began to demonstrate together at international meetings such as the Seattle WTO meeting of 1999 or Genoa G8 summit in 2001.

Generally speaking, protesters believe that the global financial institutions and agreements undermine local decision-making methods. Many governments and free trade institutions are seen as acting for the good of transnational (or multinational) corporations (e.g. Microsoft, Monsanto, etc.).

These corporations are seen as having privileges that most human persons do not have: moving freely across borders, extracting desired natural resources, and utilizing a diversity of human resources. They are perceived to be able to move on after doing permanent damage to the natural capital and biodiversity of a nation, in a manner impossible for that nation's citizens. Activists also claim that corporations impose a kind of "global monoculture". Some of the movements' common goals are, therefore, an end to the legal status of corporate personhood and the dissolution or dramatic reform of the World Bank, IMF, and WTO.

The activists are especially opposed to what they view as "globalization abuse" and the international institutions that are perceived to promote neoliberalism without regard to ethical standards. Common targets include World Bank (WB), International Monetary Fund (IMF), the Organisation for Economic Cooperation and Development (OECD) and the World Trade Organization (WTO) and "free trade" treaties like the North American Free Trade Agreement (NAFTA), Free Trade Area of the Americas (FTAA), the Multilateral Agreement on Investment (MAI) and the General Agreement on Trade in Services (GATS). In light of the economic gap between rich and poor countries, movement adherents claim "free trade" will actually result in strengthening the power of industrialized nations (often termed the "North" in opposition to the developing world's "South").

Activists often also oppose business alliances like the World Economic Forum (WEF), the Trans Atlantic Business Dialogue (TABD) and the Asia Pacific Economic Cooperation (APEC), as well as the governments which promote such agreements or institutions. Others argue that, if borders are opened to capital, borders should be similarly opened to allow free and legal circulation and choice of residence for migrants and refugees. These activists tend to target organizations such as the International Organization for Migration and the Schengen Information System.

It is sometimes also argued that the U.S. has a special advantage in the global economy because of dollar hegemony. These claims state that dollar dominance is not just a consequence of U.S. economic superiority. Globalization historians claim that dollar dominance has been achieved also by political agreements such as Bretton Woods System and OPEC dollar-only oil trade after the U.S. broke with the gold standard for the dollar.

Anti-globalization as Anti-neoliberalism

Some see the movement as a critical response to the development of neoliberalism, which is widely seen to have commenced with Margaret Thatcher's and Ronald Reagan's policies toward creating laissez-faire capitalism on a global scale by promoting the liberalization of countries' economies and the weakening of trade and business regulations. Neoliberal proponents argue the increase of free trade and the reduction of the public sector will bring benefits to poor countries and to disadvantaged people in rich countries. Most anti-globalization advocates strongly disagree, adding that neoliberal policies may bring a loss of sovereignty to democratic institutions.

"Anti-war" development

In 2003, many parts of the movement showed wide opposition to the war in Iraq. Many participants were among those 11 million or more protesters that on the weekend of February 15 participated in global protests against the Iraq war and were dubbed the "world's second superpower" by an editorial in the New York Times. Other pacifist appointments were organized by the antiglobalization movement as such: see for example the big demonstration against the impending war in Iraq that closed the first European Social Forum on November 2002 in Florence, Italy.

Anti-globalization militants worried for the proper functioning of democratic institutions as the leaders of many democratic countries (Spain, Italy, Poland) were acting against the wishes of the majorities of their populations in supporting the war. Noam Chomsky asserted that these leaders "showed their contempt for democracy". Critics of this type of argument have tended to point out that this is just a standard criticism of representative democracy-a democratically elected government will not always act in the direction of greatest current public support-and that, therefore, there is no inconsistency in the leaders' positions given that these countries are parliamentary democracies.

The economic and military issues are closely linked in the eyes of many within the movement.

Appropriateness of the Term

Some participants consider the term "anti-globalization" to be a misnomer, and one which has been used to make inaccurate criticisms of the movement. They say the term, for example, implies a negative perspective in that it simply argues for protectionism or even nationalism. In fact, they argue, the movement is actually self-consciously internationalist, organising globally and advocating for the cause of oppressed people around the world. One element that makes up the movement is the No Border network, which argues for unrestricted migration and the abolition of all national borders.

Some activists, notably David Graeber, see the movement as opposed instead to neoliberalism or "corporate globalization". He argues that the term "anti-globalization" is a term coined by the media, and that radical activists are actually more in favor of globalization, in the sense of "effacement of borders and the free movement of people, possessions and ideas" than are the IMF or WTO. He also notes that activists use the terms "globalization movement" and "anti-globalization movement" interchangeably, indicating the confusion of the terminology.

While the term "anti-globalization" arose from the movement's opposition to free-trade agreements (which have often been considered part of something called "globalization"), various participants contend they are opposed to only certain aspects of globalization and instead describe themselves, at least in French-speaking organisations, as "anti-capitalist," "anti-plutocracy," or "anti-corporate." Le Monde Diplomatique 's editor, Ignacio Ramonet's, expression of "the one-way thought" (la pensée unique) became slang against neoliberal policies and the Washington consensus.

Two main approaches to finding a common term for the movement can be distinguished: one that might be described as "anti-globalist" or "regionalist", and another that embraces some aspects of globalization (like cross-cultural exchange of information or the diminishing role of the nation state) while rejecting others (like neo-liberal economics). While proponents of both approaches often cooperate and are a reaction to the same phenomena, their differences might be actually greater than the common ground. The former approach can be described as outright anti-globalist (usually including what is perceived as "Americanization" of culture), while the latter would be more appropriately called "globalization critics". In practice, however, there is no set boundary between these approaches, and the term "anti-globalization" is often indiscriminately applied.

Another concern some activists have about the term "anti-globalization" is that it does not distinguish their position from a strictly nationalist opposition to globalization. Many nationalist movements, such as the French National Front, are also opposed to globalization, but argue that the alternative to globalization is a protection of the nation-state, sometimes, according to critics, in explicitly racist or fascist terms. Some fascist groups influenced by the Third Position have attempted to tailor their message to appeal to the anti-globalization movement. However, the far-right is overwhelmingly rejected by the anti-globalization movement, with groups such as Peoples Global Action explicitly rejecting racism, and many within the movement also active in anti-fascist groups such as ANTIFA.

INFLUENCES ON THE ANTI-GLOBALIZATION MOVEMENT

Several influential critical works have inspired the anti-globalization movement. No Logo, the book by the Canadian journalist Naomi Klein which criticized the production practices of multinational corporations and the omnipresence of brand-driven marketing in popular culture, has become a "manifesto" of the movement, presenting in a simple way themes more accurately developed in other works. In India some intellectual references of the movement can be found in the works of Vandana Shiva, an ecologist and feminist, who in her book

Biopiracy documents the way that the natural capital of indigenous peoples and ecoregions is converted into forms of intellectual capital, which are then recognized as commercial property without sharing the private utility thus derived. The writer Arundhati Roy is famous for her anti-nuclear position and her activism against India's massive hydroelectric dam project, sponsored by the World Bank. In France the well-known monthly paper Le Monde Diplomatique has advocated the antiglobalization cause and an editorial of its director Ignacio Ramonet brought about the foundation of the association ATTAC. The works of Jean Ziegler and Immanuel Wallerstein have detailed underdevelopment and dependence in a world ruled by capitalist system. Pacifist and anti-imperialist traditions have strongly influenced the movement. Critics of American foreign policy such as Noam Chomsky, the late Susan Sontag, and anti-globalist pranksters The Yes Men are widely accepted inside the movement.

Although they may not recognize themselves as antiglobalists and are pro-capitalism, some economists who don't share the neoliberal approach of international economic institutions have strongly influenced the movement. Amartya Sen's Development as Freedom (Nobel Prize in Economics, 1999), argues that third world development must be understood as the expansion of human capability, not simply the increase in national income per capita, and thus requires policies attuned to health and education, not simply GDP. James Tobin's (winner of the Bank of Sweden Prize in Economic Sciences) proposal for a Tax on financial transactions (called, after him, the Tobin Tax) has become part of the agenda of the movement.

George Soros, Joseph E. Stiglitz (another Nobel prize, formerly of the World Bank, author of Globalization and Its Discontents) and David Korten have made arguments for drastically improving transparency, for debt relief, land reform, and restructuring corporate accountability systems. Korten and Stiglitz's contribution to the movement include involvement in direct actions and street protest.

In some Roman Catholic countries such as Italy there have even been religious influences, especially from missionaries who have spent a long time in the Third World (the most famous being Alex Zanotelli). The confluence between this tradition and post-communist tradition is often perceived as odd, but not completely at odds.

Internet sources and free-information websites, such as Indymedia, are a means of diffusion of the movement's ideas. The vast array of material on spiritual movements, anarchism, libertarian socialism and the Green Movement that is now available on the Internet has been perhaps more influential than any printed book. The previously obscure works of Arundhati Roy, Starhawk, and John Zerzan, in particular, inspired a critique favoring feminism, consensus process and political secession.

ORGANIZATION

Although over the past years more emphasis has been given to the construction of grassroots alternatives to (capitalist) globalization, the movement's largest and most visible mode of organizing remains mass decentralized campaigns of direct action and civil disobedience. This mode of organizing, sometimes under the banner of the Peoples' Global Action network, tries to tie the many disparate causes together into one global struggle.

In many ways the process of organizing matters overall can be more important to activists than the avowed goals or achievements of any component of the movement.

At corporate summits, the stated goal of most demonstrations is to stop the proceedings. Although the demonstrations rarely succeed in more than delaying or inconveniencing the actual summits, this motivates the mobilizations and gives them a visible, short-term purpose. Critics claim that this form of publicity is expensive in police time and the public purse. Although not supported by many in the movement, rioting has occurred in Genoa, Seattle and London and extensive damage can be done to the area, especially corporate targets, including McDonald's restaurants and Starbucks.

Despite (or perhaps because of) the lack of formal coordinating bodies, the movement manages to successfully organize large protests on a global basis, using information technology to spread information and organize. Protesters organize themselves into "affinity groups," typically non-hierarchical groups of people who live close together and share a common political goal. Affinity groups will then send representatives to planning meetings. However, because these groups can be infiltrated by law enforcement intelligence, important plans of the protests are often not made until the last minute.

One common tactic of the protests is to split up based on willingness to break the law. This is designed, with varying success, to protect the risk-averse from the physical and legal dangers posed by confrontations with law enforcement. For example, in Prague during the anti-IMF and World Bank protests in September 2000 demonstrators split into three distinct groups, approaching the conference center from three directions: one engaging in various forms of civil disobedience (the Yellow march), one (the Pink/Silver march) advancing through "tactical frivolity" (costume, dance, theatre, music, and artwork), and one (the Blue march) engaging in violent conflicts with the baton-armed police, with the protesters throwing cobblestones lifted from the street.

These demonstrations come to resemble small societies in themselves. Many protesters take training in first aid and act as medics to other injured protesters. Some organizations like the National Lawyer's Guild and, to a lesser extent, the ACLU, provide legal witnesses in case of law enforcement confrontation. Protesters often claim that major media outlets do not properly report on them; therefore, some of them created the Independent Media Center, a collective of protesters reporting on the actions as they happen.

MAIN DEMONSTRATIONS AND APPOINTMENTS

Madrid 94: The 50th anniversary of the IMF and the World Bank, which was celebrated in Madrid in October 1994, was the scene of a protest by an ad-hoc coalition of what would later be called anti-globalization movements. They tried to drown the bankers' parties in noise from outside and held other public forms of protest under the motto "50 Years is Enough".

While Spanish King Juan Carlos was addressing the participants in a huge exhibition hall, two Greenpeace activists climbed to the top and showered the bankers with fake dollar bills carrying the slogan "No $s for Ozone Layer Destruction". A number of the demonstrators were sent at the notorious Carabanchel prison.

One of the first international anti-globalization protests was organized in dozens of cities around the world on June 18, 1999, with those in London and Eugene, Oregon most often noted. The drive was called the Carnival Against Capitalism, or J18 for short. The protest in Eugene turned into a riot where local anarchists drove police out of a small park. One anarchist, Robert Thaxton, was arrested and convicted of throwing a rock at a police officer.

The WTO meeting of 1999: The second major mobilization of the movement, known as N30, occurred on November 30, 1999, when protesters blocked delegates' entrance to WTO meetings in Seattle, USA. The protests forced the cancellation of the opening ceremonies and lasted the length of the meeting until December 3. There was a large, permitted march by members of the AFL-CIO, and another large, unauthorized march by assorted affinity groups. The protesters and Seattle riot police clashed in the streets after police fired tear gas at demonstrators blocking streets. Over 600 protesters were arrested and dozens were injured. Three policemen were injured by friendly fire, and one by a thrown rock. Many protesters destroyed the windows of storefronts of businesses owned or franchised by targeted corporations such as a large Nike shop and many Starbucks windows. The mayor put the city under the municipal equivalent of martial law and declared a curfew. As of 2002, the city of Seattle had paid over $200,000 in settlements of lawsuits filed against the Seattle Police Department for assault and wrongful arrest, with a class action lawsuit still pending.

Law Enforcement Reaction

Although local police were surprised by the size of N30, law enforcement agencies have since reacted worldwide to prevent the disruption of future events by a variety of tactics, including sheer weight of numbers, infiltrating the groups to determine their plans, and preparations for the use of force to remove protesters.

At the site of some of the protests, police have used tear gas and pepper spray, concussion grenades, rubber and wooden bullets, night sticks, water cannons, dogs, horses, and occasionally live ammunition to repel the protesters. After the November 2000 G-8 protest in Montreal, at which many protesters were beaten, trampled, and arrested in what was intended to be a festive protest, the tactic of dividing protests into "green" (permitted), "yellow" (not officially permitted but with little confrontation and low risk of arrest), and "red" (involving direct confrontation) zones was introduced.

In Quebec City, municipal officials built a ten-foot-high wall around the portion of the city where the Summit of the Americas was being held, which only residents, delegates to the summit, and certain accredited journalists were allowed to pass through. Although police claimed that violent elements in the protesters required a firm response, they allegedly fired tear gas and rubber bullets indiscriminately, dispersing peaceful assemblies and even teams of medics assisting the wounded. It is claimed they also gassed areas not involved in the protests, firing off the mountaintop where the confrontations were taking place into the city below.

Genoa Group of Eight Summit Protest

The Genoa Group of Eight Summit protest from July 18 to July 22, 2001 was one of the bloodiest protests in Western Europe's recent history, as evidenced by the death of a young citizen of Genoa named Carlo Giuliani during the demonstration and hospitalisation of several demonstrators. Police have subsequently been accused of brutality, torture and interference with non-violent protests. Several hundred demonstrators and police were injured and hundreds were arrested during the days surrounding the G8 meeting; most of those arrested have been charged with some form of "criminal association" under Italy's anti-mafia and anti-terrorist laws. As part of the continuing investigations, police raids of social centers, media centers, union buildings, and law offices have continued across

Italy since the G8 summit in Genoa. Many police officers or responsible authorities present in Genoa during the G8 summit, are currently under investigation by the Italian judges, and some of them resigned. Some have since admitted to planting Molotov cocktails in order to justify the Diaz School raids, as well as faking the stabbing of a police officer to frame activists.

International Social Forums

The slogan of the World Social Forum was "Another World Is Possible". It was here that the WSF's Charter of Principles was adopted to provide a framework for the forums.

The WSF became a periodic meeting: in 2002 and 2003 it was held again in Porto Alegre and became a rallying point for worldwide protest against the American invasion of Iraq. In 2004 it was moved to Mumbai (formerly known as Bombay, in India), to make it more accessible to the populations of Asia and Africa. This last appointment saw the participation of 75,000 delegates.

In the meantime, regional forums took place following the example of the WSF, adopting its Charter of Principles. The first European Social Forum (ESF) was held in November 2002 in Florence. The slogan was "Against the war, against racism and against neo-liberalism". It saw the participation of 60,000 delegates and ended with a huge demonstration against the war (1,000,000 people according to the organizers). The other two ESFs took place in Paris and London, in 2003 and 2004 respectively.

Recently there has been some discussion behind the movement about the role of the social forums. Some see them as a "popular university", an occasion to make many people aware of the problems of globalization. Others would prefer that delegates concentrate their efforts on the coordination and organization of the movement and on the planning of new campaigns.

INFLUENCE ON THE DEVELOPING WORLD

Some people claim that the major mobilizations have taken place mainly in the developed world, where there are strong traditions of free speech, police restraint, civil rights, and the rule of law. In these countries, one of the objectives is to demonstrate that the protesters self-govern better than they could ever be controlled by violent force: on March 15 2002 in Barcelona, 250,000 people "rioted" for days with apparently no serious injury to individuals on either side: there were far fewer casualties than would be expected in a typical European soccer riot, for example. There was, however, much damage to private and public property, which is, arguably, unnecessary in public protest.

In Argentina, during the 2001/2002 economic crisis, millions of ordinary citizens took to the streets for days with similar results to the Barcelona protests, forcing several changes in the federal government. On 19 and 20 December 2001, riots in Buenos Aires and some other large cities forced the resignation of then-president Fernando de la Rúa, though over 32 demonstrators were killed. At the same time and also during 2002, thousands of middle-class people marched against financial institutions and foreign companies banging pots and pans (this was promptly termed cacerolazo), protesting against the freezing of their bank accounts in the so-called corralito. In the months that followed, Argentinians developed some alternative neighborhood-based economic systems, social structures and local systems of autonomous self-government. A popular slogan within the uprising was, ¡Que se vayan todos! ("Everybody out [of the government]!"), indicating protesters' frustration not only with corruption in government but with the entire governmental structure.

CRITICISMS

The anti-globalization movement has been criticized on many fronts by politicians, members of conservative think tanks, mainstream economists, and other supporters of market-based economic integration.

Disorganization: One of the most common criticisms of the movement, which does not necessarily come from its opponents, is simply that the anti-globalization movement lacks coherent goals, and that the views of different protesters are often in opposition to each other. Many members of the movement are also aware of this, and argue that, as long as they have a common opponent, they should march together-even if they don't share exactly the same political vision.

Addressing Problems Incorrectly

One argument often made by the opponents of the anti-globalization movement (especially by The Economist), is that one of the major causes of poverty amongst third-world farmers are the trade barriers put up by rich nations. The WTO is an organisation set up to work towards removing those trade barriers. Therefore, it is argued, people really concerned about the plight of the third world should actually be encouraging free trade, rather than attempting to fight it. Further in this vein, it is argued that the protesters' opposition to free trade is sometimes aimed at protecting the interests of Western labor (whose wages and conditions are protected by trade barriers) rather than the interests of the developing world. This is sometime summed up as "keep the poor, poor". This contrasts with the stated goals of those in the movement, which are to improve the conditions of ordinary farmers and workers everywhere.

Anti-globalization activists counter these claims by arguing that free trade policies create an environment for workers similar to the prisoner's dilemma, in which workers in different countries are tempted to "defect" or "betray" other workers by undercutting standards on wages and work conditions. Therefore, the anti-globalization movement supports a strategy of cooperation for mutual benefit, and argues for fair trade, which is intended to provide third-world farmers with better terms of trade.

The book Globalization Unmasked claims that "the major adversaries of globalization in the dominated countries have been the peasant movements particularly in Latin America and parts of Asia." Some peasant farmers contend that free-trade policies merely aid a narrow stratum of cash-crop oriented agricultural firms in their own countries with links to multinational agribusiness, and subsidized agribusiness in developed countries. A report by Jean Ziegler, UN Special Rapporteur on the right to food, notes that "millions of farmers are losing their livelihoods in the developing countries, but small farmers in the northern countries are also suffering" and concludes that "the current inequities of the global trading system are being perpetuated rather than resolved under the WTO, given the unequal balance of power between member countries.". Critics respond that it is only natural that there are relatively fewer jobs for farmers as a nation becomes more industrialized and that actual statistics show sharply reduced poverty in the Third World.

Failure to Propose Solutions to Problems

Another criticism against the movement is that, although it protests about things that are widely recognized as serious problems, such as human rights violations, genocide and global warming, it rarely proposes detailed solutions. Proponents of the movement point to the existence of web resources like the Philadelphia IMC alternatives site and the annual World Social Forum where numerous solutions are proposed and debated and empirical data on social experiments are exchanged.

Violence: Some have also criticized the movement for engaging in violent protest. In general, movement leaders tend to encourage peaceful protest as the more productive way of getting attention and respect for their goals, although occasional protests do turn violent, sometimes due to police aggravation (such as the S11 protest). Some critics, however, see an enforced blockade of events and public throughways as a "violent" action, in and of itself. Many protesters counter that blockades are a time-honored technique of civil disobedience, and that the organizations they are protesting against are themselves guilty of crimes.

There is a debate within the movement over what is defined as violence. Many, such as anarchists who participate in the Black Bloc tactic argue that breaking windows is not necessarily a violent action unless humans beings are harmed in the process. Others, many prominent Non-governmental Organizations (NGOs) among them, dispute this view, saying that physical damage to anything is inherently violent.

Motivations: The motivations of the protesters are often questioned. Some claim key organizers are communists or anarchists who aim to start a revolution. The counter-argument is that the movement has a horizontal power structure, so that the power of individual organizers is limited, and that if violent revolution is considered a real possibility, then it is a clear sign that something is wrong with the current system.

Some critics have claimed there is strong anti-Americanism in the anti-globalization movement. They argue that protesters object to people voluntarily choosing American (or American-style) cultural products. Attempts to prevent the Americanization of French culture is held to be an example. In this sense, anti-globalization is perceived as cultural chauvinism directed against American products, corporations and individuals. These critics contend that anti-global groups routinely favour European-style economic, political and cultural systems, belying a cultural bias.

Other critics claim that anti-Semitism is rife in the movement. These charges are related to the fact that solidarity with Palestinians and criticism of Israeli government policies are common among anti-globalization activists. Within the movement, such charges are dismissed as nonsense, since the movement is explicitly anti-racist and many key organizers are Jewish. Supporters argue that criticizing Israel is not indicative of anti-Semitism, and that attempts to equate Israel's policies with the beliefs of all Jewish people is itself racist.

There is a small far right anti-globalization trend in the United States and some European nations, which exists independently of the much larger left-radical movement. Right-wing anti-globalization critics include Pat Buchanan, and some segments of the neo-Nazi movement. The latter support strong protectionist policies, an end to immigration, and frequently employ racist and anti-Semitic rhetoric. Encounters between right-and left-wing anti-globalization protesters are typically hostile and sometimes violent.

LACK OF EVIDENCE FOR CLAIMS

Critics assert that members of the anti-globalization movement use anecdotal evidence to support their views, which are not supported by worldwide economic and social statistics. These critics point to statistical trends which suggest beneficial effects of globalization, capitalism, and the economic growth they encourage. One such trend is the decrease in the percentage of people in developing countries living below $1 per day (adjusted for inflation and purchasing power), which has halved in only twenty years. A second such trend is the doubling of life expectancy in the developing world since WWII. A third such trend is the decrease in child mortality in every developing region of the world.

A fourth trend is diminishing income inequality for the world as a whole. A fifth trend is the increase in universal suffrage, from no nations in 1900 to 62.5% of all nations in 2000. A sixth trend is the shift in food supplies available; the proportion of the world's population living in countries where per capita food supplies are under 2,200 [calories per day] was 56 percent in the mid-1960s, compared to below 10 percent by the 1990s.

A seventh trend is the rising rate of literacy; between 1950 and 1999, global literacy increased from 52 percent to 81 percent, and female literacy as a percentage of male literacy increased from 59 percent in 1970 to 80 percent in 2000. There are similar trends for electric power, cars, radios, and telephones per capita as well as the percentage of the population with access to clean water.

Members of the anti-globalization movement respond that "growth is good for the poor" is an uncontroversial claim, and yet it misses the main point, which is that neoliberal policies consistent with globalization and capitalism may not actually be causing growth that has beneficial effects for the poor.

They take issue with the time period which is often normally associated with worldwide statistics, and they argue that more detailed variables measuring poverty should instead be studied. The Center for Economic and Policy Research (CEPR) has noted that from 1980-2000 there has been diminished progress in terms of economic growth, life expectancy, infant and child mortality, and to a lesser extent education.

Moreover, they have disputed the claim that the statistical trends are the effects of neoliberal policies followed by the IMF and World Bank in recent years have led to growth. Directly criticizing a world bank study, CEPR economists concluded: "Economic growth over the last twenty years, the period during which the policies advocated by the authors (and their institution) have been put into place, has been dramatically reduced. It may well be true, as Dr. Dollar argues, that "to ignore the importance of growth-enhancing policies is an injustice to the poor." But to assume that the World Bank and the IMF have brought "growth-enhancing policies" to their client countries goes against the overwhelming weight of the evidence over the last two decades."

Critics of anti-globalization note that the above study gives all nations equal weight, giving China with its 1.3 billion people the same importance as Belize with its 300,000 people. If instead giving all people in the developing world the same weight, then growth and reductions in poverty have not slowed.

They also point to the many peer-reviewed articles and research which demonstrate a correlation between economic freedom and well-being. There are two indices of economic freedom used in economic research. Both attempt to measure of the degree of economic freedom in countries, mostly in regard to lack of governmental intervention in the economy, free trade, and strength of private property rights.

They use statistics from independent organizations like the United Nations to score countries in various categories like the size of government, degree of taxes, security of property rights, degree of free trade and size of market regulations. Many peer-reviewed papers have been published using this material on the relationship between capitalism and poverty.

The more advanced capitalist countries have much higher average income per person, higher income of the poorest 10%, higher life-expectancy, higher literacy, lower infant mortality, higher access to water sources and less corruption. The share of income in percent going to the poorest 10% is the same for both more and less capitalistic countries.. Economist, Johan Norberg, author of "In Defense of Global Capitalism" concurs, arguing that the data supplied by the anti-globalization side is severely lacking in evidence. Other studies have shown similar results.

Doug Henwood, author of After the New Economy, faults the methodology of such studies, arguing that the selection of indices is arbitrary, the conclusions drawn are dubious (often neglecting the elementary fact that "correlation does not prove causation"), and concluding that the report is "meaningless.". At a more fundamental level Henwood disputes the definition of "economic freedom" used in such indices. Supporters note that this article is not peer-reviewed in contrast to many studies which do show causation.

Many supporters of capitalism do think that different policies than today should be pursued, although not necessarily those advocated by the anti-globalization movement. For example, some see the World Bank and the IMF as corrupt bureaucracies which have given repeated loans to dictators who never do any reforms. Some argue that free trade may be harmful in certain instances or that spending on education and basic health care may be very important. Some, like Hernando de Soto, argue that the most important thing for the developing world may be to develop the institutions of capitalism, like protecting the property rights and access to credit for the poor.

❑❑❑

Bibliography

Albright, K. B.: *Enhancing Kansas Communities*, Manhattan, Kansas State University, 1991.

Ash, L. E.: *Electronic Student Portfolios*, Arlington Heights, Skylight Professional Development, 2000.

Baron, Cynthia: *Creating a Digital Portfolio*, Indianapolis, Hayden Books, 1996.

Belanoff, Pat : *Portfolios: Process and Product*, Poutsmouth, Heinemann, 1991.

Beverly, D.: *Designing and Using Portfolios*, Boston, Allyn and Bacon, 1997.

Brass, Jane L.: *Community Tourism Assessment Handbook*, Corvallis, Oregon State University, 1996.

Brown, Genevieve: *The Principal Portfolio*, Thousand Oaks, Corwin Press, 1997.

Bryden, John M.: *Tourism and Development: A Case Study of the Commonwealth Caribbean*, England, Cambridge University Press, 1973.

Bullock, Ann Adams: *Developing a Teaching Portfolio: a Guide for Preservice and Practicing Teachers*, Upper Saddle River, Prentice-Hall, 2001.

Burke, Kay: *Designing Professional Portfolios for Change*, Palatine, SkyLight Training & Publishing, 1997.

Burr, Steven W: *Proceedings of the 1996 Northeastern Recreation Research Symposium*, NY, U.S. Dept. of Agriculture, 1997.

Campbell, Cignetti: *How to Develop a Professional Portfolio: A Manual for Teachers*, California, California University of Pennsylvania, 1997.

Cater, Erlet, and Gwen Lowman: *Ecotourism: A Sustainable Option?*, New York, John Wiley & Sons, 1994.

Clough, Richard: *Construction Project Management*, New York, John Wiley & Son, 2000.

David W. Marcouiller: *Ethnic Variation in Leisure and Recreational Interests*, Chicago, Council of Planning Librarians, 1994.

Davies, I.: *Competency Based Learning: Technology, Management, and Design*, New York, McGraw-Hill, 1973.

Debra, Bayles: *The Portfolio Planner - Making Professional Portfolios Work for You*, N.J., Merrill, 1999.

Dickson, Marcia: *Portfolios: Process and Product*, Poutsmouth, Heinemann, 1991.

Elizabeth, A.: *The Power of Portfolios: What Children can Teach us about Learning and Assessment*, San Francisco, Jossey-Bass, 2001.

Elizabeth, Maureen: *Digital Professional Portfolios for Change*, Arlington Heights, Skylight Professional Development, 1999.

Elkinton, Linda C.: *Back Road Adventures: A Private Enterprise Model for Nature Study on Private and Public Land*, Morgantown, West Virginia, 1990.

Fogarty, Robin: *The Mindful School: The Portfolio Connection*, Palatine, Skylight Training & Publishing, 1994.

Frame, J. Davidson: *Managing Projects in Organizations: How to Make the Best Use of Time, Techniques, and People*, San Francisco, Jossey-Bass, 1995.

Gibson, Lay James: *Economic Adaptation*, Boulder, Westview Press, 1993.

Glatthorn, Allan: *The Teacher's Portfolio: Fostering and Documenting Professional Development*, Rockport, Active Publications, 1996.

Goldman, George, and Anthony Nakazawa: *Impact of Visitor Expenditures on Local Revenues*, Corvallis, Oregon, 1994.

Hebert, E. A.: *The Power of Portfolios: What Children can Teach us about Learning and Assessment*, San Francisco, Jossey-Bass, 2001.

Helleiner, Gerald K.: *The Less Developed Countries in the International Economy*, Cambridge, Cambridge University Press, 1975.

Hilchey, Duncan: *Agritourism in New York State: Opportunities and Challenges in Farm-Based Recreation and Hospitality*, New York, Cornell University, 1993.

Hoffman, Edward: *Project Management Success Stories: Lessons of Project Leaders*, New York, John Wiley & Son, 2000.

Irby, Beverly: *The Principal Portfolio*, Thousand Oaks, Corwin Press, 1997.

Ireland, Lewis: *Quality Management for Projects and Programs*, Upper Darby, PMI, 1991.

Iso-Ahola, Seppo E.: *Social Psychological Perspectives on Leisure and Recreation*, Springfield, Illinois, Thomas, 1980.

Jensen, Clayne R.: *Leisure and Recreation: Introduction and Overview*, Philadelphia, Lea and Febiger, 1977.

Jepson, Edward J.: *Ethnic Variation in Leisure and Recreational Interests*, Chicago, Council of Planning Librarians, 1994.

Johannis, Theodore B., and C. Neil Bull: *Sociology of Leisure*, California, Sage, 1971.

Kando, Thomas M.: *Leisure and Popular Culture in Transition*, St. Louis, Mosby, 1980.

Kraus, Richard: *Recreation and Leisure in Modern Society*, New York, Meredith, 1984.

Krippendorf, Jost: *The Holiday Makers: Understanding the Impact of Leisure and Travel*, London, Heinemann, 1987.

Kuehn, Diane: *Considerations for Agritourism Development*, New York, Sea Grant, 1998.

Kusler, Jon A.: *Guidebook for Creating Wetland Interpretation Sites, Including Wetlands and Ecotourism*, New York, Association of State Wetland Managers, 1992.

Laufer, Alexander : *Project Management Success Stories: Lessons of Project Leaders*, New York, John Wiley & Son, 2000.

Linda, E.: *Electronic Student Portfolios*, Arlington Heights, Skylight Professional Development, 2000.

Lock, Dennis: *Project Management*, New York, Wiley, 1996.

Lyons, Nona: *Portfolio in Hand: Validating the New Teacher Professionalism*, New York, Teachers College Press, 1998.

Machlis, Gary E., and Donald R. Field: *National Parks and Rural Development: Practice and Policy in the United States*, Washington, DC, Island Press, 2000.

Martin, D.B.: *The Portfolio Planner - Making Professional Portfolios Work for You*, N.J., Merrill, 1999.

Mastran, Shelley: *Getting Started in Heritage Area Development*, Washington, DC, National Trust for Historic Preservation, 1997.

Morriss, Maureen: *Digital Professional Portfolios for Change*, Arlington Heights, Skylight Professional Development, 1999.

Nettles & Wyman: *How to Develop a Professional Portfolio: A Manual for Teachers*, California, California University of Pennsylvania, 1997.

Pinto, Jeffrey K. and Kharbanda, O.P.: *Successful Project Managers: Leading Your Team to Success*, New York, Van Nostrand Reinhold, 1995.

Potts, Thomas D., and Allan P. C. Marsinko: *Developing Naturally: An Exploratory Process for Nature-Based Community Tourism*, South Carolina, Clemson University, 1998.

Rosenburg, Marc J.: *E-Learning: Strategies for Delivering Knowledge in the Digital Age*, New York, McGraw-Hill, 2001.

Rothman, Hal: *Reopening the American West*, Tucson, University of Arizona Press, 1998.

Seldin, Peter: *The Teaching Portfolio*, Bolton, Anker Publishing, 1997.

Shaklee, B. D.: *Designing and Using Portfolios*, Boston, Allyn and Bacon, 1997.

Stefanakis, Evangeline: *Multiple Intelligences and Portfolios: A Window into the Learner's Mind*, Pourtsmouth, Heinemann, 2002.

Wolf, Kenneth: *Leading the Professional Portfolio Process for Change*, Arlington Heights, Skylight Professional Development , 1999.

Index

M

N

O

P

Q

R

□□□